STEAL THIS FILE SHARING BOOK

What They Won't Tell You About File Sharing

STEAL THIS

FILE SHARING

BOOK

What They Won't Tell You About File Sharing

WALLACE WANG

**NO STARCH
PRESS**

San Francisco

STEAL THIS FILE SHARING BOOK

Copyright © 2004 by Wallace Wang.

Printed in the United States of America on recycled paper

2 3 4 5 6 7 8 9 10—07 06 05

Publisher: William Pollock
Managing Editor: Karol Jurado
Developmental Editor: William Pollock
Cover and Interior Design: Octopod Studios
Technical Reviewer: Ray Hoffman
Copyeditor: Andy Carroll
Compositor: Riley Hoffman
Proofreader: Stephanie Provines

For information on book distributors or translations, please contact No Starch Press, Inc. directly:

No Starch Press, Inc.

555 De Haro Street, Suite 250, San Francisco, CA 94107

phone: 415.863.9900; fax: 415.863.9950; info@nostarch.com; http://www.nostarch.com

Library of Congress Cataloging-in-Publication Data

Wang, Wally.
  Steal this file sharing book : what they won't tell you about file sharing / Wallace Wang.
      p. cm.
  Includes index.
  ISBN 1-59327-050-X
1. Peer-to-peer architecture (Computer networks) I. Title.
  TK5105.525.W36 2004
  004.6'5--dc22

                                                              2004013806

DEDICATION

This book is dedicated to all the recording artists, movie studios, and other copyright holders who find their works traded over file sharing networks. Their creations have helped make file sharing networks as useful as they are today, so the next time you download a file that you find particularly useful, support your favorite artists, movies, authors, and so on by buying their products so they can continue to create more useful files that you and everyone else can enjoy for the future.

BRIEF CONTENTS

CONTENTS IN DETAIL

ACKNOWLEDGMENTS

Special acknowledgments go to Matt Wagner and Bill Gladstone at Waterside Productions for being the best book agents I've worked with for all these years. Without Waterside Productions working as my agent, I would have to negotiate royalties from book publishers myself, which means I'd probably be living off food stamps right about now.

Other people who deserve thanks include Bill Pollock (for having the guts to start a wonderful little publisher like No Starch Press), Karol Jurado (for always making the entire editing cycle with No Starch Press such a painless experience), and Ray Hoffman for catching any errors in print before they can embarrass me in public.

Additional acknowledgments go to all the friendly people I've met at the Riviera Comedy Club, located at the Riviera Hotel & Casino (www.rivierahotel.com) in Las Vegas: Steve Schirripa (who appears in HBO's hit show, *The Sopranos*), Bob Zany (www.bobzany.com), Gerry Bednob, Bruce Clark, Darrell Joyce, Tony Vicich, and Kip Addotta.

Other people who deserve acknowledgment include Joe Jarred, for booking comedy shows in wonderfully odd places in Pahrump and Primm, Nevada; Don Learned at the Laff Spot in Houston (www.laffspot.com); Roger Feeny at the Ann Arbor Comedy Showcase (www.aacomedy.com); Connie Ettinger at the Holly Hotel Comedy Club (www.hollyhotel.com); Doug James for his wonderful little one-nighters all over Southern California; Mark Ridley at the Comedy Castle (www.comedycastle.com); Russ Rivas at Laffs Comedy Club (www.laffscomedy.com) in Albuquerque, New Mexico; and Berri-Lee at the River Palms Hotel (www.river-palms.com) in Laughlin, Nevada, right across the Colorado River from Bullhead City, Arizona, the only town where dental care is still a mystery to most of its inhabitants.

Patrick DeGuire also deserves acknowledgment for helping me form Top Bananas Entertainment (www.topbananas.com)—our company devoted to providing clean, quality stand-up comedy for the wonderful people in San Diego. Other people who deserve acknowledgment include Chris (the Zooman) Clobber, Dante, Dobie "Mr. Lucky" Maxwell, and Leo (the man, the myth, the legend) Fontaine just because they like seeing their names in print.

Final acknowledgments must go to Cassandra (my wife) and Jordan (my son) for putting up with all the time I've spent staring into the computer screen for days at a time. Of course, I must also acknowledge Bo, Scraps, Tasha, and Nuit (our cats) for making my life more interesting by the minute every time they cough up a hairball or spray the furniture in yet another out of the way location that isn't easily accessible for cleaning.

Wallace Wang
San Diego, CA

PART 1

LEARNING ABOUT FILE SHARING

1

FINDING THE FILES

A computer file can be anything from a single song to a photograph, a full-length motion picture, the complete text from a book, or a computer program that sells for thousands of dollars. Because a computer file is made up of electronic data, all it does is fill up the space on your hard drive. And large hard drives are really cheap today, which means you can fill them up with many, many files at relatively little cost. Storing this stuff is just not an issue.

There is one thing stronger than all the armies in the world, and that is an idea whose time has come.

—Victor Hugo

Computer files can also be copied with perfect accuracy and transferred flawlessly to nearly any computer in the world. In most industries, such qualities might be admirable, but in the computer industry, those same qualities spell trouble for copyright holders. If someone can make multiple copies of a song, a book, or a computer program at no cost, what will stop people from blatantly copying everything they own and passing it around to all their friends?

The answer is simple: nothing. And that's spelled trouble for the computer industry. Of course, people have been illegally copying music with tape recorders and CD burners for years, but cassette tapes and CDs aren't as easy to distribute as a single file that you can email or post on a file sharing network for millions of people to copy at once.

Similarly, photocopying has threatened the copyright on books, but photocopying an entire book is usually more trouble (and more expense) than it's worth. Plus, most people like their books bound, rather than in loose sets of not always perfectly copied pages.

The same can be said for the video cassette recorder, which spawned the copying of videos. But as with audio tapes, each copy of a video cassette loses some of its original quality. It's also simply too troublesome for the average user to duplicate videos on a mass scale and distribute them.

But once you store something in a computer file, copying suddenly becomes easy and fast for everyone. Instead of asking, "Can it be copied?" people ask, "Where can I find it?" And the answer is usually somewhere online where people can copy and distribute files fast.

THE INTERNET: A GRAB BAG OF FILES

If something can be copied, it probably already has been, and it's just a matter of knowing where to look for it on the Internet. Although most people think of the Internet as nothing more than pretty websites and email, it's really a network that connects computers.

The Internet has revolutionized the way people share files. In the old days, sharing files meant physically handing a copy of a floppy disk to another person, but with the Internet, sharing files can be as simple as pressing a button.

With people able to share files so easily, sharing files no longer requires technical knowledge as much as it requires motivation. Some people share files because they like the idea of "getting back" at big corporations by not paying for the copyrighted files that they duplicate and distribute to others. Others share because they just want a copy of a particular song or program, and they don't want or can't afford to pay for it. Still a few people share files in blissful ignorance of the fact that duplicating copyrighted files is actually illegal.

So over the past decade, people have found various ways to share files, always staying just one step ahead of the law. Here's a look at some of the more popular methods of file sharing.

BBS

Before the Internet, people used to share files through electronic bulletin board systems, otherwise known as BBSs. Basically, a BBS was nothing more than a computer hooked up to one or more phone lines that allowed anyone from around the world to call in. Once you called into a BBS, you could download files to your computer or upload files from your computer to the BBS for other people to copy.

While BBSs were once popular, their technical limitations prevented widespread file sharing. First, each caller had to pay their own phone charges to connect to a BBS, which meant that most BBS users tended to live in the city where the BBS was located, although some of the larger and more popular BBSs attracted the occasional long distance or overseas user.

Since the only way to connect to a BBS was through a telephone line, people found sharing files through a BBS inconvenient because telephone lines are notoriously slow for transferring huge files. Although people could still share files through a BBS, the files spread slowly and could take days, months, or even years just to reach someone else in another part of the country.

The Internet pretty much wiped out BBSs as a popular way to share files, but some people still maintain BBSs in areas where Internet access is still sporadic (such as Third World countries) or because a BBS can offer more privacy and anonymity than a website. To find a BBS in your area, enter **BBS** in your favorite search engine or browse through the USBBS site (http://www.usbbs.org) to view a listing of BBSs in the United States and Canada.

EMAIL

Email lets you send a message to a particular address on the Internet. As long as you type the recipient's email address correctly, your message will likely take no more than a few hours (if not minutes) to reach its destination.

Of course, you don't need to send only text in your email. Email can also include files as attachments. So if your friend wants a copy of a Madonna song, you can email that song to him as an audio file, and that's that.

While trading files through email is easy and relatively safe from prying eyes, it does limit you to trading files with people whose email addresses you already know. If you want a copy of an Eminem song but none of your friends have it, you're out of luck. So while email offers near-certain delivery, the variety of files you can get is limited by the number of friends you have and their tastes in files. For technical reasons, many Internet service providers (ISPs) also limit the maximum size of files you can send by email. If too many people start sending massive files by email, they could overload the storage space on their ISP's computers. For these reasons, file trading by email remains a common but not dominant way to share files with others.

NEWSGROUPS

Trading files by email limits your choices to specific email addresses and the limited number of files each of your email correspondents possesses. To avoid this problem, many people trade files through newsgroups, which act like the electronic equivalent of a massive bulletin board. Instead of sending a message to a specific person, you send your message to a newsgroup for anyone to view.

Each newsgroup focuses on a specific topic, such as computer programming, skydiving, or rap music. Visitors can quickly find a topic that interests them, and then read and write messages from and to other people interested in the same topic. Anyone can read a message posted in a newsgroup, which means you can meet and communicate with people all over the world.

This turns out to be great for file trading, too, because you're no longer limited to trading files with a small circle of friends. Now you can trade files with people you don't know and who you may never meet. (In fact, you may never *want* to meet many of the people who hang out in newsgroups.)

For example, in many music-related newsgroups, people leave messages asking for a particular song. If the timing is right, someone with that particular song may read that message and either send that file by email or, more likely, post it in the newsgroup for anyone to copy.

Still, newsgroups are fairly unreliable for file trading. Merely asking for a song won't guarantee that anyone will ever give it to you. And after you request a song, it may take hours, days, weeks, or even longer before the song actually appears in the newsgroup—if it appears at all. Of course, if you wait long enough in the right newsgroup, you'll probably find what you're after. But that limits newsgroup file sharing to people with a lot of patience, a trait not usually found among file traders. Generally, file sharing within newsgroups consists more of browsing and taking what you find rather than searching for a particular file. Newsgroups may well be the best resource for browsing the different genres of music and finding new music to audition. Many music lovers browse through newsgroups to sample different songs and styles that they might never have listened to before.

DOWNLOADING FROM WEBSITES

If someone has files that you want, you may never know, unless you ask them by email or find it through a newsgroup. But what if you don't want to ask or you don't want people to ask you? You can find your files at a website or post them to a website for others to download.

If you create a website, you can post all the files that you own, allowing anyone to browse through your collection and copy the files they want. Of course, few people freely give away their collection of files without expecting something in return, so many such sites will only let you download a file if you first give them some files in return. Like newsgroups, these file downloading sites can be convenient because you simply browse through their file collection and download the ones you want.

The main drawback with file trading through an FTP or website is that it's easy for the recording industry (such as the RIAA in the United States) or the government to find out who's running a specific site and come after you. Offering copyrighted files through a website can blatantly advertise your law-breaking activities in much the same way as selling illegal drugs from your front porch in full view of the neighbors. Someone is going to turn you in.

Although they were rampant during the Internet's early years, websites created for file sharing don't last long today. Some amateurs still run them, often on free, anonymous web hosting services like Yahoo! GeoCities, but they're usually shut down within a few weeks or days. Some even host their sites on computers located in Third World countries to avoid breaking the laws of American or European countries.

DOWNLOADING FROM FTP SITES

Before websites appeared, many people transferred files through FTP (File Transfer Protocol) sites, which contained files stored in different directories. To have full access to an FTP site, you need to use a special FTP program. (Many web browsers allow you to read and download from FTP sites, but not save files to the sites.) The FTP program runs on your computer and lets you navigate through the directories and files stored on another computer so you can download the files you want, as shown in Figure 1-1.

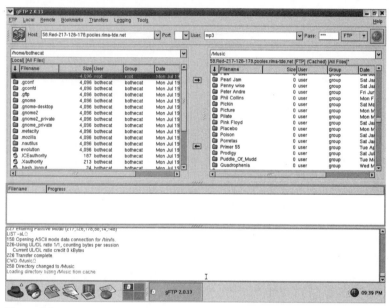

Figure 1-1

An FTP program lets you browse another computer's drives and folders for the files you want.

Like websites, it's risky to run a file trading FTP site because it's simple to track down the computer hosting the site. As a result, many such FTP sites won't allow people to download files until they first upload some.

By forcing people to upload files, these FTP sites ensure that government or industry officials can't access their sites since doing so would mean they would have to violate the very copyright infringement laws they're trying to enforce. And if these officials can't actually download a copyrighted file from an FTP site, they can't prove that the site is actually trading copyrighted files rather than just legitimate files that "happen" to use the names of copyrighted files, such as popular songs.

Still, despite the risk of running an FTP site, FTP downloading is still heavily used in conjunction with IRC file-sharing channels that post the login information required to access these FTP sites.

INSTANT FILE TRANSFER: IRC

When you ask for a file by email, it can be frustrating to wait for an answer. So for instant communication, many people are turning to Internet Relay Chat (IRC) to swap files. IRC acts like a real-time version of newsgroups, except that whatever you type appears instantly on the computer screens of other people around the world. Like the instant messaging services you may be used to (like AIM and Yahoo! IM), IRC is a way to chat online.

Like newsgroups, IRC organizes people into channels based on specific topics, such as classical music or computer graphics. Once you join a channel based on a specific topic, such as jazz, you can ask someone for a particular file or just browse through the files someone offers and start downloading right away.

As with newsgroups, IRC is a holdover from the Internet's early days. It's awkward and cumbersome compared with newer file sharing methods. Users can't simply load a program and begin grabbing files. Instead, they must learn new navigation methods, moving to the right channel at the right time. Sometimes users must type complex commands to locate and download the files they want. Figure 1-2 shows a typical IRC chat room filled with messages from different users.

Unlike newsgroups messages that someone can read a day or two later, IRC messages disappear fairly quickly. As a result, many people use IRC channels to post access instructions for visiting web or FTP file trading sites or to plant special programs, called file server bots, that allow others to download files from another computer.

IRC channels are often places where file traders meet, offer their file collections for downloading, and then start swapping files. Many IRC users are technically savvy people who don't mind typing arcane commands to chat or swap files. For most people, instant messaging services are much more popular, because they offer simpler point-and-click methods for finding and downloading files.

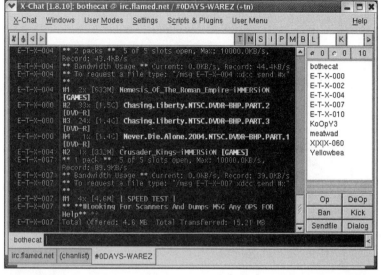

Figure 1-2

Sharing files through IRC requires a file server bot, which advertises which files it offers such as the Crusader Kings video game or the *Chasing Liberty* or *Never Die Alone* movies.

INSTANT FILE TRANSFER: INSTANT MESSAGING

Instant messaging services have adopted the real-time communication of IRC and slapped a pretty graphical user interface over it. So instead of typing cryptic commands to chat, as you would with IRC, instant messaging lets you chat by typing messages and clicking buttons to send or receive files.

Like IRC, instant messaging services divide users into chat rooms, with each chat room focusing on a specific topic. Users can also set up temporary private chat rooms to lock out strangers and invite only their friends in. While some chat rooms focus exclusively on chatting, others include some file sharing.

Despite the larger number of people using instant messaging (as compared with IRC), there's still no guarantee that you'll find a particular file within a chat room. Some people won't have the file you want, others won't want to take the time to trade files with a stranger, and still others may have the file you want but may not have seen your request. While file trading within instant messaging can be done, it happens more often between friends than between complete strangers.

FILE SHARING NETWORKS—WHERE THE REAL FILE SWAPPING HAPPENS

File sharing networks have soared in popularity because they make it really easy to find tons of files and download multiple files at one time. File sharing networks, like FastTrack, eDonkey, and Gnutella, are easy, fast, and convenient, making them a natural choice for trading.

To use a file sharing network, you have to run a special program (called a *client*) on your computer. When you search for a particular file, the client scans the Internet to find other computers running the same client program. Once it finds them, your client scans the directories of the other client programs and gives you a list of files matching your search and the associated usernames the people whose computers contain the files (see Figure 1-3). When you ask to copy a file, your computer simply downloads that file from another computer.

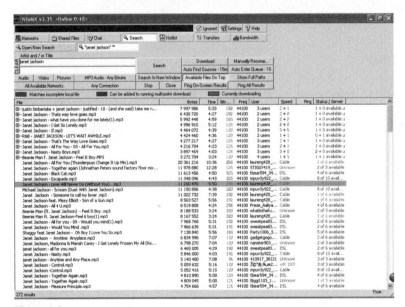

Figure 1-3

When you search for a file, your client program displays a list of files along with the usernames of the computers where the files can be found.

The size of the file sharing network constantly changes as people come and go. As a result, if you begin downloading a file from someone who then disconnects from the network, you may not get the file you want.

By the same token, the more people connected to a file sharing network, the more likely someone will have the song you want, but then you have the added problem of having so many more people trying to access the same files all at once.

Because file sharing networks are so easy to use, they're today's most common method for trading files. They are also the authorities' primary target, attracting lawsuits from recording industry and government authorities intent on shutting down the illegal flow of copyrighted materials.

TRADING FILES MANUALLY

Although most people trade files over the Internet because it's fast and convenient, you can still find people trading files the old-fashioned way by passing around copies of files manually. Although trading pirated files this way can be slow, it has huge side benefits: it's anonymous and more profitable.

At the simplest level, many people freely copy CDs or DVDs for their friends. While this is technically illegal, it's highly unlikely that the police will bust you for owning a single illegal DVD copy of *The Lord of the Rings*. People often "share" programs by passing a program's installation CD around an office so everyone can install the program on their computer.

CORPORATE PIRACY

On a somewhat larger scale, many businesses buy a single legal copy of a program and then install that program on multiple computers to save money. Such frugalness often backfires when a disgruntled employee notifies the authorities, and the company winds up getting fined for pirating software.

Want to punish your current employer? Try one of these:

Business Software Alliance (BSA)	888-NOPIRACY
Corel Corporation	888-761-6907
Macromedia	800-343-3325
Microsoft Anti-Piracy Hotline	800-R-U-LEGIT

SMALL-SCALE PIRACY

Of course, not everyone who uses pirated files may be aware of it. To entice people to buy a computer, many small computer dealers throw in free software worth hundreds of dollars, including the operating system (probably Microsoft Windows), antivirus programs, or office suites. Unfortunately, such copies may not be legitimate if they don't come with manuals, the original CDs, or a license with a registration number on it.

The computer dealer's only cost to copy and install these programs on a computer is the time it takes, unless they get caught. Customers buying computers with pirated software installed may believe that they're getting a bargain on legitimate software.

PIRACY FOR PROFIT

While loading pirated software on a computer may increase sales, the real money in piracy comes from selling counterfeit CDs or DVDs. Sophisticated counterfeiters often duplicate the CD or DVD graphics from the original disc and box, and then shrink-wrap the whole thing to lend it the appearance of legitimacy. Then they sell their counterfeit goods at flea markets, swap meets, subway stations, and online auctions, or even to unsuspecting dealers. Many software pirates are even so bold as to advertise their counterfeit goods by mail order or through a website. If someone offers to sell you anything that's priced way below the original retail price, be careful. Chances are good that what's being offered is a counterfeit CD or DVD.

Beyond the cost of actually buying the software (maybe) and duplicating it, such counterfeiters spend very little money, so they can sell their bogus copies well below the software's real retail price. Small-scale counterfeiting operations have snared thousands of dollars worth of illicit profits. Large-scale counterfeiting rings, often operating out of Asia, can earn millions in a single year.

As an alternative to selling pirated software, other people have jumped into the market selling registration key databases. (If you want to buy a CD full of registration keys for popular programs, visit http://www.hackerscatalog.com.)

Because registration key databases are just numbers and letters, the people who sell them aren't technically selling pirated software; it's up to you to pirate the software you want, look up the program name and version number in the registration key database, and then type the valid registration number into the program.

THE THIEVES' MINDSET

With such rampant file copying occurring on and off the Internet, you might wonder why people do it, if they know it's against the law. Of course, people break the speed limit, cheat on their taxes, and accept bribes for the same reason they might copy files illegally—because it's a low-risk, high-reward activity.

One reason some people copy files illegally is because they don't see their activities as harmful. When they copy a CD or give a duplicate to a friend, they don't see anyone getting hurt in the process. What they don't see are the copyright owners losing money every time someone copies a CD or DVD instead of buying a legitimate copy (assuming, of course, that they would have bought the pirated CD/DVD in the first place, which is not necessarily the case).

Beyond those who see copying as harmless and innocent, there are many more people who copy CDs and DVDs knowing full well that they're breaking the law. In some cases, they feel that the law is too restrictive or unfair. After all, if you buy a legitimate copy of a computer program stored on a CD, why shouldn't you be able to make multiple copies for backup purposes and install that same program on several different computers that you may use at work or at home?

Many people copy DVDs because they believe they have the right to make a backup copy in case their original DVD gets ruined. Some also copy them to get around the DVD region coding.

When manufacturers sell DVDs, they encode them to play only in DVD players within a certain region, such as North America or Europe. So if you buy a DVD in Asia and bring it home to North America, there's a chance that the DVD won't play at all. DVD manufacturers claim that regional coding reduces piracy, but customers complain that it hurts them even more. After all, why should someone buy two copies of the same DVD just to watch it on DVD players made by two different countries? So these people see no problem with copying a DVD that they may already own, just to get it to run in a different DVD player.

In the realm of music, people copy CDs for many reasons. Some just want to hear one hit single and won't spend $18 or more to buy an entire CD just to get the one song they want. Others believe that the recording industry has cheated consumers for years by conspiring to artificially inflate CD prices, so stealing music is a way to get back at the recording industry for all the millions they already stole from their customers.

While many musicians complain that music trading over the Internet cuts into their CD sales and royalties, many others make very little from the sales of a studio CD and instead earn the bulk of their income from concerts and merchandise sales. So to these musicians, swapping music doesn't steal from them; it steals from the record labels who are already stealing from the musicians anyway.

Older people may have vinyl records and may simply want to hear their favorite albums on their computer or through a portable MP3 player. Because they already bought the album once, they don't want to buy a second copy on a CD when they could just copy the music off the Internet instead. File sharing is also much more convenient than "burning" a CD from their vinyl album.

Sometimes people copy for more practical reasons: they can't find what they want on CD or DVD, so they have to resort to scouring the Internet to find the file they want. You can find music by the Rolling Stones or Elvis Presley practically everywhere. But if you want to find music by some obscure 18th-century composer, or ragtime melodies from the turn of the century, you may not be able to buy those songs no matter how much you're willing to pay. If you can't buy it, there's still a chance that you can steal it, and with the Internet's vast reach, there's also a good chance someone somewhere will have exactly what you want if you just know where to look.

A small minority of people collect copyrighted files from the Internet just because they can. Such collectors enjoy the thrill of getting the latest Hollywood blockbusters, recording artists' newest albums, or Microsoft's latest programs before anyone else has a copy. Such collectors relish the idea of having every song the Beatles ever recorded or every episode of the *Star Trek* TV series. Collectors rarely profit from their collections. They just enjoy the challenge of gathering the most complete collection possible for their particular sphere of interest.

Another class of file swappers have simply lost respect for copyright because corporations overuse it, stamping blanket copyright notices on anything they produce. Jason Mazzone recently lamented this practice in the Washington D.C.–based newspaper, *Legal Times* (http://www.legaltimes.biz):

> *False claims to copyright are everywhere. Copyright belongs to the author of a work and expires 70 years after the author's death. Yet copyright notices appear on modern reprints of Shakespeare's plays, Beethoven piano scores, and greeting card versions of Monet's water lilies. Corporations that sell to libraries microfilmed versions of early newspapers and other documents too old to be copyrighted routinely attach a copyright notice to their products.*

You can read the full article by Jason Mazzone, "Too Quick to Copyright," at http://www.brooklaw.edu/faculty/news/mazzone_legtimes_2003-11-17.pdf.

Countries also continually extend the length of copyright terms, leaving less and less material to fall into the public domain. And when software companies no longer sell software but "licenses" to use the software, many people feel that there's no longer a way to "own" something legally. So they resort to stealing the files they want from the Internet or their friends.

To save money, many college students swap pirated textbooks that have been electronically scanned. (And some students even get a copy of the test questions that come with the teacher's manual of a textbook and share those over the Internet as well.) In some countries, textbooks are often unavailable at any price, so piracy may be the only way to get a copy of a particular book.

There's a final reason why people copy files. It's easy, and chances are they'll never be caught. So if everybody's doing it, why shouldn't they?

In fact, there's a good chance that someone will scan this book into a PDF file and pass it around the Internet. While many people may copy this book without ever intending to buy it, a handful of people may be interested and willing to pay for the convenience of reading an actual printed book instead of reading it off a computer screen, so sometimes file sharing can be a free form of advertising as well.

2

THE PEER-TO-PEER FILE
SHARING NETWORKS

Between 1999 and 2001, Napster defined the entire world of peer-to-peer file sharing networks until lawsuits shut them down. Despite limiting trading only to audio files and forcing every user to access a central server to find the files they wanted (which allowed the authorities to shut down Napster just by shutting down this central server), Napster proved both the technical feasibility and popular acceptance of peer-to-peer file sharing networks for the masses.

Behind every great fortune there is a crime.

—Honoré de Balzac

While Napster (http://www.napster.com) has reincarnated itself as a legal, subscription-based file sharing service (see Chapter 16 for more information), the free-wheeling, rebellious spirit of file sharing lives on in a host of copycat networks struggling to define themselves in the void left by the original, free version of Napster (which was put out of business by lawsuits launched by the recording industry). With so many options available, there's sure to be one file sharing network that will appeal to you.

HOW FILE SHARING WORKS

The whole idea behind file sharing is to connect everyone in a network so that every computer can copy files from any other computer over the Internet. The types of files you share can be anything from programs and pictures to music and movies. If you can store it in a file, you can share it over a file sharing network.

To connect to one of the many file sharing networks available, you need a file sharing program. In technical terms, a file sharing program turns your computer into both a *client* and a *server*. As a client, your computer can search a file sharing network to find and copy files from any other computer on the network. As a server, your computer can provide files to anyone else on the network. Once you've installed a file sharing program on your computer, you're ready to start searching for files.

NOTE: *Visit See What You Share on P2P (http://www.seewhatyoushare.com) for a look at what people share online: everything from ordinary pictures to police reports to military records listing individual soldier's home and cell phone numbers.*

SEARCHING FOR A FILE

Searching for a file is like using a search engine on the Internet. At the simplest level, just type in a word or phrase that describes what you want to find, such as a song title or a musician's name, and the file sharing network returns a list of matching files, as shown in Figure 2-1.

Figure 2-1
Searching for a file can be as simple as typing in a song or artist name.

Unfortunately, if you type in a song title or artist name, you're likely to get a long list of irrelevant files. For example, searching for the music group Heart will also turn up songs from recording artists like Black Heart and Brave Heart; songs with names like "Broken Heart" and "Atom Heart Mother"; and even videos like "Wild at Heart." To avoid this problem, file sharing programs let you limit your search to specific types of files, such as audio or video, as shown in Figure 2-2.

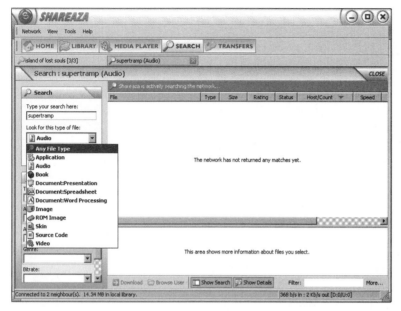

Figure 2-2
Many file sharing programs let you specify the type of file you want to search for, such as a
program or an audio file.

Once you've identified the specific file types you want (audio, video, programs,
and so on), you can enter more specific information, such as the name of the
recording artist and a specific album, as shown in Figure 2-3.

Once your file sharing program displays a list of files that match your
search criteria, you choose the files you want, and your computer starts transferring them across the network from some stranger's computer to yours.

That's the theory, anyway. The reality is that you may get cut off in the middle of a file transfer, especially if the person whose computer contains the file
you want suddenly turns their computer off. Other times, you may get the file you
want, only to find out that the file has been misnamed, so instead of seeing the
latest *Star Wars* trailer, you've really downloaded a pornographic movie instead.
Even worse, sometimes the file you get is exactly what you want, but the sound
or video quality is so poor that it's practically useless. When downloading files,
be prepared for a lot of frustration—but if you use a computer on a regular basis,
you should already be used to that.

Figure 2-3
You can narrow your search criteria to specific details,
such as the names of recording artists and albums.

LINKING TO A FILE

Besides poor-quality files, misnamed files, and files that contain only part of
what you really want, you also have to worry about bogus files that the recording
industry plants on file sharing networks to frustrate anyone who uses them. To
avoid these problems, many file sharing networks now provide another way to
download files—*hash links*.

    File sharing networks (several of which are discussed in "The Different
File Sharing Networks" section that follows) tend to support different types of
hash links:

ed2k links	eDonkey2000 network
.torrent links	BitTorrent network
Sig2dat links	FastTrack network
Magnet links	Gnutella network and newer versions of Kazaa

Basically, a hash link uses a file's contents and size to generate a mathematical result that uniquely identifies that particular file. Once someone calculates
this mathematical value for a file, they post a link to the file on a website. When
people visit that web page and click the hash link, the hash link loads up a file
sharing program and starts downloading the desired file.

Hash links offer two huge advantages to the file sharing community. First, listing hash links isn't illegal, because websites aren't offering any copyrighted information for downloading; they're just providing links to copyrighted files that someone else's computer may be holding. Second, hash links verify that you're getting the file you really want and not some misnamed or deliberately altered bogus file instead.

Many websites specialize in listing hash links for unique files, such as the following:

The Asia Cinema Forum (http://www.acfmovies.com)
Asian movies

IMAXmovies (http://www.imaxmovies.tk)
IMAX films

ShareTV (http://www.sharetv.net)
Old episodes from television shows, like *Six Feet Under* and *M*A*S*H*

ShareMonkey (http://www.sharemonkey.com)
Music, movies, video games, and software

Isoheaven (http://www.isoheaven.com)
Movies, television shows, and video games

To find more websites that offer hash links, visit one of the following hash link search engines:

FileDonkey	http://www.filedonkey.com
isoHunt	http://s1.isohunt.com
Whatabig	http://www.whatabig.com

So the next time you're searching for a file, you can search for a particular file by name or visit a website that lists hash links. But be quick about it. Despite the legal "gray area" in posting hash links, the government did step in and shut down one of the earliest and largest hash link websites called ShareReactor. Don't be too surprised if, by the time you get to a hash link website, the authorities have already shut it down.

THE DIFFERENT FILE SHARING NETWORKS

When it comes to file sharing, there are the networks themselves, and there are the programs that actually run on your computer (the client programs). A file sharing network is like a television network, while a client program is like a television that tunes in only to a particular network. Each file sharing network has its own dedicated client program; if you want to use the FastTrack file sharing network, you need to use the Kazaa client. The client is what you use to search for and download files from the file sharing network.

Because the file sharing networks don't share files among themselves, your chances of finding a particular file are much better if you tap into one of the larger networks or use multiple clients to tap into multiple networks. (Just don't run two client programs that use the same network, or you'll just be searching the same network twice.) Here are some of the more popular file sharing networks:

- Gnutella and Gnutella2 (G2)

- FastTrack

- eDonkey and Overnet

- DirectConnect

- MP2P

NOTE: Be careful when choosing a client program to tap into a file sharing network. Many client programs are free but come loaded with adware or spyware programs that may bombard you with pop-up ads or track your movements on the Internet.

THE GNUTELLA AND GNUTELLA2 (G2) NETWORKS

Gnutella emerged shortly after the demise of the original Napster. Napster's fatal flaw was relying on a central server to connect computers together, as shown in Figure 2-4. By shutting down this central server, the authorities managed to shut down the entire Napster network.

To prevent this from happening again, Gnutella eliminated the central server and created a completely decentralized network where all computers on the network could communicate directly with each other, as shown in Figure 2-5. Unlike Napster, every computer on the Gnutella network can work independently, so shutting down one computer can never kill the entire network.

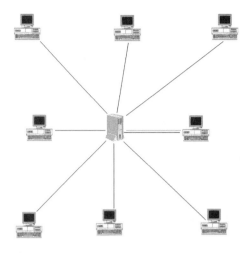

Figure 2-4
When searching on Napster, every file request first had to go
through a central server, which could be shut down.

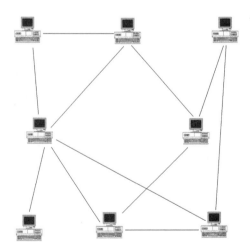

Figure 2-5
When searching on Gnutella, every file request goes through
every computer connected to the Gnutella network. This
makes it impossible for the authorities to shut down the entire
network just by removing a single computer.

Gnutella improved upon Napster in another way. While Napster allowed people to share only music files with each other, Gnutella allows people to share all types of files, including music, videos, pictures, and programs.

Strangely enough, the Gnutella network owes part of its existence to the unwitting generosity of America Online, which purchased Nullsoft, publishers of the popular Winamp MP3 player. The programmers at Nullsoft examined Napster's flaws and created the Gnutella network as an alternative, which they named after a combination of GNU and Nutella, the chocolate-hazelnut spread.

When Nullsoft posted the source code to Gnutella on its website on March 14, 2000, America Online yanked the program within hours, but more than 10,000 people had already downloaded copies and spread them across the Internet. Other programmers studied the way Gnutella worked and created their own client programs to access the Gnutella network. By releasing the source code to Gnutella, Nullsoft's programmers ensured that the Gnutella network would continue to thrive and develop without the need for further intervention and support from the original programmers. As a result, more file sharing programs tap into the Gnutella network than any other file sharing network in the world.

Gnutella is one of the oldest, largest, and most popular of the file sharing networks, but searching it can be slow. When you request a file, your request goes through every computer connected to the Gnutella network, and they can number in the thousands. Still, many client programs tap into Gnutella for its vast library of file sharing offerings (see Figure 2-6). The following are some popular Gnutella client programs:

Morpheus	http://www.morpheus.com
BearShare	http://www.bearshare.com
Acquisition	http://www.acquisitionx.com
LimeWire	http://www.limewire.com
FreeWire	http://www.freewirep2p.com
Deepnet Explorer	http://www.deepnetexplorer.com
XoloX	http://www.xolox.nl

NOTE: For a current list of Gnutella clients, visit http://www.gnutelliums.com or http://www.gnutella.com/connect.

Figure 2-6

The LimeWire client is just one of many clients that can connect to the Gnutella network.

Once Gnutella had been running for a while, people began to notice some problems. The more computers that were connected to Gnutella, the slower file searches got, because every file request had to go through each computer. Having to constantly deal with file requests from other computers meant that each computer wasted much of its time processing requests.

To improve upon Gnutella, a programmer designed a new network, based on Gnutella, but dubbed Gnutella2 or G2 (http://www.gnutella2.com). Like the original Gnutella, Gnutella2 remains open source, so anyone can create a client to connect to Gnutella2. The latest version of Morpheus can now connect to both the original Gnutella and the newer Gnutella2 networks. The following clients can connect to both Gnutella and Gnutella2:

Kiwi Alpha	http://www.kiwialpha.com
Gnucleus	http://www.gnucleus.com
Shareaza	http://www.shareaza.com (also connects to BitTorrent and eDonkey2000)

THE FASTTRACK NETWORK

While Gnutella offers an open source network that allows anyone to connect, FastTrack is a closed, proprietary network that only a limited number of clients can access: Kazaa (in various versions), iMesh, and Grokster, as shown in Figure 2-7.

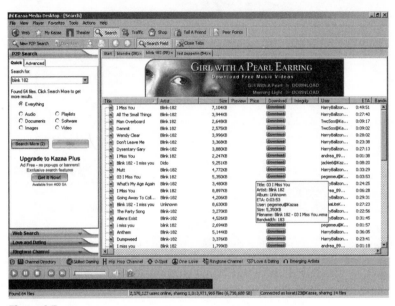

Figure 2-7
Kazaa is one of the most popular, and most sued, file sharing programs in the world.

A Dutch company, called Kazaa BV, created FastTrack shortly before the demise of the original Napster. Based partially on the open source Gnutella protocol, FastTrack improves upon Gnutella by speeding up file searching.

Rather than search every computer for a file like the Gnutella network does, FastTrack routes every file request through *Supernodes* (shown in Figure 2-8). Supernodes essentially divide the larger network into smaller ones, so searching occurs much more quickly—each Supernode only has to search part of the network. Once a Supernode finds your file, it connects you to that particular computer so you can download the file.

FastTrack also introduced two other innovations: the ability to resume interrupted downloads and the ability to download a file from multiple sources, both of which can prove especially useful for downloading massive files, such as full-length movies. Finally, FastTrack's protocol included encryption, which meant that if anyone wanted to create a client program to connect to FastTrack, they had to pay a license fee. Upon its release, FastTrack quickly ran afoul of the recording industry, who successfully sued Kazaa BV. The company soon sold the rights to the FastTrack network to a collection of offshore companies, where the main investor was an Australian company called Sharman Networks.

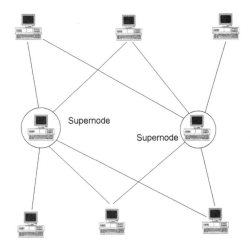

Figure 2-8
FastTrack uses Supernodes, which divide a large network into several smaller ones to speed up file searching.

Further problems occurred between FastTrack's new owners, Sharman Networks, and the file sharing client Morpheus. When Morpheus refused to pay the licensing fee to stay connected to FastTrack, Sharman Networks rewrote the encryption protocol, effectively shutting out millions of Morpheus users. In retaliation, Morpheus rewrote its client to connect to the Gnutella network instead.

As the most popular file sharing network, FastTrack's popularity has also made it the number one target of the recording industry. Not only does the recording industry prowl around the FastTrack network, ready to serve subpoenas to people sharing large numbers of files, but they also flood the FastTrack network with bogus files to discourage people from using FastTrack at all. If you use FastTrack, you're more likely to be sued by the recording industry than if you use a less popular file sharing network.

Despite these problems, the growing popularity of the FastTrack network means that you can probably find a file on this network that you might not find on any other network. Just be aware that the following "official" FastTrack clients come loaded with spyware that can replace your home web page and bombard you with a flurry of pop-up ads:

Kazaa	http://www.kazaa.com
Grokster	http://www.grokster.com
iMesh	http://www.imesh.com

For a while, anyone who wanted to connect to FastTrack without getting bombarded by pop-up ads used an unauthorized program dubbed Kazaa Lite. Kazaa Lite offered the same features as Kazaa, but without the intrusive *adware* and *spyware*. (Technically, adware just feeds your computer with a constant stream of advertisements, while spyware keeps track of websites you visit and secretly feeds this information to another computer without your knowledge.)

Naturally the copyright owner of Kazaa, Sharman Networks, wasn't too pleased with Kazaa Lite, because Kazaa Lite could still use FastTrack while avoiding the advertising that supports the network. Sharman Networks periodically changed the encryption method needed to connect to FastTrack, but with a little reprogramming, Kazaa Lite kept getting reconnected again. For Kazaa, which makes its money by allowing people to trade copyrighted files illegally, to threaten Kazaa Lite with violating their copyright to the FastTrack network seems just a little bit ironic.

To use Kazaa without the advertising, grab a copy of Diet K (http://www.dietk.com), a free add-on program that strips away the advertising embedded in Kazaa. While Sharman Networks can periodically change encryption methods to lock out Kazaa Lite users, they can't lock out anyone using Diet K, because they're still using Kazaa.

Two additional ad-free, unauthorized FastTrack clients are Mammoth (http://mammoth.sourceforge.net) and iMesh Light (http://www.imesh-light.com). While Mammoth is an open source project, iMesh Light is a version of iMesh but with the adware stripped away.

Because FastTrack remains proprietary, programmers have created an open source alternative dubbed OpenFT (http://gift.sourceforge.net). Despite their similarities, OpenFT is a separate file sharing network from FastTrack, so if you want the features of FastTrack but without the adware and spyware embedded in Kazaa, you might want to rely on OpenFT instead.

THE EDONKEY2000 AND OVERNET NETWORKS

Although Gnutella and FastTrack allow people to swap any type of file, the most popular files are usually music files that contain individual songs. While you can still find individual songs over the eDonkey2000 (often abbreviated as ed2k) and Overnet networks, you're much more likely to find files that contain movies, complete albums, video games, pirated software, and ISO disc images (which capture the contents of an entire CD in a single file), as shown in Figure 2-9.

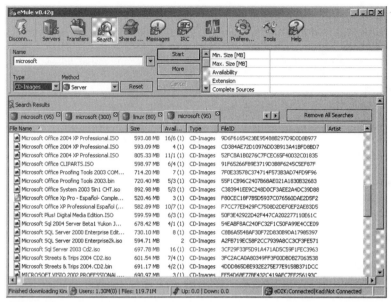

Figure 2-9

A quick search on the eDonkey network reveals plenty of CD images of popular Microsoft programs, including Office 2004, SQL Server, and Streets & Trips.

What makes both eDonkey and Overnet popular for sharing large files is their ability to download a file from multiple sources. By downloading a file from multiple sources, both eDonkey and Overnet ensure that if one computer with your desired file disconnects from the network, you can still download the rest of that same file right away from another computer.

To avoid the confusion caused by similarly named files, both networks examine the contents and size of each file and create a unique calculation known as a *hash checksum*. This checksum helps identify identical files that may appear on the network under different file names. That way you won't waste time downloading a movie like *The Matrix* only to find out that it's really a misnamed file of another movie called *Threat Matrix*.

To improve the sharing of large files, both eDonkey and Overnet allow you to start sharing a file before you've completely downloaded it. So if you're downloading a 400MB file, you can start sharing it as soon as you receive just part of that file. Anyone copying that file off your computer may receive their file at nearly the same time that you do without having to wait until you download the complete file first.

Despite their different names, the same people designed both the eDonkey and Overnet networks. The main difference is that eDonkey relies on a central server (much like the original Napster did) while Overnet does not.

Overnet can connect to both the Overnet and eDonkey networks. However, with eDonkey's growing popularity, Overnet's technology is gradually being phased into eDonkey.

Here are some popular client programs for accessing the eDonkey network:

OneMX	http://www.onemx.com
eMule	http://www.emule-project.net
eDonkey	http://www.edonkey2000.com

To access the Overnet network, just use the official Overnet client program (http://www.overnet.com).

THE DIRECTCONNECT NETWORK

Unlike the Gnutella and FastTrack networks, the DirectConnect network is more of a loose collection of central servers than a single unified network. Instead of sharing files among themselves, each server only shares files with people who connect directly to that particular server (hence the network's name). Figure 2-10 shows a list of servers as seen within the DC++ client.

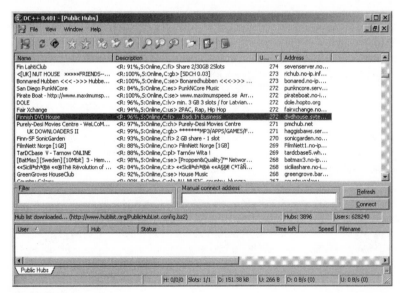

Figure 2-10
Before you can share files over the DirectConnect network, you must find a server that will grant you access to the network.

Each DirectConnect server runs more like a private clubhouse that sets its own rules for who can get access and what trading ratio you need to meet before you're allowed to download anything. Typically, most DirectConnect servers won't grant you access unless you agree to share a minimum volume of files, such as 10GB or 20GB. So before you can connect to a DirectConnect server and start sharing files, you must have a library of files to share.

By allowing anyone to create their own server, DirectConnect gives users the chance to specialize in certain types of files, such as jazz MP3 files or black-and-white, silent, full-length movies. Once you find a favorite server that provides the type of files you want, DirectConnect can be much easier to use than other types of networks. As a novice to DirectConnect, though, you'll have to spend some time browsing through different servers until you find the ones that you like best. Plus, you'll need to amass a collection of files to share, just to get access to any DirectConnect server.

Three programs for connecting to the DirectConnect network include:

DirectConnect	http://www.neo-modus.com
DC++	http://dcplusplus.sourceforge.net
DCGui	http://dcgui.berlios.de

THE MP2P NETWORK

While other networks offer video, program, and graphic files, the Manolito P2P (MP2P) network originally focused on nothing but MP3 music files. If all you want to find is music, then you'll find the Manolito network is a treasure trove for finding rare and bootleg music that you probably won't find anywhere else. Although people have recently started sharing other types of files besides music over this network, MP3 music files still dominate the file offerings.

While most file sharing networks have only one official client program, the MP2P network actually has three official clients, although Piolet (shown in Figure 2-11) doesn't come bogged down with adware like the other two clients, Blubster and Rockitnet:

Blubster	http://www.blubster.com
Piolet	http://www.piolet.com
Rockitnet	http://www.rockitnet.com

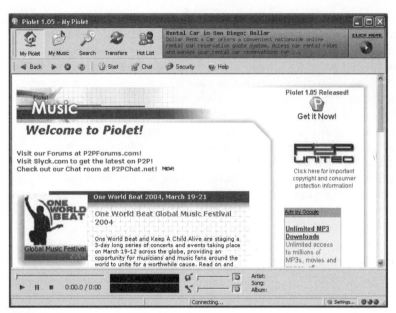

Figure 2-11
Piolet is advertiser-supported, but the ads only appear in a banner within the program; they're
not embedded in hard-to-remove adware.

ADDITIONAL FILE SHARING FEATURES

With so many different client programs available to tap into the same file sharing networks, each client program may offer different features to entice people
to use their program instead. Some client programs claim faster searching and
downloading. Others include a built-in media player, so you can play your downloaded files immediately without having to load a separate media player, such as
iTunes or Windows Media Player.

Other client programs offer parental controls to limit your kids from searching for specific words (and finding certain types of files to download, such as
pornography), file shredders to destroy all traces of a downloaded file after you
delete it (to prevent the authorities from examining your hard disk to see what
copyrighted files you might have copied in the past), and proxy server access,
so you can connect to a file sharing network through another computer (called a
proxy) to help mask your IP address.

Some other popular features to look for in a client program include the
absence of adware and spyware, the ability to access multiple file sharing networks, and anonymity while you are connected to a file sharing network.

ADWARE VS. FREEWARE

Creators of file sharing networks have a dilemma. On the one hand, they want to give their client programs away for free to encourage as many people as possible to use it and join. On the other hand, they also need to find a way to make a profit. So to compensate for giving away software for free, many companies create client programs that include *adware*, also known by the more insidious name *spyware*.

The idea is that when you install a free program such as a file sharing client program, you also agree to install the companion adware or spyware programs. By selling advertising, software companies can continue to give away their client programs for free and still make money. (Once you install adware/spyware on your computer, you may suddenly notice pop-up ads springing up on your screen whether you're using the file sharing network or not.)

To help you determine whether a particular client program comes embedded with adware or spyware, visit Spyware Info (http://www.spywareinfo. com/articles/p2p). Before installing a client program, browse its website to see if it reveals whether it's freeware or advertisement-sponsored. You can often detect adware/spyware in a client program during the installation program because a screen will pop up and ask if you agree to install and run a program to display ads, as shown in Figure 2-12.

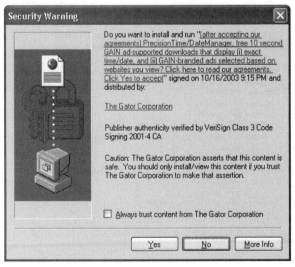

Figure 2-12
If a screen pops up and asks if you want to install additional software besides a client program for a network, chances are good that you'll be installing adware/spyware.

Most people accept adware/spyware as the price they need to pay for using a particular file sharing network, but now that you know you can find free client programs without adware/spyware, you should use those alternatives instead, unless you enjoy getting bombarded with pop-up ads whenever you use your computer.

MULTINETWORK ACCESS

Most client programs can connect to only one file sharing network, so if you can't find a particular file on one file sharing network, you often have to run a second or a third client program to access a different network. To avoid this inconvenience, a handful of client programs offer the ability to access multiple file sharing networks, as shown in Figure 2-13. This means you can use a single client program to search for a file, no matter which file sharing network it may be stored on.

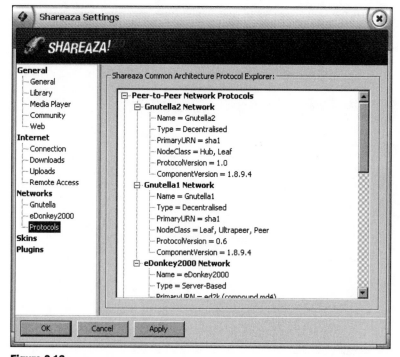

Figure 2-13
Programs like Shareaza can connect to multiple file sharing networks, such as Gnutella and eDonkey2000.

Here are some popular multinetwork client programs:

MLdonkey (http://www.nongnu.org/mldonkey)   Accesses Gnutella, Gnutella2, OpenNap, FastTrack, Overnet, and DirectConnect

giFT (http://sourceforge.net/projects/gift)   Accesses FastTrack, OpenFT, and Gnutella

Poisoned (http://gottsilla.net)   Accesses Gnutella, FastTrack, and OpenFT

iSwipe (http://www.hillmanminx.net/iswipe)   Accesses Gnutella, FastTrack, OpenNap, and OpenFT

Shareaza (http://www.shareaza.com)   Accesses Gnutella, Gnutella2, eDonkey2000, and BitTorrent

One problem with multinetwork client programs is that they may not offer all the features that a client program that is specifically designed for one file sharing network might offer. While not as well known as dedicated client programs like Kazaa or Morpheus, multinetwork client programs probably represent the future of file sharing clients, given their reach across multiple networks, which greatly increases the chance that you'll find the file you want.

ANONYMITY AND ENCRYPTION

File sharing by itself isn't illegal; it's what people trade that could be illegal. With the recording industry and government authorities cracking down on people trading copyrighted files, many client programs offer special anonymity and encryption features to mask your IP address so nobody can trace you. To ensure anonymity, these more specialized client programs rely on their own file sharing networks, which means that they aren't as popular, so the file selection isn't as great as the older, more established networks such as FastTrack or Gnutella.

Filetopia (http://www.filetopia.org), EarthStation 5 (http://www.es5.com), and Mnet (http://mnet.sourceforge.net) rely on encryption to keep others from detecting what types of files you may be trading, as shown in Figure 2-14. Encryption can mask either your IP address or the type of files you're sharing. Just remember that there is no such thing as true anonymity over the Internet; encryption makes users more difficult to identify, but not impossible.

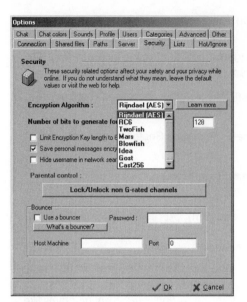

Figure 2-14
A program like Filetopia offers different ways to encrypt
your information from prying eyes.

SPECIALIZED FILE SHARING NETWORKS

In the computer world, nothing stays the same for long, and peer-to-peer technology is no different. Although FastTrack and Gnutella may be two popular file
sharing networks right now, there's no guarantee that another file sharing network won't suddenly surge in popularity and push more established file sharing
networks into the background. So if you're the adventurous type who wants to
explore some of the smaller and newer file sharing networks, take some time to
experiment with the file sharing networks listed in this section.

UP-AND-COMING FILE SHARING NETWORKS

For an alternative file sharing network, take a peek at Soulseek (http://www.
slsknet.org), which specializes in sharing complete music albums. Soulseek
is completely free, and it doesn't secretly install adware on your computer. To
make money, the publishers of Soulseek offer a unique incentive: the more
money you donate, the closer you get to the front of the line when waiting to
download files.

BitTorrent (http://bitconjurer.org/bittorrent) specializes in distributing large files, such as full-length movies, to multiple people. Like an ordinary file sharing network, BitTorrent allows someone to post a large file for many different people to download. To speed up the downloading process, when multiple users download the same file, BitTorrent gives each user a different part of the file. Once everyone has downloaded a different part of the same file, BitTorrent redirects them to download the other parts of the file from other users. By spreading the file sharing process among multiple users, everyone can download a single large file quickly with less risk of getting cut off before they can download the entire file from a single computer.

Another programmer created MUTE (http://mute-net.sourceforge.net) after watching how ants scatter and regroup when disturbed, yet always manage to reach their final destination. MUTE applies the same theory as BitTorrent to file sharing. Instead of directly linking two computers to swap files, the MUTE network routes pieces of the files through several computers before they reach their destination. MUTE works much like spreading a message through a crowded room: if you give the message to seven people, and they spread the message to seven more, and so on, the message eventually reaches the right person.

In order for the recording industry to keep track of who's sending and receiving what file, they would have to monitor every single computer on the MUTE network, carefully tracing each piece of the file as it moves from computer to computer before reaching its final destination. MUTE remains optimized for smaller networks to preserve speed, but it shows how programmers are applying more sophisticated construction techniques to preserve user privacy.

Sometimes a client program starts out on an established network, but then decides to break away to form its own private network instead, whether for political or technical reasons. WinMX (http://www.winmx.com) originally connected to the OpenNap network, which was an open source version of the original Napster network. When the recording industry started shutting down OpenNap, WinMX slipped away, formed its own network, and continues to thrive to this day.

Ares (http://www.aresgalaxy.org) originally connected to the Gnutella network and then realized that Gnutella's technical limitations would also limit the future of Ares, so Ares broke away and created its own network, too. Some unique features that Ares offers include the ability to deal with interrupted file downloads (Ares just starts downloading the missing parts of a file rather than forcing you to download the whole thing over again) and multisource downloads (so you can download the file you want as quickly as possible).

BUILDING YOUR OWN NETWORK

Whether you use an old or a new file sharing network, there's always the danger that government authorities may be secretly monitoring your activities. While a handful of file sharing networks use encryption to hide the types of files you've shared, and proxy servers to mask your IP address, nothing is foolproof. So rather than risk trading files among any of these public file sharing networks, why not start a private file sharing network instead?

With a private file sharing network, you can control who can join and who can't, so you can swap files of any type within your trusted circle of friends and coworkers (without any possible snooping by government authorities or recording industry infiltrators).

If you already chat with friends through ICQ, you can use a program like ICQ File Share (http://www.npssoftware.com) to swap files with your ICQ chat buddies. If you don't use ICQ, try one of these instead:

BigSpeed	http://www.bigspeed.net
Aimini	http://www.aimini.com
HotP2P	http://playapp.com/hotp2p

Perhaps the most intriguing private file sharing network is one created by Nullsoft, the company that created the Gnutella file sharing network. Just like they did when they released Gnutella over the Internet, Nullsoft once again managed to irk its parent company, America Online, when it posted a program dubbed WASTE (http://grazzy.mjoelkbar.net/waste/mirror), which allows users to set up private file sharing networks with encrypted file transfers. Named after an underground postal system in the Thomas Pynchon novel *The Crying of Lot 49*, WASTE combined private file sharing networks with encryption. This combination pretty much ensured that even government authorities couldn't snoop on a WASTE network without a great deal of difficulty in locating the network in the first place, and then cracking the encryption once they found the network.

Not surprisingly, America Online quickly yanked WASTE off Nullsoft's website, but other programmers had already taken the WASTE source code and are likely to create alternatives and variations. Now if you visit Nullsoft's website, you'll see the following dire warning:

NOTICE OF UNAUTHORIZED SOFTWARE

An unauthorized copy of Nullsoft's copyrighted software was briefly posted on this website on or about Wednesday May 28, 2003. The software was identified as "WASTE" (the

"Software") and includes the files "waste-setup.exe", "waste-source.zip", "waste-source.tar.gz" and any additional files contained in these files.

Nullsoft is the exclusive owner of all right, title and interest in the Software. The posting of the Software on this website was not authorized by Nullsoft.

If you downloaded or otherwise obtained a copy of the Software, you acquired no lawful rights to the Software and must destroy any and all copies of the Software, including by deleting it from your computer. Any license that you may believe you acquired with the Software is void, revoked and terminated.

Any reproduction, distribution, display or other use of the Software by you is unauthorized and an infringement of Nullsoft's copyright in the Software as well as a potential violation of other laws.

Thank you.

Nullsoft

Although you can find plenty of files on websites, FTP sites, and newsgroups, most people are likely to find file sharing networks easier and faster to use. To maximize your chances of finding a particular file, connect to the more popular file sharing networks along with some of the smaller, less popular ones, as well. Chances are good that the next time you want to find a certain file on the Internet, the first place you'll look will be through a file sharing network.

3

NAVIGATING NEWSGROUPS

Before the Web offered point-and-click access to information, Internet users shared information through Usenet (Unix User Network or Users Network) newsgroups. Newsgroups provided a place to swap scholarly talk about mostly academic and scientific topics, but eventually people created two previously vetoed newsgroups: "Sex" and "Drugs." To complete the trilogy, a programmer named Brian Reid added a third newsgroup called "Rock and Roll":

We live in a rainbow of Chaos.

—Paul Cézanne

```
From: mejac!decwrl!reid (Brian Reid)
Message-Id: <8804040154.AA01236@woodpecker.dec.com>
Date:  3 Apr 1988 1754-PST (Sunday)
To: backbone@purdue.edu, chiefdan@vax1.acs.udel.edu, hoptoad!gnu
Subject: Re: soc.sex final results
In-Reply-To: Gene Spafford <spaf@purdue.edu> / Sun, 03 Apr 88 18:22:36 EST.
          <8804032322.AA15650@arthur.cs.purdue.edu>
To end the suspense, I have just created alt.sex
That meant that the alt network now carried alt.sex and alt.drugs.
It was therefore artistically necessary to create alt.rock-n-roll,
which I have also done. I have no idea what sort of traffic it
will carry. If the bizzarroids take it over I will rmgroup it or
moderate it; otherwise I will let it be.
Brian Reid
T5 (5th thoracic)
```

To some Internet historians, the creation of these three "alternative" newsgroups sparked the beginning of anarchy within the previously tame world of newsgroups. Unlike the traditional newsgroups, which offer academic or friendly discussions, many alternative newsgroups skirt the boundaries of the law, letting people swap everything from copyrighted audio and video files to live viruses and hacking tools. Because of the relatively underground nature of these alternative newsgroups, you can often find rare bootleg recordings of your favorite artists lurking around newsgroups that you might never find anywhere else on the Internet.

GETTING STARTED WITH NEWSGROUPS

Usenet offers more than 50,000 different newsgroups to choose from, but before you can read them, let alone download any files from them, you need the following:

- A newsgroup server (which most Internet service providers offer free with your Internet service)

- A newsgroup reader program (such as Thunderbird, free from http://www.mozilla.org)

- A subscription to one or more newsgroups (these are free)

CHOOSING A NEWSGROUP SERVER

A newsgroup server is simply a computer that constantly adds, deletes, and updates messages from all over the Internet. When you connect your computer to the newsgroup server computer, you can start downloading files or exchanging messages with other people.

Newsgroup servers aren't hard to find. Most ISPs run their own newsgroup servers, so if you have your own Internet service, you probably already have free access to newsgroups. However, the quality differs widely among different servers.

For instance, very few ISPs carry every available newsgroup. Some won't carry newsgroups that offer blatantly pornographic images, while others filter out newsgroups where people regularly engage in heavy file sharing. When viewing the newsgroups that your ISP offers, be aware that you're not seeing every available newsgroup—just the ones your particular ISP happens to carry.

Another issue is the server's *retention rate*. A newsgroup is like a constantly flowing river of uploaded files and messages. Servers that keep a large chunk of this river available have a *high* retention rate—files may remain for several weeks or months before being deleted to make room for newer ones.

Servers that just offer a recent portion of the newsgroup content, by contrast, have a *low* retention rate, so the files may only be available for a few hours or a day or two at the most. The higher the retention rate, the greater your chances of finding the files you want to download.

To improve the quality of their newsgroup access, serious newsgroup users often subscribe to special newsgroup servers that charge a fee, but offer access to a larger number of newsgroups, unlimited file downloading, high retention rates, fast and reliable service, and spam filtering so your newsgroups don't get overwhelmed with irrelevant ads and messages. (Like email, spam clogs many newsgroups.) When examining the following news servers, check their current prices, retention rates, and file transfer speed to find the one that's best for you:

Anonymousnewsfeed.com	http://www.anonymousnewsfeed.com
Binaries.net	http://www.binaries.net
Newsfeeds.com	http://www.newsfeeds.com
Newscene	http://www.newscene.com
NuthinButNews.com	http://www.nuthinbutnews.com
Supernews	http://www.supernews.com
Tera News	http://www.teranews.com
UseNetServer	http://www.usenetserver.com
Usenet.com	http://www.usenet.com

While most news servers carry a similar variety of newsgroups, some specialize in adult content that other ISP newsgroup servers won't offer, as shown in Figure 3-1:

Adult Newsgroup Service	http://www.adult-news.to
Gigantic Usenet Binaries Archive	http://www.guba.com
The Usenet Binaries Newsreader	http://www.usenetbinaries.com
XXX-News	http://www.xxx-news.to

Figure 3-1
Some newsgroup servers specialize in newsgroups that offer X-rated pictures and videos.

With so many newsgroup servers to choose from, you're certain to find one with the features you need. To keep up with the latest on various news servers, visit SMR-Usenet (http://www.smr-usenet.com) or Slyck (http://www.slyck.com) for reviews and comments about particular ones.

SMR-Usenet provides newsgroup tutorials and information about different newsgroup servers, such as a listing of the fastest servers and price comparisons of popular newsgroup servers. Slyck provides tutorials and information about file sharing that focuses on both file sharing networks and newsgroups (see Figure 3-2).

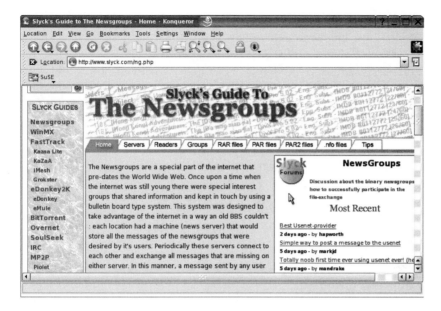

Figure 3-2
The Slyck website offers tips, tutorials, and hints for grabbing files from both newsgroups and file sharing networks.

SELECTING A NEWSGROUP READER

Most email programs can read information on newsgroups in addition to email, so if you have Outlook Express, you already have a primitive newsgroup reader. Most full-featured browsers, like Opera (http://www.opera.com) and Mozilla (http://www.mozilla.org), also have limited, built-in newsgroup readers. Mozilla also offers a free, separate email/newsgroup reader called Thunderbird, which you can download from the Mozilla website, too. However, these programs are designed more for exchanging messages on newsgroups, not swapping files. If you plan to do some serious downloading from newsgroups, you'll definitely want a dedicated newsgroup reader, instead.

Dedicated newsgroup readers, like GrabIt, shown in Figure 3-3, offer: point-and-click downloading (missing from the simple newsreaders), as well as scheduling (which tells your computer to access certain newsgroups at specific times), specialized file searching (to help you search newsgroups for particular MP3s), and multisession access (which allows your computer to connect to multiple news servers to ensure speed and reliability when downloading large files, such as movies). Here are some popular Windows newsreader programs:

Agent	http://www.forteinc.com
Binary Boy	http://www.binaryboy.com
GrabIt	http://www.shemes.com
Pluckit	http://www.pluckit.com
TIFNY	http://www.tifny.com

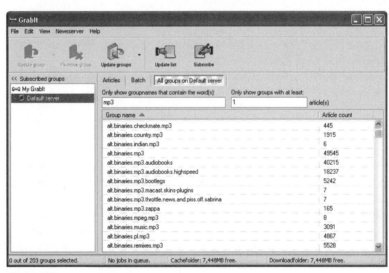

Figure 3-3
GrabIt can help you find and download files from a newsgroup.

SUBSCRIBING TO A NEWSGROUP

To start accessing newsgroups, you simply tell your newsreader the name of the newsgroup server you want to visit (such as news.ispname.com). To do this, you typically have to click the Tools menu and then click Account Settings or Account Options, and then enter the specific newsgroup server name to use, as shown in Figure 3-4.

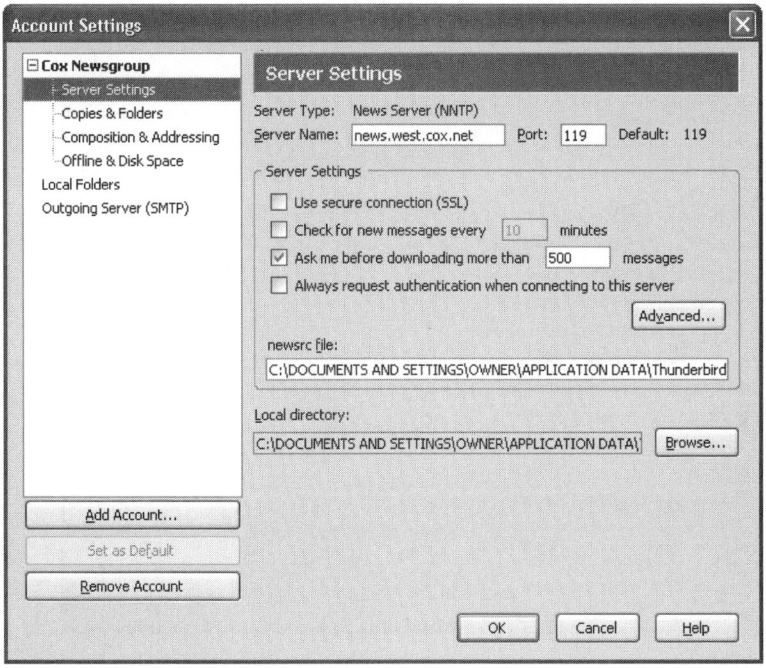

Figure 3-4
Most newsgroup readers let you specify the newsgroup server name in a dialog box that you can access with the Account Settings or Account Options command in the Tools menu.

Once you're connected, your newsgroup reader will show you every possible newsgroup available through that particular newsgroup server. (Just remember that your newsgroup reader only displays the newsgroups carried by the server you're connecting to, not every possible newsgroup available on the Internet.) Few people have time to search through 50,000 newsgroups, so tell your news-reader to list only those newsgroups with specific words in their name, such as "sounds." That way your newsgroup reader only shows newsgroups like alt.binaries.sounds.mp3.pop or alt.binaries.sounds.country.mp3, as shown in Figure 3-5.

Once you've narrowed down your list of newsgroups to the ones that seem interesting, you can choose which ones you want to access. While you can read messages and download files from a newsgroup without subscribing to it, many people subscribe to their favorite ones in order to track the different messages posted over time.

If you get tired of a newsgroup and don't want to read its messages any more, simply unsubscribe from it.

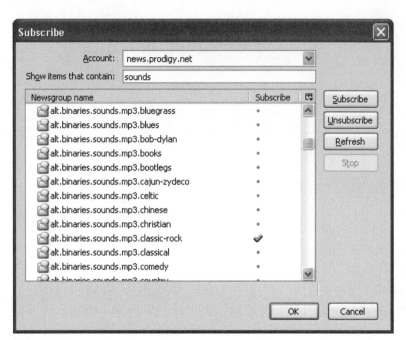

Figure 3-5
By searching for specific words in a newsgroup name, you can get a shortened list of newsgroups that you might want to subscribe to.

FINDING FILES IN NEWSGROUPS

To find specific types of files, visit Bincrawler (http://www.bincrawler.com),
a specialized search engine that helps you find files buried within different
newsgroups.

Besides using a newsgroup search engine like Bincrawler, you can also
browse through individual newsgroups manually. You can find newsgroups that
specialize in audio files, video files, pirated software, pornography, and so on.

For example, the easiest place to find and download music is in the alt.
binaries.sounds.mp3 newsgroup. The reason for this is *crossposting*, which
means that a single file can appear in multiple newsgroups.

Normally, people post songs in one newsgroup, such as posting Iron
Butterfly songs in the alt.binaries.sounds.mp3.1960s newsgroup. One problem
with posting files in a single newsgroup, though, is that some people might not
know that certain newsgroups even exist. For example, you may search the alt.
binaries.sounds.mp3.1980s newsgroup and never find your favorite Billy Joel

songs, only to realize that an entire library of Billy Joel songs is available in the alt.binaries.sounds.billy.joel newsgroup, instead.

To increase the chances that people will find the files they want, many people crosspost any files they upload, which simply means that they post the same file in multiple newsgroups. So instead of just choosing a single newsgroup to post a file to, crossposting means you type multiple newsgroup names, separated by a comma, as shown in Figure 3-6. Crossposting ensures that nearly every song posted in a newsgroup will eventually appear in the alt. binaries.sounds.mp3s newsgroup, as well as in more specialized newsgroups.

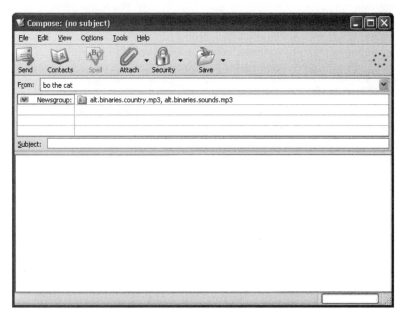

Figure 3-6
To crosspost a file, type the names of two or more newsgroups, each separated from the next by a comma.

Unfortunately, the alt.binaries.sounds.mp3s newsgroup is so popular that files rarely stay online for more than a few days. If you don't visit the alt.binaries. sounds.mp3s newsgroup within a few days of somebody posting your desired file, the server may have automatically deleted that file to make room for newer ones.

So when you are searching for MP3 files, try to find a specialized newsgroup that is likely to offer what you want, such as alt.binaries.sounds. mp3.elvispresley. If you can't find such a specialized newsgroup, try searching for the MP3 file in the more general newsgroup categories, such as alt.binaries.sounds.mp3.1960s. As a last resort, you can try the catch-all MP3 file newsgroup, alt.binaries.sounds.mp3s.

NAVIGATING NEWSGROUPS

Although there are thousands of newsgroups to choose from, you can often decipher the type of information each one contains by examining the newsgroup name. For example, the newsgroup named sci.space is a science-related newsgroup focusing on space interests such as space exploration; comp.privacy is a computer-related newsgroup focusing on privacy issues. The following table lists the most common newsgroup names you'll encounter along with a brief description of the type of information each one contains.

WORD	TYPE OF INFORMATION COVERED	TYPICAL NAME
comp	Computer-related topics	comp.privacy
news	News about Usenet itself	news.announce
rec	Recreational activities	rec.audio.misc
sci	Science-related topics, except for computers	sci.space
soc	Sociology topics	soc.culture.bolivia
talk	Chat forum for discussing and debating different ideas and topics	talk.atheism
alt	Alternative topics	alt.binaries.movies
misc	Miscellaneous topics that don't fit anywhere else	misc.jobs.offered

To see a massive list of newsgroups (including newsgroups from other countries), visit ftp://ftp.isc.org/pub/usenet/config/newsgroups.

THE ALT.BINARIES NEWSGROUPS

Although you can probably find files scattered among several thousand different newsgroups, most people post files in newsgroups with the word "binaries" in their names, such as alt.binaries.sounds.mp3.audiobook or alt.binaries.movies. ("Binaries" is just a technical term for any type of computer-readable, such as a program, a digital photograph, an audio file, or a video file.) If the newsgroup doesn't contain the word "binaries," it probably just contains text messages.

Fortunately when looking for files to download, you can sort the newsgroups alphabetically, starting with the phrase alt.binaries. To get idea of the variety of different newsgroups available that trade files on particular topics, take a look at the following, each of which contains more specialized newsgroups:

alt.binaries.multimedia	Videos (TV shows, mostly)
alt.binaries.pictures	Photographs
alt.binaries.sounds.mp3	MP3 files
alt.binaries.cd.image	Images of CDs (mostly PC software)
alt.binaries.warez	Pirated software, sorted by platform and category

Once you've jumped to the beginning of a newsgroup section, you can find similar, more specialized newsgroups within your chosen category. (Chapters 9 through 15 contain more information about finding different types of files in newsgroups and from other sources.)

SHARING FILES THROUGH A NEWSGROUP

Newsgroups were originally designed to contain nothing but plain-text messages. To get around that restriction, programmers created special ways to convert binary files—music or programs, for instance—into text, so that the files can appear in a newsgroup.

Dedicated newsreader programs can automatically encode and decode binary files as you upload or download them so you probably won't even notice all the work going on in the background. When you download an MP3 file from a newsgroup, for instance, your newsreader automatically decodes it and places it on your hard drive as an MP3 file. However, a new encoding scheme appeared in 2001, and a few newsreaders still don't support it. Known as yEnc (http://www.yenc.org), the scheme packs more information into less space, which is beneficial to the newsreader but which doesn't save any time uploading or downloading. Many newsreader programs include built-in yEnc encoding and decoding, but ordinary email/newsreader programs like Microsoft's Outlook Express do not. If your newsreader doesn't offer built-in yEnc encoding and decoding, you can visit the yEnc website and download a separate yEnc encoder/decoder.

DOWNLOADING FILES

Once you've found a particular newsgroup to explore (such as alt.binaries. sounds.mp3.album.new), the next step is to find files to download. The biggest obstacle is that files are almost always broken into pieces. Because newsgroups were designed for simple exchanges of short messages and small programs of 300KB to 450KB in size—that was all computers could handle back then—the basic structure of the newsgroup posting system has never changed. To post today's larger files onto newsgroups, newsreader programs must break them apart and post them as consecutively numbered pieces. When you download them, the newsreader downloads each part, decodes the pieces, and reassembles them in the proper order to reconstruct the binary file.

Luckily, dedicated newsreader programs handle these huge chores automatically during the upload or download process. When you choose a file to download, a dedicated newsreader program automatically fetches the pieces, reassembles them, and places the file onto your hard drive without any help from you. (It automatically does the same, in reverse order, when you upload a file.) With a newsreader program, downloading from newsgroups is nearly as easy as downloading any other file from the Internet.

That's not true for newsreader programs that don't support automatic file encoding and decoding, like Outlook Express. Outlook Express forces you to locate every piece of a posted file manually, and then list them in consecutively numbered order. Only then can Outlook Express take over, downloading, decoding, and reassembling the file for you.

To help you find every piece of a file, newsreader programs automatically number every piece consecutively while they upload: The subject heading for each piece of a file lists something like "(07/12)," meaning that that particular file is the 7th part of a total of 12 files. (Tell your program to sort the files by their Subject, which will line up all the pieces in numerical order and make them easier to grab.)

For instance, Figure 3-7 shows what the alt.binaries.sounds.mp3 newsgroup looks like in Outlook Express, showing the O'Jays song "Back Stabbers" listed as a 12-part file, with each part consecutively numbered.

Figure 3-8, by contrast, shows how the same song appears in the more sophisticated Agent newsreader. Notice how Agent doesn't show all of the file's 12 parts—it automatically gathers them, hides the details, and simply displays the "Back Stabbers" song on a single line. When each file is listed on a single line, you can easily see which files you want without having to worry about missing a piece of a file.

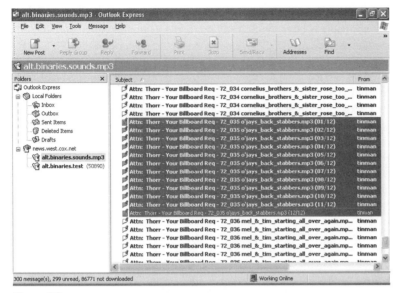

Figure 3-7

Outlook Express lists all the different parts of a binary file, then leaves it up to you to locate each part.

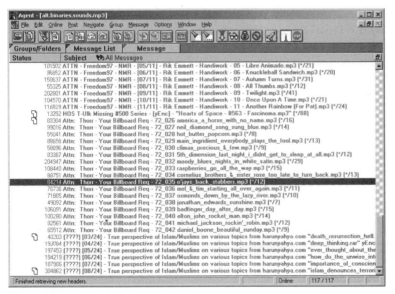

Figure 3-8

A specialized newsreader, like Agent, locates all the parts of a large file automatically.

To download the song in the Agent newsreader, you just right-click the "Back Stabbers" song and choose the Save all Attachments option. Agent automatically downloads each part of the file, decodes it, and saves it as an MP3 file on your hard drive.

To download the song in Outlook Express, by contrast, you must highlight every part of the listed file (as shown in Figure 3-7), right-click the highlighted files, and choose the Combine and Decode option. Then Outlook Express displays a window, shown in Figure 3-9, listing all the files you've selected. Click the Move Up or Move Down buttons to sort the files in consecutively numbered order. When you click the OK button, Outlook Express then downloads each part, decodes it, reassembles them in order, and saves the file as an MP3 file. If the parts are out of order or you couldn't find some of the file's parts, the file won't download correctly.

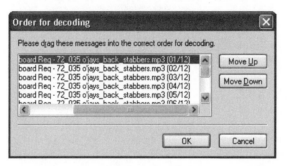

Figure 3-9
After selecting every part of a file in Outlook Express, line them up
in numerical order, then click OK to download them.

One more problem plagues Outlook Express and other old newsreaders. They can't handle the yEnc compression format, which compresses files more efficiently than older compression methods (like UUencode and Base64). Most newsreader programs quickly added yEnc to their arsenal and automatically decode yEnc-encoded files, just as they decode any other file. But if you download a yEnc-encoded file in Outlook Express or in another newsreader that doesn't offer built-in yEnc encoding and decoding, your downloaded files arrive as gibberish, like the example shown in Figure 3-10. (The words "ybegin" and "ypart" in the first two lines are the giveaway that you've downloaded a yEnc-encoded file.)

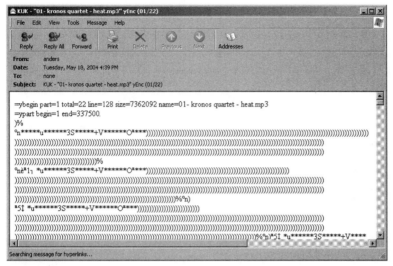

Figure 3-10

You can identify a yEnc-encoded file by the words "ybegin" and "ypart" in the first two lines of the message.

If you've downloaded a yEnc-encoded file in Outlook Express or another newsreader that doesn't support the format, you must save the message as a plain-text file. Click the File menu and choose Save As, making sure you save the file in the text file format. Once you've stored all your yEnc-encoded files as text files, use a third-party conversion program, like yEnc32 (http://www.yenc32.com) to quickly convert the text file to its original form, such as an MP3 file.

NOTE: *Although Outlook Express is free, it's generally considered one of the worst programs to use for accessing newsgroups.*

DEALING WITH MISSING FILE PARTS

One major problem with downloading files from newsgroups is that if the file you want consists of 23 separate parts, but you can only find 15 of those parts, downloading just part of the file will be worthless. (To keep you from wasting time downloading incomplete files, dedicated newsreader programs like Agent can display a "broken" icon next to the file's name, alerting you that it's missing some parts and is not worth downloading.)

NOTE: There is one exception when you don't absolutely need all the parts of a file. If some of the files you find contain PAR or PAR2 files, easily identified by the word PAR in the file's name, you can actually re-create missing parts of the original file. Although these are occasionally found with music uploads, PAR and PAR2 files are much more prevalent in the movies newsgroups, so we'll look at them in Chapter 10.

After using Outlook Express or other primitive newsreaders designed mostly for exchanging messages, it's easy to see why most people quickly move to a dedicated newsreader program for downloading files from newsgroups.

UPLOADING FILES TO A NEWSGROUP

Unlike file sharing networks, newsgroups don't pressure visitors to share files. In fact, they prefer that users *don't* post files. That way, only experienced newsgroup posters upload files, keeping the quality levels high. (Most MP3 uploaders rip their *own* CDs, for instance, and then post the entire CD on a newsgroup, with all the tags filled out correctly.) Also, remember that newsgroup posts only last for a few days. If everybody started posting files, the files wouldn't last long enough for anybody to download them. So leech as much as you want—it's definitely considered good behavior.

Uploading a file with a newsreader program is just like sending a piece of email with an attached file. Most newsreaders handle everything automatically: encoding, breaking into parts, numbering each piece correctly, and posting to the appropriate newsgroup.

Before you can start posting, though, you need four things:

- The name of your ISP's outgoing mail server

- The name of the newsgroup that receives the files

- A descriptive subject header

- The name of the files to upload

To upload a file, follow these steps:

1. Set up your newsreader program with the name of your ISP's outgoing mail server (generally something like smtp.ispname.com). You usually enter this name into your newsreader program on the same page where you entered your news server's name.

2. Click the newsreader program's Post a New Message button. When the message window appears, type in the name of the subscribed newsgroup where you want the post to appear. (Most newsreaders automatically fill in the name of the newsgroup you're currently visiting.)
3. Type a subject header that describes your post: `01 - Usher - Burn.mp3`, for instance.
4. Attach the file you want to post. The newsreader automatically encodes the file and posts its pieces to your chosen newsgroup.

NOTE: *Don't attach several files to the same post; use a separate post for each file. This makes it easier for people to download one file without having to download all the rest. Most newsreaders let you create queues to upload several files in one session.*

Of course, if you're using Outlook Express, there's one extra step. Newsreader programs are smart enough to encode the file, break it into pieces, and upload each piece—all automatically. Outlook Express must be told to break it into pieces automatically. To do that, follow these steps:

1. Click the Tools menu, and click Accounts.
2. Click the News tab.
3. Click a Newsgroup account, click Properties, and click the Advanced tab.
4. Click in the box that says Break Apart Messages Larger Than, and set the larger-than value to 350KB. (Outlook Express normally uses a value of 60KB, which is much too small.)
5. Click OK.

Once you've done that, posting a newsgroup file in Outlook Express is just like sending a friend an email that contains an attachment. (Don't bother trying to post in yEnc when using Outlook Express. If you want to use yEnc, upgrade to a newsreader that can handle yEnc automatically, such as Power-Post 2003, available at http://www.cosmicwolf.com.)

HIDING YOUR IDENTITY IN NEWSGROUPS

Posting a file doesn't necessarily reveal your name, but the post still shows your IP (Internet Protocol) address, which is a unique numeric address that identifies your computer on the Internet. Once the authorities know your IP address, they can track down your physical location just as easily as if they had your street address.

To protect their identity when posting messages and files, many people use anonymous remailers, which strip away the sender's email and IP addresses (making the sender anonymous) before forwarding a message to a newsgroup or email address. The Global Internet Liberty Campaign (http://www.gilc.org/speech/anonymous/remailer.html) provides an anonymous remailer, but you can always search your favorite search engine for **anonymous remailer** to find more.

For most people, anonymous remailers may prove cumbersome, so many people now subscribe to newsgroup servers that offer anonymous posting, which strips away your IP address without going through an anonymous remailer. For the really paranoid, you could use both an anonymous remailer and a news server that strips way your IP address.

NEWSGROUP ETIQUETTE

When file swapping on newsgroups, you're joining a gang of very efficiently organized thieves and pirates, so it's best to keep a low profile.

Many binary groups have an adjacent "discussion" group. The "d" attached to alt.binaries.sounds.mp3.d, for instance, designates it as a discussion group where people talk about items they've posted in alt.binaries.sounds.mp3, such as announcing dates when they'll post certain files.

Don't make the mistake of posting binaries in a discussion group. While this may seem like an innocent mistake to you, it's considered a glaring breach of etiquette to serious users. Without Usenet's strict categories, the system would soon be useless to everybody, so Usenet veterans are often quick to chastise newcomers who unknowingly break these important rules. And they won't necessarily chastise nicely.

Newsgroups can only hold a limited amount of messages, so the more people post messages, the less time each message remains available before newer messages push the older ones aside. As a result, most binary newsgroups ask users to limit the number of files they upload. While posting six CDs at a time may seem like you're doing the group a favor, the sheer size of the postings will erase older messages before other people can read them. Be sure to adhere to upload limits.

NOTE: *In terms of security, hundreds of people post files in newsgroups, which often scroll off after a week or two. File sharing network users, by contrast, constantly share their entire music collection. That makes file sharing network users much easier to monitor and, subsequently, sue for damages.*

And finally, don't post a question until you've read the newsgroup's Frequently Asked Questions (FAQ) file first. If you can't find a newsgroup's FAQ, it's considered polite to ask, "Where can I find the FAQ for this group?" When you locate the FAQ, study it thoroughly. Asking a question that's already answered in the newsgroup's FAQ will mark you as an amateur and a target for others to attack. Not physically, of course, but verbally and with near-rabid intensity.

You'll find a fairly complete and updated set of FAQs at http://www.faqs.org/faqs. For a group of FAQs sorted by newsgroup categories (like alt, comp, rec, and others) visit http://www.faqs.org/faqs/by-newsgroup. The faqs.org site also keeps a list of the most popular FAQs (http://www.faqs.org/toprated.html).

Finally, don't post anything until you're sure you understand the mechanics involved and the acceptable quality rates. Before posting in a newsgroup, visit alt.binaries.test and post your file there. If it appears correctly, then try posting it in a regular newsgroup.

NOTE: *When visiting newsgroups, you'll probably run across the usual spam advertising everything from lower mortgage rates to Viagra to pornography. More serious are malicious people who post viruses and Trojan horses in a newsgroup to attack unsuspecting users. The Melissa virus began life in 1999 as a post in alt.sex, which wound up infecting 100,000 computers on its first weekend and crashing email servers worldwide. See Chapter 7 for more information on protecting your computer while file hunting. And please don't download those files named "Christina Aguilera naked 7234."*

4

INSTANT MESSAGING AND ONLINE CHAT ROOMS

For many people, email isn't fast enough. Forget about the fact that you can send a message to anyone in the world and often get a reply back within minutes. Email may be useful, but once you send out your message, you have to wait for someone to read it and write back.

That's why instant messaging is so popular. Unlike email, where you have absolutely no idea if any of your messages are actually getting through to the people you're sending them to, instant messaging lets you write messages directly to others and have them respond within seconds. Best of all, you can only send messages to people when they're online at the same time as you are, so you know without a doubt that your messages are being received.

Still, given the unpredictable and chaotic nature of instant messaging conversations, you're less likely to find people trading files with one another than to find them trading thinly veiled but barbed insults. But while strangers may not trust each other enough to share files indiscriminately, many people use instant messaging services to create private chat rooms so they can share files with their friends, away from the prying eyes of any government authorities.

INTERNET RELAY CHAT (IRC)

Although the idea of chatting with your friends online might seem like a recent invention, it's actually been around since the early days of the Internet. The early real-time chatting system, called Internet Relay Chat (or IRC), is often overlooked by many people because it isn't quite as straightforward or as easy to use as newer, more user-friendly instant messaging services, such as AOL Instant Messenger (AIM) or Yahoo! Messenger.

Hackers typically choose IRC channels over products like AIM or Yahoo! Messenger because IRC channels are unregulated and generally unmoderated. Think Wild Wild West; and they can be wild.

GETTING AN IRC CLIENT

To chat over IRC, you first need to run an IRC client program on your computer (such as the one shown in Figure 4-1), which you use to contact an IRC server.

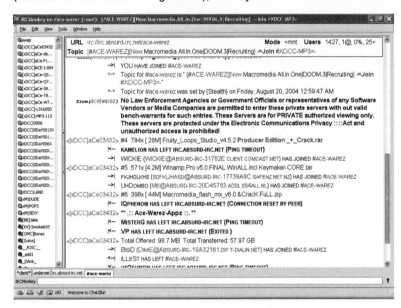

Figure 4-1
An IRC chat room shows you the nicknames of all the people in the room, along with the messages they've already typed.

These are some popular IRC clients for different operating systems:

Windows IRC client programs

mIRC	http://www.mirc.co.uk
Pirch	http://www.pirch.com
Visual IRC	http://www.visualirc.net

Macintosh IRC client programs

| Ircle | http://www.ircle.com |
| Snak | http://www.snak.com |

Linux IRC client programs

BitchX   http://www.bitchx.org

XChat   http://www.xchat.org

CONNECTING TO AN IRC NETWORK

Once you have an IRC client program on your computer, the next step is to connect to an IRC network. Three of the most popular IRC networks used for file trading include Undernet (http://www.undernet.org), Rizon (http://www.rizon.net), and EFnet (http://www.efnet.org). An IRC network is nothing more than a collection of computers, called *servers*, which manage all the messages that people type to each other.

Initially, there was just a single computer that formed the first IRC network, so if you wanted to chat with anyone over IRC, you had to connect to this one IRC server to connect to the IRC network.

Naturally, a single computer couldn't handle all the messages that people all over the world wanted to type, so people started adding additional servers to the IRC network. So instead of connecting to a single IRC server, you could connect to the IRC server closest to you. Whichever server you connected to would relay messages to all the other servers in the IRC network, creating the illusion that everyone was still chatting on the same computer.

Over the years, people running different IRC servers have formed their own IRC networks. As a result, there are now hundreds of different IRC networks, and each is isolated from the other. So if you connect to the DALnet IRC network, you can't chat with someone connected to the EFnet IRC network, and vice versa.

IRC networks tend to fall into several categories:

Popular   These are the large networks where people from all over the world chat and swap website and FTP addresses for finding different types of files.

Subject   These are smaller networks that concentrate on a particular topic, such as computers or health.

Local   These are small networks, often centered within a particular geographical region or country; they are popular in non–English-speaking countries.

For a list of different IRC networks, visit http://www.irchelp.org/irchelp/networks.

Once you find an IRC network you want to connect to, you need to find a server that belongs to that particular IRC network. IRC client programs typically store a list of servers that you can choose from, as shown in Figure 4-2.

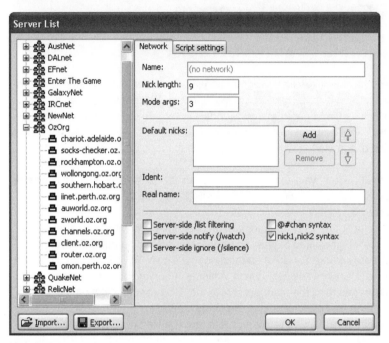

Figure 4-2
Most IRC clients have a list of servers for different IRC networks.

While IRC servers can be located anywhere in the world, it's usually best to connect to one that's closest to you (your connection may be a bit faster and more reliable that way). Once you find a server that connects you to a particular IRC network, your next step is to find a particular channel to visit.

CHOOSING AN IRC CHANNEL

If everyone joined a single IRC network, there would be so many people typing messages all at once that nobody would be able to chat with each other. Rather than force everyone to chat within one big network, IRC networks divide everyone into different channels, where you can chat with others. Channels will typically cater to different interests—from sailing and Linux programming to pornography and music piracy.

While most channels are open to the public, you can also create private ones. That way you can invite (and block) people from these private channels, just as you would a private club, and within these private channels you can share files that you might not want other people to know you have.

Most IRC networks contain hundreds of different channels. To find a particular channel that caters to your interests, visit an IRC search engine, such as the following:

IRCSpy.com	http://ircspy.com
XDCCSearch.com	http://www.xdccsearch.com/html
PacketNews	http://packetnews.com
SearchIRC	http://searchirc.com
IRC Search Engine	http://irc.netsplit.de/channels

For example, if you enter **MP3** into SearchIRC, you can find a list of channels and networks where people discuss (and presumably trade) MP3 files, videos, and software, as shown in Figure 4-3.

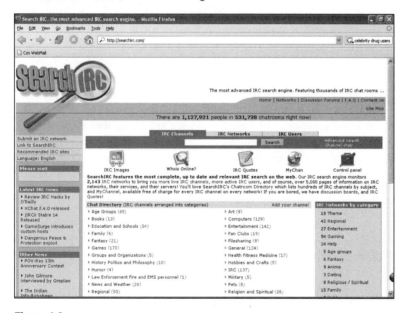

Figure 4-3

An IRC search engine can help you find a specific IRC network and channel where people are trading music, movies, or games.

To learn more about IRC, pick up a copy of *The Book of IRC* by Alex Charalabidis, published by No Starch Press.

DOWNLOADING FILES FROM IRC

Like newsgroups, IRC is best for grabbing whatever files happen to be available at the moment. While you could strike up a conversation with someone in an IRC channel, request a file, and have them send it to you, you're more likely to find files such as music, videos, programs, games, electronic books, and pictures in IRC through file server bots, which are special programs that people set up in an IRC channel to share files with other people. File server bots essentially automate the process of sharing files through an IRC channel without forcing the person sharing the files to constantly monitor an IRC channel and respond to file requests manually.

NOTE: One of the earlier file server bots was called Fserve, but the currently used file server bots are called XDCC. If you find a file server bot on an IRC chat room, chances are good it will be an XDCC bot.

To find a file server bot, just start up your IRC client program (such as mIRC) and visit an IRC search engine such as PacketNews (http://www.packetnews.com), myDownloader (http://www.xdccspy.com), or IRCSpy (http://www.ircspy.com). Search for the type of file you want, such as the name of a particular movie *(Spider-Man 2)* or song title, or just a generic description of what type of file you want to find, such as the phrase **MP3**. The IRC search engine will display a list of IRC networks, channel names, and files currently offered for copying, as shown in Figure 4-4.

Once you see a file that you want, you have to tell your IRC client program to connect to the listed IRC network and the particular channel where the files are being traded. In Figure 4-4, the Absurd-IRC network and the #mad-mp3 channel is where you can find an MP3 file of a song by Nirvana, identified by its pack number, #32.

After you've connected to the Absurd-IRC network and switched to the #madmp3 channel, you can start downloading the file by typing the following:

```
/msg [xddc]giga-bot[evil] xdcc send #32
```

The preceding command tells the file server bot to start sending you file #32. While this process may seem complicated, most IRC search engines let you click on the song you want (such as pack #32), which automatically copies the correct command needed to start downloading the song. Just switch to the correct IRC network and channel, and paste the command into the IRC channel to start downloading your file.

HOW INSTANT MESSAGING WORKS

Although there are several different instant messaging services available, joining one service won't necessarily allow you to chat with anyone who uses another instant messaging service. The problem lies in the way instant messaging works.

To use an instant messaging service, you run a special instant messaging client program on your computer. This client program connects directly to another computer, called a server, run by the instant messaging company.

To find out if someone is online, your client program sends a message to the server, which in turn checks to see if the person you want to reach is connected. If so, the server connects you directly to them. At this point, your computer communicates directly with the other person's computer; your client doesn't send your messages to the server again. Once connected to another computer, you can type messages, send video images back and forth, and (of course) send files to each other.

Instant messaging lets you chat with one person at a time. Although you can chat with multiple people, each conversation can only be read by you and the other person. If you want to chat with several people at once, you can create a separate chat room where everyone can type and read messages from everyone else.

Chat rooms are like private clubhouses where you can invite others to join and chat about whatever you choose, be it gardening, sports, or trading MP3 files from your favorite bands. Many people create private chat rooms, which can only be accessed with a password. That way they can create a chat room, swap files and information, and then disband before the authorities even realize that the chat room existed in the first place.

Popular instant messaging services, like MSN Messenger or ICQ, are proprietary, which means that you can't peek at the source code to see how the instant messaging service works. In case you don't like the idea of tying yourself to a proprietary instant messaging service, try the open source Jabber (http://www.jabber.org). Like the other instant messaging services, Jabber offers real-time chatting and file sharing, but it uses open standards, so anyone can freely access it without worrying about getting shut out periodically.

TALKING TO MULTIPLE SERVICES AT ONCE

Although instant messaging services work alike, they don't communicate with each other, so if you have a friend who uses ICQ, but you use MSN Messenger, you won't be able to chat with each other unless you use the same instant messaging program. If you have friends who use ICQ and other friends who use MSN Messenger, you can either load both instant messaging programs or use one of the following instant messaging client programs that can tap into multiple instant messaging services, as shown in Figure 4-7:

Ayttm	http://ayttm.sourceforge.net
Gaim	http://gaim.sourceforge.net
Trillian	http://www.ceruleanstudios.com
Miranda IM	http://www.miranda-im.org

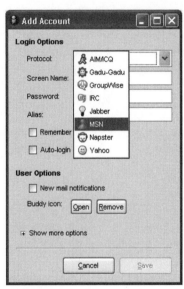

Figure 4-7
A program such as Gaim can connect to
several different instant messaging services.

Of course, the instant messaging services (ICQ, Yahoo!, MSN, and AIM) don't like programs that let you talk to more than one service at once; they want to lock you to theirs. Because instant messaging services, such as ICQ or AIM, are free, the companies make their money by slipping in ads to all of their subscribers. If you use a program like Trillian, you won't see the ads that ICQ or AIM want you to see.

To discourage people from using unauthorized programs like Gaim and Trillian to access their networks (thus avoiding the advertising), many instant messaging services occasionally shut out unauthorized programs. Although this is usually only until the programmers can figure out how to make their programs work with the service again, it can be inconvenient. That doesn't mean that you shouldn't try them—just be prepared for some potential frustration.

PEER-TO-PEER INSTANT MESSAGING PROGRAMS

Many people use instant messaging programs like AIM to meet new people and chat with old friends. But if you tend to chat with the same circle of friends, you could set up your own private chat rooms on services like Yahoo! Messenger or ICQ, or set up your own private instant messaging service altogether.

Private instant messaging networks let you turn your computer into a server. This way your friends can connect to your computer using one of the following instant messaging programs without fear of some recording industry spy snooping and tracking down the IP addresses of the people doing the most trading of copyrighted MP3 music files:

MeetGate	http://www.meetgate.com
P2P Instant Messenger	http://www.ufasoft.com
PalTalk	http://www.paltalk.com

STILL PARANOID? ENCRYPT YOUR MESSAGES

The truly paranoid who feel that even their own private instant messaging networks could be spied upon encrypt their messages so that nobody will know what they're saying or what files they're trading. Encryption basically scrambles the content of your files so only you (and anyone who knows the password to decrypt the file) can unscramble it again. Most encryption can scramble a file so thoroughly that even governments using supercomputers can't crack the encryption to peek at the content of a file.

If you're using a public instant messaging service like ICQ or AIM, you might want to use SurfSecret IMSafe (http://www.surfsecret.com) to encrypt your messages.

While private instant messaging services, such as PalTalk or MeetGate, offer more privacy, you may want to go one step further and set up a private instant messaging network that uses encryption, with one of these programs:

CryptoHeaven	http://www.cryptoheaven.com
Super Cipher P2P Messenger	http://www.brooksyounce.com/design.htm
Sealquest Messenger	http://www.sealquest.com

CryptoHeaven even offers encrypted offline storage, so if you don't want to risk getting caught with incriminating files on your hard disk, store them in CryptoHeaven's encrypted file vaults (for a fee), and nobody will be able to access them without the right password (including you, if you forget your own password).

IS BIG BROTHER WATCHING?

The threat of the recording industry or the government spying on instant messaging activities is probably remote, but that doesn't mean that someone closer to you isn't spying on you. Your boss, your spouse, or your parents may be curious to know what you're doing, especially if you're not supposed to be using instant messaging, or if they just want to know who you're chatting with.

For example, Chat Watch (http://www.zemericks.com) can record instant messaging conversations and email the conversations to whoever installed the program on that computer. Programs like EmployeeWatcher (http://www.matewatcher.com) and MateWatcher (from the same publisher) can also record every key that you type at the keyboard and take pictures of your screen as you chat, in addition to recording instant messaging conversations. ICQ Sniffer (http://www.ufasoft.com) can even intercept messages sent through ICQ, email, or IRC.

While such programs can help you spy on someone's instant messaging or IRC conversations, you might want to capture *everything* they might type, whether it's a message in a word processor or passwords entered into a website. To capture every keystroke, you can get a program called a *keylogger*. The Keylogger.org website (http://www.keylogger.org) lists some popular keyloggers.

To protect yourself against keyloggers, you can run spyware removal programs, such as McAfee AntiSpyware (http://www.mcafee.com). To guard specifically against keyloggers, grab a copy of Anti-keylogger (http://www.anti-keyloggers.com).

Whether you use a public instant messaging service or set up your own private instant messaging network, anything you view, send, or type could be recorded by someone else, so be careful if you plan to share copyrighted files.

5

FINDING FILES ON WEB AND FTP SITES

In the early days of the Internet, people didn't have file sharing networks for swapping files with each other. Instead, if you wanted to share files over the Internet, you had to use File Transfer Protocol—FTP for short. FTP is just a standard method for transferring files from one computer to another.

Before the file sharing networks took over, many people used to share files (legal and otherwise) through websites and FTP sites. Websites that offer FTP transfer simply display a list of files available, and you click the file you want to copy, as shown in Figure 5-1.

I can't understand why people are frightened of new ideas. I'm frightened of the old ones.

—John Cage

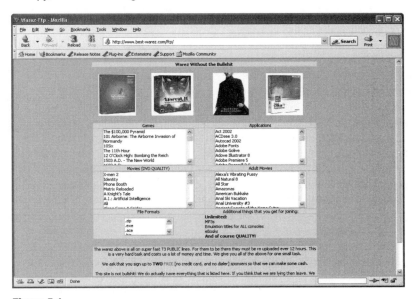

Figure 5-1

The graphical nature of a web page lets you point and click on the files you want to copy, such as the movie *The Matrix Revolutions* or Microsoft Office XP.

FTP sites, on the other hand, don't have the luxury of displaying graphics or point-and-click interfaces (FTP sites were around long before the World Wide Web popped up); they simply display lists of files within a cryptic hierarchy of directories and subdirectories, as shown in Figure 5-2. Essentially, you can think of an FTP site as a website without the pretty graphical appearance.

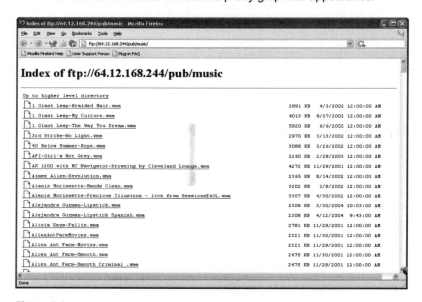

Figure 5-2
An FTP site displays files organized in directories and subdirectories.

Web and FTP sites often contain freeware or shareware programs, software drivers, and scientific papers. Of course, many people also use web and FTP sites to share copyrighted information, including MP3 music files, pornographic photographs, full-length videos, and the latest versions of popular programs such as Adobe Photoshop, Microsoft Office, or Macromedia Dreamweaver.

Setting up a website to distribute illegal material can be risky, but many people use free web hosting services, such as GeoCities (http://geocities.yahoo.com) or Tripod (http://www.tripod.lycos.com), which they can operate anonymously. Still others don't mind taking the risk of setting up a web or FTP site to distribute copyrighted files, because the authorities don't have time to examine every web or FTP site on the Internet to search for illegally distributed files. To avoid prosecution, many of these web and FTP sites are located in countries like Russia, Germany, or India, which protects them to a large extent from prosecution by American companies and authorities.

If you're willing to take some time and do a little more work, you can often find most any file you want on various web and FTP sites around the Internet with little legal risk to yourself (unless, of course, you start sharing your copyrighted files with others).

TYPES OF SITES

When exploring FTP sites and websites, you're likely to run across three different types:

Leech sites   These provide free, unlimited access to all the files you want. They're also extremely rare.

Ratio sites   These force users to upload a certain number or size of files before the FTP or website administrator will allow you to download anything. A typical ratio might be 1:10, which means you need to upload 1MB of files, and in return, you'll be able to download up to 10MB of files.

Banner sites   These display banner ads (sometimes many obnoxious ones) that you must click before you can get access to the FTP site or website. Web and FTP site administrators get a certain amount of money for each banner ad their site displays, so these sites tend to force users to view dozens of such ads, usually offering pornography. The worst part is that many of these are themselves scams; even if you click all the banners, there's no guarantee that you'll ever get access to the desired site or that it has anything other than banners. In fact, we estimate that close to 99 percent of these sites are scams.

NOTE: Many banner sites do nothing but display an endless series of banner ads at you without ever giving you access to anything useful.

FINDING A FILE SHARING SITE

Normally when you want to find something on the Internet, you can use a search engine such as Google or Yahoo! While search engines can find a list of potential sites to visit, you may have to visit several different sites just to find one that isn't shut down, especially if you're looking for illegal music files, software, or full-length movies.

If you're lucky enough to find a website that contains what you want, you may have to wade through several layers of pop-up ads trying to entice you into looking at pictures of naked celebrities having sex (like who cares). Finally, you find a file that you want to download, but the link is dead, so you have to visit another website. Repeat this process several more times, and you can see why the recording industry views web and FTP sites as only a minor threat to their profit margins compared to the danger that file sharing networks pose.

Fortunately, there are faster, less frustrating ways to find what you want on the Internet. Rather than waste time browsing multiple sites listed by a single search engine, use a specialized search engine or a multi–search engine program to query multiple search engines simultaneously.

SPECIALIZED SEARCH ENGINES

If you type the string **mp3** in a search engine, chances are good that you'll find not only websites that offer MP3 files, but also newspaper articles about MP3 files, programs for creating MP3 files, and even pornographic sites that use popular search strings like **mp3** to entice people to take a peek at what they have to offer.

To avoid bombarding you with a list of irrelevant websites, many search engines allow you to search only for MP3 files related to what you want to find, as shown in Figure 5-3.

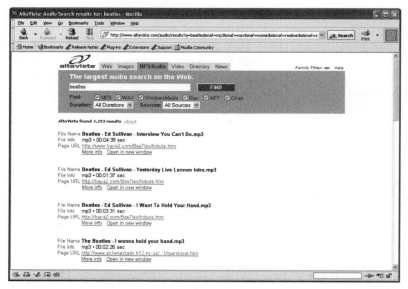

Figure 5-3

By narrowing your search just for MP3 files within a search engine, you can quickly find illegally traded music files on the Internet.

To find music files on the Internet, visit one of these specialized search engines:

MP3.box	http://mp3.box.sk
Big Search Engine Index	http://www.search-engine-index.co.uk
Music Search Engine	http://mp3-music-search-engines.com
SongCrawler	http://songcrawler.com

MP3 FILE FINDING PROGRAMS

You can also use specialized MP3 file searching programs to find the music files you want. Simply enter a song title or recording artist's name into one of these file searching programs, and the program searches multiple MP3 search engines for you and shows you the addresses of the web or FTP sites where you can get the file you want (see Figure 5-4).

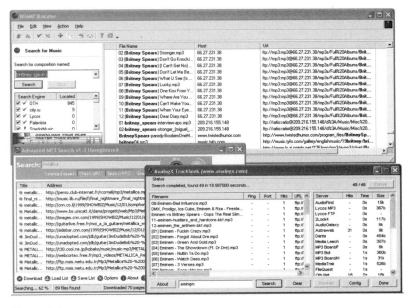

Figure 5-4
File finding programs can locate MP3 files on both web and FTP sites.

While specialized music search engines can often find MP3 files stored on websites, MP3 file finding programs are better for finding music files stored on FTP sites. These are some popular MP3 file finding programs:

2 Find MP3	http://www.npssoftware.com/2findmp3
WinMP3Locator	http://www.winmp3locator.com
Advanced MP3 Search	http://www.search-mp3.org
MediaGrab	http://www.eastbaytech.com

COPYING FILES TO YOUR COMPUTER

Once you've found your favorite MP3 files, your next step is to visit the web or FTP sites that holds the files you want. If you used a search engine, you can just click the appropriate links.

COPYING FROM WEBSITES

On the website, you may simply see a list of URLs, something like this one:

```
http://my.dreamwiz.com/maluchi/sound/music.mp3
```

This is the address of a web page that contains the file you want. You know it's a web page (rather than an FTP site) because it starts with the letters http (which stand for Hypertext Transfer Protocol). Enter this address into the address bar in your web browser, and you'll jump straight to the web page that contains the link to the MP3 file you want. If you right-click this link (on a Macintosh, hold down the CTRL key and then click the mouse), a pop-up menu appears, as shown in Figure 5-5. Click Save Target As (or something similar, depending on the specific browser you're using) to display a dialog box in which you can specify where you want to save your file. Choose a folder and click Save. Your computer should download the file and save it to the folder you've chosen.

NOTE: *Downloads from popular sites take longer, as you're competing with lots of other visitors for the server's time. Sometimes, you'll only find a message saying that the server is too busy, and to try again later.*

Figure 5-5

When you right-click a link that represents a file, a pop-up menu appears, allowing you to save
that file on your own computer.

COPYING FILES FROM AN FTP SITE

You can always identify an FTP address by the letters `ftp` at the beginning of the
address, like this:

`ftp://66.130.118.79:7777/MP3%27s/Madonna/Madonna-prayer.mp3`

In this example, the FTP site address is the series of numbers listed as
`66.130.118.79:7777`, and anything beyond the slash is the file path on the server
where the file is stored. None of this really matters too much, because all you
want to do is find the file.

You access an FTP site with an FTP program. (You can access an FTP
site through a browser, but it's not always fast, easy, or reliable.) A popular
Windows FTP client program is WS_FTP (http://www.ipswitch.com). A popular
Macintosh FTP client program is Fetch (http://fetchsoftworks.com).

NOTE: Copying files off an FTP site varies depending on the FTP client program you're using. Basically, you have to click the files you want to copy, specify where you want to store that file on your own computer, and then click the command to transfer the file.

Once you have the FTP program set up, enter the FTP site's address into it, and you should see the list of folders and files on the site, as shown in Figure 5-6. The left pane in that window lists all the folders and files on your computer. The right pane lists the folders and files stored on the FTP site.

When you access an FTP site, you're essentially peeking into the files and folders stored on another computer. While most FTP sites prevent you from moving, renaming, or deleting any files or folders, you can freely browse through the files and choose the ones you want to copy to your own computer.

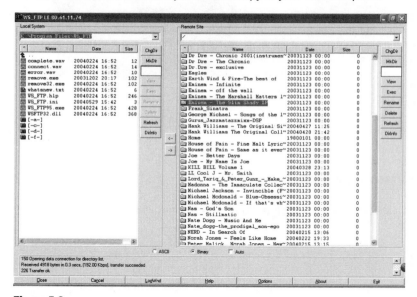

Figure 5-6

An FTP client program displays the folders and files stored on your computer and on the FTP site.

To get the files you want, click through the folders in the right pane (the files on the FTP site), select the ones you want to copy, and then choose a folder on your machine (in the left pane) where you want to store those files.

Some FTP sites require you to enter a username and password to access them, while others allow anonymous access. Try anonymous access if you don't know whether you need a password or not. But if you can't get in, chances are good that you need a username or password.

If you find an FTP site through a search engine or a file finding program, you may find a cryptic listing like this:

```
ftp://oth:oth@spidermp3.no-ip.com/MP3%20%28M-Z%29/Madonna/
Ray%20Of%20Light/08-Shanti%20-%20Ashtangi.mp3
```

The text `oth:oth` (presented in bold above) in front of the @ symbol identifies the username and password you must use to access that particular FTP site. In this case, the username is `oth` and the password is also `oth`, although the username and password will not always be identical. In this example, the FTP site address is `spidermp3.no-ip.com`.

Understanding upload/download ratios

Once you have an FTP site address and a password, you may still be unable to copy any files from the FTP site unless you upload files from your computer to the FTP site first. For example, a typical message you may see upon entering an FTP site for the first time might look like this:

```
To obtain download rights, you have to upload at least one
complete album from my request list. Only complete albums are
accepted. Create a new directory in the upload directory and
upload the album. Leave your email in a text file. If everything
is all right, I'll contact you informing you of the username/
password of your download account. For each complete album you
upload, I'll grant you seven days access to my site with no
download limit.
```

Once you upload some files that the FTP site administrator wants, you should get a password that allows you to download anything from the FTP site. If you don't upload anything first (as this message requires), you won't be able to download anything at all.

PROS AND CONS OF WEB AND FTP SITES

Copying files from a file sharing network can be simple. Copying files through a website is slightly trickier, and copying files from an FTP site can be the clumsiest method yet. Given the obstacles in copying files from a web or FTP site, why would anyone want to do it?

The main reason to copy files from a web or FTP site is anonymity. If the recording industry is going to sue anyone, it will be the person running the web or FTP site, not the people who copy files from it.

Of course, downloading from a website isn't completely anonymous either, because your browser gives information to websites, such as your monitor's resolution and operating system, so that web pages are displayed correctly. More importantly, your browser must give away your IP address, which uniquely identifies your computer on the Internet. By giving your IP address away, your browser tells a website where to send text and graphics to display them. If your browser didn't give away your IP address, any website you visited would have no idea which computer wanted to view its web pages. (Visit www.whatismyip.com to see how your browser gives away your IP address every time it connects to a website.) Unless you use an anonymous browsing service like Anonymizer (http://www.anonymizer.com), which strips away your IP address and other identifying information, downloading files from any website will always reveal your identity.

NOTE: *Many file trading websites may do something known as* drive-by downloading, *which means that just visiting the site can install spyware on your computer without your knowledge.*

Another reason why web and FTP sites are still popular for file sharing is that you can often find obscure files that you may never find on most file sharing networks. FTP sites usually offer every song from an album, and you can copy them all in one visit; file sharing networks, on the other hand, usually only offer the most popular songs from a particular album.

While file sharing networks may attract all the publicity, don't overlook web and FTP sites for finding the files you want. With less legal risk, web and FTP sites offer a slower but safer alternative for file sharing.

PART 2

STEALING FILES

6

PROTECTING YOUR IDENTITY

With the RIAA hunting down individuals who share pirated music files, the Business Software Alliance (BSA) targeting people who pirate software, and the FBI looking for anyone who breaks copyright laws, the prospect of sharing files over the Internet may seem about as dumb as selling crack from the trunk of your car while parked behind a police station. Of course, file sharing itself isn't illegal as long as you own the copyright on the files (they're your photos, music, poetry, and so on), or if the files are in the public domain.

Hiding yourself from the world doesn't exactly hide the world from you.

—Unknown

But even though the RIAA may threaten and sue, millions of people are still sharing files. They're just getting a little bit smarter about doing so and playing the odds. Rather than stop sharing files that violate copyright, most file sharers simply adopt different ways of sharing to avoid detection and prosecution. While the authorities may be able to catch and prosecute blatant violators, they are less likely to find, let alone spend the time to prosecute, the less flagrant offenders. As a result, people can always skirt the law selectively, much like accelerating down an isolated stretch of highway in the middle of the night when you figure there's no cop around.

But the RIAA isn't the only danger people face when sharing files. One major and very real danger is of downloading and running a crippling computer virus that will wipe out your entire hard disk. (See Chapter 7 to learn more about protecting your computer from viruses and other malicious programs.)

No matter what files you share, you should always take precautions to protect yourself and your computer as much as possible.

HIDING YOUR IDENTITY

Share a copyrighted file or two and you're breaking the law. Share a few hundred and you'll likely attract the attention of the authorities.

The first step people take when they are worried that the police may raid their house because of their file sharing activities is to mask their identity online so that nobody will know who is doing the illegal file sharing. The first way of masking your identity is to keep your real email address secret; the second is to mask your IP (Internet Protocol) address.

HIDING YOUR EMAIL ADDRESS

Once the authorities know an email address, they can monitor the account holder's activity to see what the person does and receives over the Internet, much the same way they can tap a telephone line and eavesdrop on telephone conversations.

The simplest way to keep your email address a secret is to never share it with anyone you don't trust. An email address can identify either the company that you work for (such as billgates@microsoft.com), the Internet service provider (ISP) you use (such as jsmith@aol.com), or the company that hosts your email account (such as bigman1239@lycos.com).

Many people skirt this problem by using a free email account on Hotmail (http://www.hotmail.com) or Yahoo! (http://www.yahoo.com). Unlike ordinary email accounts that can link you to a specific company or ISP, web-based email accounts can be created anonymously (just type in a false name and address when you create the initial email account) and can be accessed by any computer (such as a public Internet kiosk), anywhere in the world. To ensure their anonymity, many file sharers abandon their free email accounts periodically and create new ones.

MASKING YOUR IP ADDRESS

An IP address is a unique string of numbers, such as 65.3.158.155, that identifies your particular computer on the Internet, much like a street address can identify your specific location in a city.

Hiding your IP address can be tricky, because every time you connect to a website, a file sharing network, or even an IRC chat room, your computer sends your IP address so other computers will know where to send the information you request. As a result, your computer constantly broadcasts your IP address to dozens of different computers every time you access the Internet, and once someone knows your IP address, they can find you.

Don't believe us? Visit the Shields UP website (http://www.grc.com), shown in Figure 6-1, to see the information your computer is sending. (You may have to click around a bit to reach the right page on the site.)

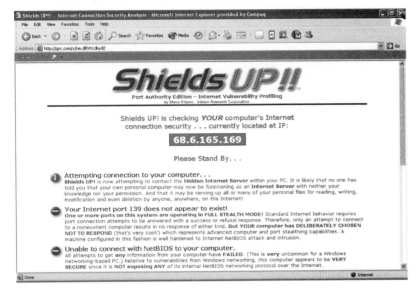

Figure 6-1
The Shields UP website can show you the type of information that your computer sends out over the Internet, such as your IP address.

Dynamic and static IP addresses

Depending on your type of Internet connection, you may have a *dynamic* or a *static* IP address. If you connect to the Internet through a telephone line, you have a dynamic IP address. If you connect to the Internet using a cable or DSL modem, you may have either a static or dynamic IP address.

As the names imply, a dynamic IP address changes each time you connect, while a static IP address is always the same each time you connect. If yours is a dynamic address, every time you connect to your ISP, they assign you a randomly selected IP address. When you disconnect and then reconnect, your computer gets a totally new IP address.

If yours is a static IP address, it's always the same when you connect to the Internet, much like your street address remains the same as long as you live at that location. It shouldn't surprise you then that once someone knows your static IP address, they can easily find your computer on the Internet. But it may surprise you to learn that they can track down a dynamic IP address, too.

While dynamic IP addresses might seem to hide your identity, don't count on it. Why? Your ISP likely keeps records on who used which particular IP address at any given time, and if the authorities suspect a specific IP address at some particular time, all they have to do is view your ISP's records to see who was using that particular dynamic IP address at that time, which will probably lead them right back to you.

Similarly, when you use a file sharing program, you probably won't be able to hide your IP address because the computer you're communicating with needs to know where to send that file. It knows where to send it because your computer tells it, and that makes the file sharer an easy target for the major music companies who hire people to search these networks for IP addresses that are sharing large numbers of files (say 1,000 or more), or that are sharing popular music. Once they find that IP address, they can eventually track it down to the offending computer.

SECRETS OF ANONYMOUS FILE SHARING

Whether you're a privacy freak or you're actually doing something wrong, you have three choices if you want to maintain your anonymity over a file sharing network:

- Use a special firewall, such as PeerGuardian, to mask your IP address.

- Use a file sharing program that encrypts your IP address.

- Use a proxy server to strip away your IP address.

KEEPING YOUR IP ADDRESS SECRET WITH PEERGUARDIAN

If you can't keep your IP address a secret from a file sharing network, you can keep it secret from the people most likely to be trying to track you down—if you know *their* IP addresses.

PeerGuardian (http://www.methlabs.org) knows those addresses; it contains a database of IP addresses that belong to various law enforcement agencies and music companies (see Figure 6-2). When someone with one of these known IP addresses tries to examine the files on various computers to determine the number and names of the songs available, PeerGuardian jumps in and blocks your IP address so they can't examine your files. PeerGuardian lets in anyone whose IP address is not in their database.

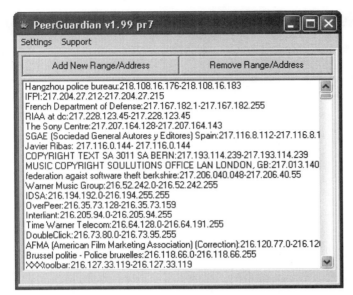

Figure 6-2

PeerGuardian maintains a database of suspicious IP addresses that it blocks
over a file sharing network, such as those belonging to the RIAA, Warner Music,
and the French Department of Defense.

HIDING YOUR IP ADDRESS AND YOUR ACTIVITIES ON AN ENCRYPTED FILE SHARING NETWORK

Can PeerGuardian really protect you from prying eyes? Maybe, but don't
count on it, because those same agencies can change their addresses or use
dynamic ones. Alternatively, consider using only file sharing networks that use
encryption to ensure anonymity, such as Filetopia (see Figure 6-3).

Such file sharing networks protect your privacy in two ways. First, instead
of connecting directly to another computer to share files, networks such as
MUTE reroute your connection through multiple computers. Doing this makes it
nearly impossible for anyone to determine which two computers may be communicating at any given time, thus ensuring your anonymity.

Second, these networks also encrypt any files sent between computers so
no one can tell what type of information people may be passing along to each
other. Anonymity protects your identity while encryption protects the contents of
any files that you share.

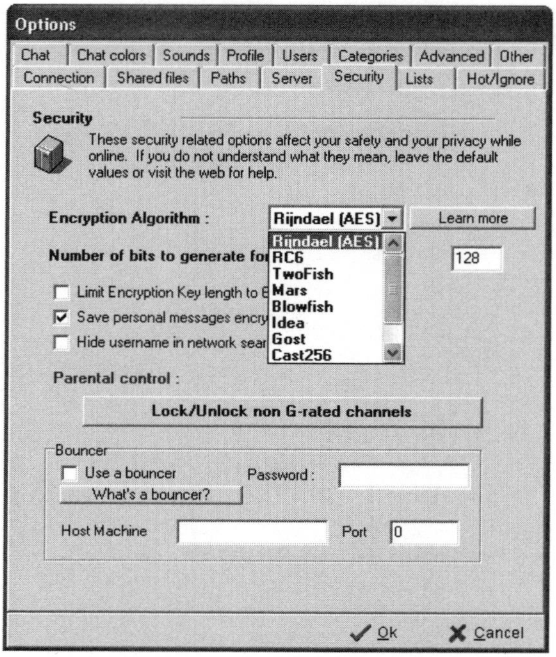

Figure 6-3

Filetopia gives you a choice of different encryption algorithms to mask your identity when you are connected to the Filetopia peer-to-peer network.

Because an anonymous file sharing network could mask the identity of blatant file sharers, the recording industry targeted Madster (formerly called Aimster), which allowed people to encrypt files and send them over instant messaging services. In court, Madster claimed that they could not block files swapped using their software because they could not tell which ones might violate copyright. However, the appeals court called this argument "willful blindness" and ordered Madster shut down anyway.

Until they shut down every possible file sharing network, though, try using one of the following:

Freenet   http://freenet.sourceforge.net

Filetopia   http://www.filetopia.org

GRL ISN   http://www.grltechnology.com

While it's nearly impossible to shut down a file sharing network that doesn't route everything through a central server (which proved to be the downfall of the original Napster), organizations such as the RIAA can still try to sue the companies that produce the file sharing programs in the first place, such as Kazaa. However, that won't happen with EarthStation 5 (http://www.earthstation5.com), a file sharing company located in war-torn Palestine.

To keep their users anonymous, EarthStation 5 uses encryption (which hides the contents of the files you're sharing) and proxy servers (which masks your IP address so people can't find you on the Internet) to ensure everyone's identity is as secure and private as possible (see Figure 6-4).

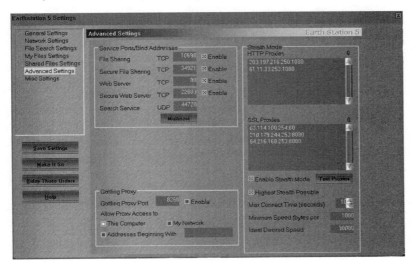

Figure 6-4
EarthStation 5 offers a stealth mode to mask your IP address from any intruders.

If the authorities try to shut down EarthStation 5, they'll have to visit the less than comfortable lands inside the Palestinian territory. Between missile strikes, car bombings, and random shootings, few authorities are going to care, let alone enforce, any laws against EarthStation 5, so EarthStation 5 is likely to escape the wrath of the RIAA and other Western-based organizations for the foreseeable future.

HIDING YOUR IP ADDRESS WITH AN ANONYMOUS PROXY SERVER

When you use file sharing networks like Morpheus or Kazaa, anyone on that network can see the IP address that identifies every computer. To avoid broadcasting your IP address to anyone who might be looking for it, try masking it by using a *proxy server*.

A proxy server acts as a middleman that (theoretically, at least) strips away your IP address. Instead of connecting to another computer directly, and thus giving away your own IP address, you connect to a proxy server, which then contacts the other computer for you. All the other computer sees is the IP address of the proxy server.

By the same token, when you connect through a proxy server and then copy files from another computer, the file you're downloading first goes to the proxy server and then to your computer. Proxy servers thus slow down file sharing programs, but they also protect your identity so that no one (except the proxy server computer) knows your IP address.

For a list of proxy servers, visit one of the following websites:

The Proxy Connection	http://theproxyconnection.com/httplist.html
Socks 5 Proxy List	http://www.atomintersoft.com/products/alive-proxy/socks5-list
OpenProxies	http://www.openproxies.com
ProxyKing	http://www.proxyking.com
StayInvisible.com	http://www.stayinvisible.com/index.pl/proxy_list

You'll find both free and commercial proxy servers on these lists. The free ones may be slow because so many people use them, and not all of them will strip away your IP address, so if you value your time and privacy, pay to use a faster, anonymous proxy server instead.

NOTE: *Pay attention to the locations of different proxy servers. A proxy in Taiwan or Brazil probably won't care if what you're doing skirts American laws, but one in Utah or New York just might.*

Hiding behind a proxy server

Once you find a proxy server that you think you can trust, you need to configure your file sharing program to use it. Most file sharing programs allow you to configure a proxy server to mask your IP address, although finding the specific command to do so may not be easy.

To configure Kazaa to use a proxy server, click Tools > Options, and in the Desktop Options dialog box, click the Firewall tab, as shown in Figure 6-5. There you can enter the IP address of the proxy server you want to use.

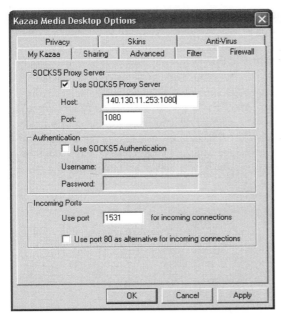

Figure 6-5
Using a proxy server with Kazaa to mask your IP address.

Hiding behind a wireless hotspot

For the ultimate in identity masking, log on to one of the many free wireless *hotspots* around the country. By using a public wireless Internet connection with a laptop, the only IP address anyone will see will be the one that belongs to the wireless hotspot itself, and not to your computer.

You'll find free wireless Internet access available at various parks, libraries, hotels, and restaurants in cities worldwide. Many businesses don't bother to password-protect their wireless systems, which leaves them open to visitors too.

Downloading files takes some time, so drop by with fully charged batteries (or a power cord if you can find an outlet), and keep your screen dimmed while downloading to slow the battery drain. And bring something to read while you wait.

The following websites list where free wireless hotspots are located:

The Wi-Fi-FreeSpot Directory   http://www.wififreespot.com

FreeNetworks   http://www.freenetworks.org

WiFiMaps   http://www.wifimaps.com

OTHER WAYS OF HIDING YOUR IDENTITY

The precautions listed in this chapter can minimize your visibility over the Internet when you use a file sharing program. For added security, many people use file sharing networks at their job (so any file sharing activities get traced to their employer and not to any particular individual).

For even greater protection, you can turn off file sharing on your computer, as shown in Figure 6-6. That means you can still copy files from other people's computers, but no one can examine, let alone copy, any files on your computer. Of course, if everyone stops sharing files to protect themselves, that essentially shuts down the file sharing networks, which is what organizations like the RIAA want everyone to do in the first place.

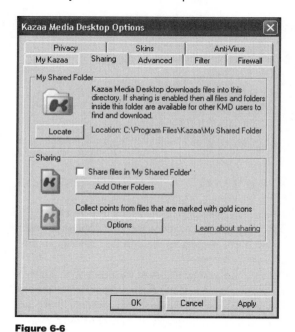

Figure 6-6

If you refuse to share files over a file sharing network, the authorities can't see if your computer contains any copyrighted files.

As another alternative, just share a handful of files and when you download new files, move them to a separate folder that you won't share with others. Now if the RIAA examines your computer, they'll think that you're not sharing enough files to make you a worthwhile target.

Another way to mask your identity is to do all your illegal file sharing activity on somebody else's computer, preferably someone you don't like. That way if the authorities do track your IP address, it will lead them directly to anyone but you. An additional way to protect yourself involves taking advantage of the way the RIAA tracks copyright violators. They don't target people copying files; they target people sharing files.

Remember, don't break the law; just creatively skirt around the legal boundaries like any law-abiding politician would do.

7

PROTECTING YOUR COMPUTER

One of the biggest problems with file sharing is keeping your IP address private so organizations like the RIAA can't find and sue you. The second biggest problem with file sharing is keeping your computer safe. Not only do you have to worry about downloading bogus MP3 files that contain static or verbal insults, urging you to buy music legally, but you also have to worry about the more insidious files you might download by mistake: viruses, worms, Trojan horses, pop-up ads, and spyware.

In any country there are people who have to die. They are the sacrifices any nation has to make to achieve law and order.

—Idi Amin Dada

CATCHING MALICIOUS FILES

Every time you copy and share files, you risk infecting your computer, and if you copy files from several sources, you will undoubtedly run into a nasty file at some point.

To fully protect your computer, you need all of the following programs:

– An antivirus program

– A firewall

– An anti–Trojan horse program

– An anti-spyware program

STOPPING A VIRUS

Viruses act like parasites that attach themselves to otherwise harmless files, so that when you copy the infected file to your hard disk, the virus starts infecting your computer. Once a virus has infected your computer, it may display an annoying message, interfere with the normal use of your computer (such as fouling up the mouse or stopping the keyboard from working), or delete files—

it could even wipe out your entire hard disk. While not all viruses will threaten your files, all viruses are unwanted.

To protect yourself against viruses, use an antivirus program that can detect and remove viruses before they can cause any problems. But don't rush out and buy a commercial antivirus program like Norton or McAfee; use one of the free ones instead. Try one of these:

AVG Anti-Virus	http://www.grisoft.com
avast	http://www.avast.com
AntiVir	http://www.free-av.com

These companies can't compete against Norton or McAfee for shelf space in the stores, so they give away their antivirus programs to get more people to use them free for noncommercial home use. The more people who use their products, the more likely it is that some of them will eventually decide to purchase the commercial version for their businesses or workplace.

Once you install an antivirus program, the program constantly checks every file that you send or receive. If the antivirus program detects a virus stored in a file, it gives you the option of erasing the file and killing the file transfer. (See the help information that comes with your particular program for details on setting it up properly.) Always use your antivirus program to scan files that you download *before* you open them.

As an alternative to buying an antivirus program, you can also use a free online antivirus scanner, like one of these:

Trend Micro	http://housecall.trendmicro.com
BitDefender	http://www.bitdefender.com/scan/licence.php
RAV AntiVirus	http://www.ravantivirus.com/scan

NOTE: *There is no perfect antivirus program because hackers write new viruses all the time. No matter what type of antivirus program you use, keep its virus database updated constantly so the antivirus program will know how to recognize and destroy the latest viruses that have been released over the Internet. Even the best antivirus program is useless if you don't regularly update its virus database.*

STOPPING A WORM

Unlike viruses, worms can travel on their own without attaching themselves to another file, so it's entirely possible that your computer could get infected with a worm if you just connect to the Internet. While many antivirus programs can detect and remove worms after they infect your computer, you still need a *firewall* to keep worms from slipping into your computer in the first place.

Every computer connects to the Internet through a physical connection, such as a telephone line, a cable connection, or a DSL (Digital Subscriber Line) connection. But once you're connected to the Internet, you may want to perform several tasks at the same time, such as sending and receiving email while you browse websites and chat with friends through an instant messaging program. To sort all this data out, every computer divides its Internet connection into *ports*, which act like doorways into your computer, and every port serves a specific function, such as retrieving web pages or sending and receiving email.

When your computer receives data from the Internet, it has no idea what that data might be, so to avoid confusing each other, computers agree to send only specific data to certain ports. That way when a computer receives data in port 80, it knows that data will always be a web page sent from another computer.

The more ports that are open on your computer, the more ways there are for a worm to sneak in and infect your computer. To protect your computer, a firewall simply shuts down any open ports that you don't need at the moment, effectively blocking worms from infecting your computer. Because every computer needs to open some ports just to connect to the Internet, a firewall also screens data coming and going through open ports, to make sure that none of the data is malicious.

If you're running Windows XP, you have a free, but limited, firewall. To turn it on, follow these steps:

1. Click the Start button, and click Control Panel. A Control Panel window appears.
2. Click Network, and Internet Connections. Another Control Panel window appears.
3. Click Network Connections.
4. Click the dial-up, LAN, or high-speed Internet connection that you want to protect, and then, in the Network Tasks pane, click the Change Settings of This Connection option. A Connection Properties dialog box appears.

5. Click the Advanced tab, and under Internet Connection Firewall, click the Help Protect My Computer and Network by Limiting or Preventing Access to This Computer from the Internet check box. If a check mark appears, the firewall is turned on. If a check mark does not appear, the firewall is turned off.

The Windows XP firewall is better than nothing (and Windows XP's Service Pack 2 beefs it up considerably), but for a more comprehensive firewall that can block incoming hacker attacks and prevent any spyware or Trojan horses on your computer from communicating to the outside world, you need a full-featured firewall that lets you control every possible port leading in and out of your computer. Rather than buy a firewall program, though, try a free firewall program first.

To get as many people to use their products as possible, many firewall companies give away free versions for home use in hopes that people will like their products so much that they'll either purchase the commercial version that offers more features, or recommend that particular firewall for use at work. Here are some of the free firewalls available:

Outpost Firewall	http://www.agnitum.com
Sygate Personal Firewall	http://soho.sygate.com
Kerio Personal Firewall	http://www.kerio.com
Look 'n' Stop	http://www.looknstop.com
ZoneAlarm	http://www.zonelabs.com

NOTE: A firewall can block your computer from accessing many file sharing networks. To prevent this problem, you may need to configure your firewall to allow a specific file sharing program to access the Internet without interference. See the program's instructions to find out how to do this.

STOPPING A TROJAN HORSE

A Trojan horse masquerades as one program but really contains a secret payload. Sometimes this secret payload can be a message, a silly picture, or more commonly, a hidden program known as a *remote access Trojan* (RAT).

Once a RAT sneaks onto your computer, it can open a port and allow someone anywhere in the world to access your computer and control it. While many antivirus programs can detect and remove Trojan horses, you might want to use a dedicated anti–Trojan horse program in addition to any antivirus programs you may be using.

Dedicated anti–Trojan horse programs can detect and remove a wider variety of Trojan horse programs than most antivirus programs. Most anti–Trojan horse programs also include a real-time scanner that can prevent a Trojan horse from doing anything as soon as it tries to run.

Two popular anti–Trojan horse programs are TDS-3 (http://www. diamondcs.com.au) and TrojanHunter (http://www.misec.net). While neither program is free, they do offer a trial version to evaluate before you have to pay. For a free anti–Trojan horse program, grab a copy of a^2 (http://www.emsisoft. com/en). If you like the free, but limited, version, you may want to pay for the more advanced version.

In addition to an anti–Trojan horse program, you can also use your firewall to block certain ports that RATs use. By blocking these ports, you can keep a RAT from transmitting any data from your computer to the Internet, which effectively stops it from doing anything at all. Figure 7-1 shows a typical dialog box for configuring a firewall to block certain ports on your computer.

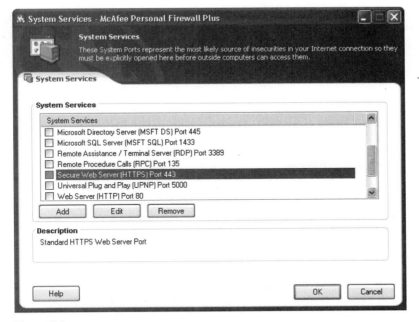

Figure 7-1

McAfee Personal Firewall lets you specify which ports to keep open and which ports to keep closed unless they are explicitly opened by a trusted program.

STOPPING SPYWARE/ADWARE

Unlike viruses that can attach themselves to a file, spyware (which is related to the less malicious, but similar type of program dubbed "adware") is something that is deliberately inserted into a file.

NOTE: *Technically, adware refers to programs that display advertisements on your screen while spyware refers to programs that secretly monitor your activities and send personal information about your computer back to another computer on the Internet. Because both types of programs are often unwanted, most people refer to adware as spyware and vice versa.*

Why should you care about spyware/adware when file sharing? Because when you install many shareware or freeware programs, such as file sharing programs, you may see a cryptic licensing agreement in small print that explains how third-party programs may subject your computer to ceaseless bombardments of pop-up advertising (although they don't put it in quite those terms).

Because reading the fine print licensing agreements in a tiny dialog box on your computer screen may be less than inviting (a fact that most corporations count on), here's part of the licensing agreement displayed when you try to install the Blubster file sharing program.

> *PLEASE READ THE GATOR CORPORATION PRIVACY STATEMENT AND END USER LICENSE AGREEMENT (COLLECTIVELY "Terms and Conditions") CAREFULLY AND MAKE SURE YOU UNDERSTAND THEM. THEY CONTAIN IMPORTANT INFORMATION THAT YOU SHOULD KNOW BEFORE ACCEPTING ANY GAIN-Supported Software (DEFINED BELOW).*
>
> *THESE Terms and Conditions MAY BE TERMINATED AT ANY TIME BY REMOVING ALL GAIN-Supported Software FROM THE COMPUTER ON WHICH THEY RESIDE USING THE ADD/REMOVE PROGRAMS MENU IN THE MICROSOFT(r) WINDOWS(r) CONTROL PANEL, AND DESTROYING ANY OTHER COPIES OF GAIN-Supported Software THAT MAY HAVE BEEN MADE. SOON AFTER ALL GAIN-Supported Software HAS BEEN REMOVED THE GAIN AdServer WILL REMOVE ITSELF AUTOMATICALLY. http://webpdp.gator.com/gain/32/about-gain-01.html, INCORPORATED HEREIN BY REFERENCE, GENERATES A LIST OF GAIN-Supported Software THAT RESIDES ON THE COMPUTER THAT IS USED TO ACCESS THE LINK.*

The Gator Corporation

Privacy Statement and End User License Agreement

("Terms and Conditions")

The Gator Corporation ("TGC") provides personal computer users with a winning proposition: the ability to get advertising-supported versions of popular software applications (often valued at up to $30) free-of-charge or at a reduced cost. Downloading or installing these ad-supported software applications requires acceptance of these Terms and Conditions which allows TGC to download and install the "GAIN AdServer" software, which delivers advertising, software, and various informational messages to computer screens ("GAIN Ads").

The whole idea behind spyware/adware is to monitor what type of information may be stored on a hard disk, such as cookies from a shopping website that identifies the types of books recently ordered, or the cached list of websites recently visited. Based on this information, spyware/adware sends a message to another computer, which uses this retrieved information to determine what types of advertisements to display on your computer through a multitude of additional browser windows known as pop-up ads (which are discussed in the following section).

Even if you delete the program that included the spyware, you may not end up removing the spyware itself. To remove spyware, you must use a special anti-spyware program that will scan your hard disk for traces of known spyware and, once it finds a spyware program, give you the option of wiping it out (see Figure 7-2).

Here are some popular anti-spyware programs:

Pest Patrol	http://www.pestpatrol.com
AntiSpyware	http://www.mcafee.com
Spyware Eliminator	http://www.aluriasoftware.com
Spy Sweeper	http://www.webroot.com

Two popular (and free) spyware-removal programs:

| **Ad-Aware** | http://www.lavasoft.nu |
| **Spybot** | http://www.safer-networking.org |

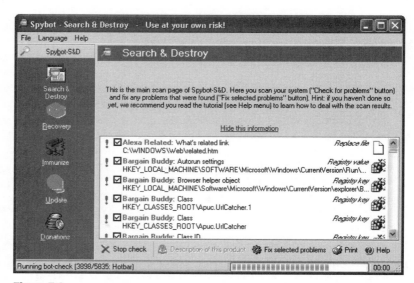

Figure 7-2
An anti-spyware program, such as Spybot, can identify all the spyware programs currently stored on a hard disk and give you the option of removing them.

STOPPING POP-UP ADS

The moment you install a peer-to-peer program on your computer, get ready to start seeing strange things happen. Many peer-to-peer programs offer two versions: a free one that includes built-in advertising (known as adware), or a commercial one that costs money but does not include any advertising.

If you choose the free version of a peer-to-peer program, such as Kazaa, you may suddenly start noticing ads popping up in separate windows every time you connect to the Internet. Shutting down each window individually will prove troublesome, so you have two choices: buy a program to block pop-up ads, or switch to a browser that includes a feature to block pop-up ads. (Unfortunately, if you switch to a different browser while running Microsoft Windows, many pop-up ads will just load Internet Explorer to create pop-up ads all over your screen anyway.)

Windows XP's second Service Pack adds a pop-up ad blocker and auto-matically turns it on. Once you've installed Service Pack 2 through Windows Update, make sure the blocker's turned on: choose Pop-up Blocker from Internet Explorer's Tools menu, and make sure there's no check mark next to Turn Off Pop-Up Blocker.

To shut off pop-up ads in Mozilla, a free browser available for Windows, Linux, and Mac OS, follow these steps:

1. Select Edit > Preferences to display the Preferences dialog box.
2. Click the plus sign that appears to the left of the Privacy & Security category, and then click Popup Windows.
3. Click in the check box next to Block Unrequested Popup Windows, and then click OK, as shown in Figure 7-3.

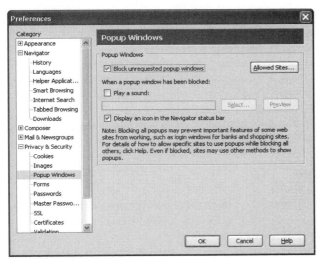

Figure 7-3

Mozilla allows you to block pop-up ads from appearing. Unfortunately, pop-up ads can still appear on your Windows computer if they use Internet Explorer (before you install Service Pack 2), even if you make Mozilla your default browser.

To shut off pop-up ads in Safari, the browser that comes with Mac OS X, click Safari > Block Pop-Up Windows, or press COMMAND-K.

You can also buy pop-up ad blocking programs such as the following:

STOPzilla	http://www.stopzilla.com
Ad Blocker Pro	http://www.3bsoftware.com
Pop-Up Stopper	http://www.panicware.com
Guidescope	http://www.guidescope.com
12Ghosts Popup-Killer	http://www.12ghosts.com
Muffin	http://muffin.doit.org

Many firewalls, such as the paid version of ZoneAlarm, can also block pop-up ads. Too, both Yahoo! and Google offer free pop-up blockers if you install their toolbars in your browser.

PROTECTING DATA ON YOUR COMPUTER

No matter how carefully you use antivirus programs, firewalls, pop-up ad blockers, and anti-spyware programs, a new virus, worm, Trojan horse, pop-up ad, or spyware/adware program may still slip past your defenses. At the very least, such programs will just be a nuisance, cluttering up your hard disk or possibly slowing down your computer. At the worst, they could crash your computer or delete files from your hard disk despite your precautions.

The last thing you want to do is risk messing up any hard disk that contains important information. So if you're going to engage in the high-risk behavior of sharing files, separate your important data from your file sharing activities. That way if you download a strange file that turns out to be the latest virus, or if a spyware/adware program latches on to your computer and wrecks it, your important data will still be safe.

MAKING BACKUPS

Computers are inherently unreliable beasts, whether you have to worry about viruses or other malicious programs, so the first rule for any computer user is to back up important data. Backups can be as simple as storing important files on a floppy disk, or as complicated as having a separate tape backup unit that automatically backs up your files

Other popular ways to backup files include connecting an external hard disk to your computer (so if your computer dies, you can just plug the external hard drive into another computer and transfer all of your files), storing files on a CD or DVD, or capturing your files, operating system, and operating system settings as a disc image file. By backing up your entire hard disk to a disc image file, you can restore your entire computer, operating system settings, files, and programs, to a new hard disk within minutes. Some popular programs that can save your hard disk as a disc image include Norton Ghost (http://www.symantec.com) and SecurePC (http://www.farstone.com).

NOTE: When you back up your files, make sure you don't accidentally back up any viruses, Trojan horses, or spyware in the process. If you do, and you restore your files from a backup together with these malicious programs, you'll just end up with the same problems once again.

USING SEPARATE COMPUTERS

The safest way to protect your data is to use two separate computers: one for your ordinary, everyday activities, such as tracking your finances and writing letters, and a second one to download files from file sharing networks. Whenever you download a new file, check it for viruses or Trojan horses on your second computer, and if the file appears safe, then copy it to your main computer. If a virus or tenacious spyware/adware program causes problems, just wipe clean the hard disk on your downloading computer, reinstall your operating system, and start from scratch. Almost any computer of recent vintage will do—you can probably pick up a suitable Pentium III or similar system for a few hundred dollars or less.

USING REMOVABLE HARD DISKS

Not everyone has the space or money to afford a second computer, even if they buy a used one. As another alternative, install removable hard disks in your computer. Removable hard disks are nothing more than trays that slide in and out of your computer, and inside each tray is an ordinary hard disk. That way you can have one removable hard disk holding your important data, and a second removable hard disk that contains all the files you download from the Internet.

To find a removable hard disk kit to install in your computer, visit one of these sites or try a search in Froogle (http://www.froogle.com):

Kingwin	http://www.kingwin.com
DataCity	http://www.datacity.net
StarTech.com	http://www.startech.com

And if you've got a removable hard disk, you can just yank it out and hide it if the police start banging on your door.

PARTITIONING YOUR HARD DISK

If you can't afford multiple hard disks, you can do the next best thing and partition a single hard disk. From the computer's point of view, partitioning essentially divides a single large hard disk into several smaller disks. That way, one part of your hard disk can store just your operating system, a second part of that same hard disk can store your valuable data, and a third part of that hard disk can store all your file sharing programs.

Now if a virus attacks your computer, it will likely only damage the files stored in a single partition. With multiple partitions, it's even possible to install Windows XP on one partition and Linux (or even a second copy of Windows XP) on a second partition. When you boot up your computer, you can choose which operating system to use, which gives you a chance to isolate your important data from your operating system and file sharing programs that may be burdened with spyware or viruses.

You'll need software to partition your hard disk and allow you to boot up from multiple operating systems stored on different partitions. Pick up a copy of one of these programs:

PartitionMagic	http://www.symantec.com
System Commander **or Partition Commander**	http://www.v-com.com
Ranish Partition Manager	http://www.ranish.com

CREATING A VIRTUAL COMPUTER

Using removable hard disks or partitioning a single hard disk can be cumbersome, so for another way to isolate your file sharing programs from the rest of your computer, consider using a virtual computer program instead. Virtual computer programs emulate an ordinary PC, so you can run another operating system in a separate window on your computer. This way, it's possible to run Windows 2000 on Mac OS X, or Linux on a computer that runs Windows XP, as shown in Figure 7-4.

With a virtual computer program, you can save your important data on your hard disk and then create a virtual computer running a second copy of your operating system (or a different operating system altogether) where you can run your file sharing programs. If a virus or spyware program gets loose on your virtual computer, it can't migrate to your real computer and mess up any data.

NOTE: *The music industry once sued a woman for illegally sharing copyrighted music over the Internet, but they later retracted their claim when they discovered she used a Macintosh, yet the file sharing program they claimed she was using only ran on Windows. Of course, she could have been using a Macintosh to run a program like Virtual PC to run Windows.*

Figure 7-4
With a virtual computer program, such as Virtual PC, you can run multiple operating systems simultaneously to isolate data from each operating system.

Virtual computer programs run noticeably slower than the same operating system running on a computer all by itself, but a virtual computer program gives you the advantage of running two or more operating systems simultaneously, so you can run Windows XP in the background and both Red Hat Linux and Windows 98 in two separate windows on your screen.

Two popular virtual computer programs are VMware (http://www.vmware.com) and Virtual PC (http://www.microsoft.com). VMware can run on either Windows or Linux, while Virtual PC can run on either Windows or Mac OS 9/X. To learn more about VMware, pick up a copy of *The Book of VMware* by Brian Ward, published by No Starch Press.

DESTROYING THE EVIDENCE

With the major music companies using their financial muscle to sue anyone caught trading files illegally, the final step in protecting your computer and yourself involves wiping out any evidence that you've ever had questionable files stored on your computer at all. Two ways to hide your questionable files from view are encryption and secure deletion.

ENCRYPTING YOUR FILES

Encryption basically scrambles your files so no one can tell what type of data may have been stored inside them. To make encryption easy to use, programs such as the following ones can automatically encrypt everything in a folder:

Encrypted Magic Folders   http://www.pc-magic.com

CryptoExpert   http://www.secureaction.com

To use any files stored in an encrypted folder, you enter a password. When you're ready to leave your computer, just enter your password again, and these programs magically encrypt your folders once more, protecting the folder and file contents from prying eyes.

SECURELY DELETING YOUR FILES

In addition to encryption, consider securely deleting your files when you don't need them anymore. Encrypted files can still be cracked, but deleted files can never be used as evidence if their contents can't be recovered.

When you delete a file, use a secure deletion method. When you delete files in the normal way, your computer doesn't physically erase the file from your hard disk—it just erases part of the file name and marks the space that the file used on the disk as blank so that it can be used for something else. As far as your operating system knows, the file no longer exists, but with a simple utility program, such as Norton Utilities, you can recover previously deleted files rather quickly if they haven't yet been written over.

On the other hand, secure deletion programs erase the file from a hard disk and then rewrite random data over that area of the hard disk several times. The more times you write random data over a file, the harder it will be for anyone to recover that file ever again.

Here are some popular secure deletion programs:

AbsoluteShield File Shredder   http://www.sys-shield.com

Mutilate File Wiper   http://home.att.net/~craigchr/mutilate.html

CyberScrub   http://www.cyberscrub.com

Autoclave   http://staff.washington.edu/jdlarios/autoclave

Protecting your computer from viruses and other threats requires vigilance, but armed with the proper tools, you can protect most of your file sharing activities from interfering with your regular data. However, no matter how many precautions you take, or how careful you may be, every time you connect to the Internet, you're putting your computer and data at risk. Although you can protect your computer using a variety of tools and techniques, none can guarantee true security, so be aware of the dangers whenever you engage in any type of file sharing.

8

THE FILE FORMATS

Much to our frustration, computer files can be stored in hundreds of different formats. Practically every program creates its own file format because each software company wants their file format to dominate and control the market, while possibly earning extra licensing fees at the same time. For example, Apple originally snubbed rival Microsoft by designing its popular iPod to use a different audio file format than the "standard" audio file format (Windows Media Audio or WMA) that Microsoft supports. Microsoft, hoping to make money on their own WMA audio format, designed Windows Media Player so it only converts songs to WMA, not to the vastly more popular MP3 format. (People must purchase a separate MP3 encoder before Windows Media Player will create MP3 files.)

Property is theft.

—Pierre-Joseph Proudhon

Besides there being so many file formats created by different software publishers, new file formats often pop up for other reasons. Some formats compress files to make them faster to swap and easier to store. Others simply break files into several pieces so they can be posted (and downloaded, one at a time) in a newsgroup. Sometimes people change file formats just so their software can read that particular file, leading to programs that specialize in doing nothing but converting files from one format to another.

Although you're likely to stumble across many different file formats, you'll find that most programs, such as music and video players, can recognize different file formats or convert one file format to another. To identify the format of a file, take a peek at the file's three-letter file-name extension.

If you're using Windows, open the Windows Explorer program, click the Tools menu, and click Folder Options to display the Folder Options dialog box. Click the View tab and remove the check mark next to Hide Extensions for Known File Types, as shown in Figure 8-1.

If you're using a Macintosh, click on a file and press COMMAND-I to display the properties of that file, such as the file extension and the type of file it may be. To further help identify the type of data a file contains, the Macintosh displays files with descriptive icons, such as showing musical notes for a music file or displaying the icon of the program that created the file, as shown in Figure 8-2.

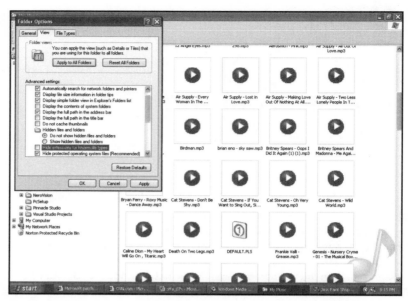

Figure 8-1

The Folder Options dialog box lets you set Windows to display file extensions that are normally hidden from view.

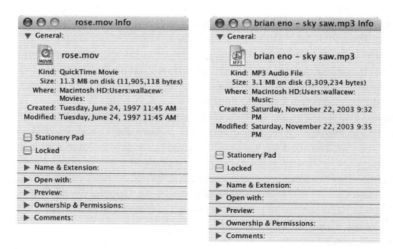

Figure 8-2

A Macintosh can identify both the extension of a file and the kind of file it may be, such as an MP3 audio file or a QuickTime movie file.

If you're using Linux, right-click a file, and when a pop-up menu appears, click Properties to display the properties of that file, such as the file extension and the type of file it may be. To further help you identify the type of data a file contains, Linux displays both the file extension and a descriptive icon, such as musical notes to identify an audio file, as shown in Figure 8-3.

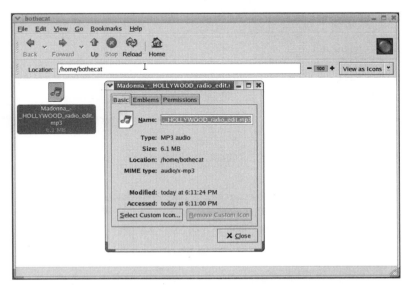

Figure 8-3
Linux can display both the extension of a file and the kind of file it may be, such as an MP3 audio file.

NOTE: *File extensions generally identify the type of data the file contains, but you can give a file any file extension you want. So it's actually possible to give a word processor document a file extension of .mp3. Most people don't do that, to avoid confusing others, but some viruses and Trojan horses use this trick to disguise themselves.*

To help you understand the different file formats you may see, this chapter summarizes the more popular file formats and explains why they exist in the first place.

MUSIC FILE FORMATS

Commercial audio CDs preserve all the fidelity of recorded music, but the size of each song is huge, making them awkward for storing and trading. To solve this problem, most people compress audio files using something called *lossy compression* (like the MP3 format), which smashes a huge audio file into a smaller file size while preserving as much sound fidelity as possible. As an alternative, you can also compress files using *lossless compression* (like the WAV format), which compresses audio files very little but maintains excellent sound fidelity.

With so many audio file formats available, it's possible to get an audio file that your music player won't recognize. To solve this problem, you can convert audio files from one format to another with an audio conversion program such as one of the following:

dBpowerAMP Music Converter	http://www.dbpoweramp.com
Audio MP3 WAV WMA OGG Converter	http://www.audio-converter.com
Awave Audio	http://www.fmjsoft.com

NOTE: *Converting between file formats nearly always removes some of the audio quality in the process, so if you need a different format for a specific audio player, it's best to either re-rip the CD or to download the file in the format you need.*

LOSSY COMPRESSION MUSIC FORMATS

The most common audio file formats are known as lossy formats because they compress audio files into much smaller sizes by physically removing parts of the original audio file—usually sounds that can't be heard clearly anyway, to reduce the size of an audio file. Although discriminating ears can tell the difference in quality between files compressed with lossy compression (such as MP3 files) and an original audio CD, most people don't mind the minor loss in audio quality, especially if they're listening to music through earbuds on a subway or airplane.

Because trading large files over the Internet takes time, most people are willing to sacrifice a little audio quality to save a lot of space by compressing music into one of many lossy file formats. Several of these lossy file formats are described in the following sections.

MP3

Type of file: Lossy compression
Usual contents: Individual songs
Copy protection: No

Official website: Fraunhofer IIS (http://www.iis.fraunhofer.de/amm)
Programs used: Nearly every music-playing program and device

MP3 (MPEG Audio Stream, Layer III) is by far the most popular format for sharing music. MP3 was one of the first compression formats available, and it can often shrink a song's size by nearly 90 percent, making for speedy Internet transfers.

Although newer compression formats now create smaller, better-sounding audio files, MP3 remains popular because it's supported by nearly every music player and it doesn't contain any copy protection, which allows users to copy and distribute as many copies as they want. With so many songs stored in the MP3 file format, few people are willing to switch to yet another format until the newer format offers substantial improvements over MP3.

To find a program that can extract songs from an audio CD and store them as MP3 files (a process known as *ripping*), visit MP3Machine (http://www.mp3machine.com), which offers shareware, freeware, demo, and trial MP3 rippers for Windows, Macintosh, and Linux. Popular CD rippers include the following:

FreeRIP	http://www.mgshareware.com
CoffeeCup MP3 Rip & Burn	http://www.coffeecup.com
Easy CD Ripper	http://www.8to32.com

Many jukebox programs also offer MP3 ripping capabilities, such as Musicmatch Jukebox (http://www.musicmatch.com) for Windows, and iTunes (http://www.apple.com/itunes) for Windows or Macintosh. Microsoft's Windows Media Player can create MP3 files from CDs, but only after you buy an MP3 encoder plug-in from one of these companies:

CyberLink	http://www.gocyberlink.com
InterVideo	http://www.intervideo.com
Sonic CinePlayer	http://www.cineplayer.com

You can also rip MP3 files from an audio CD if you have a CD/DVD burning program, such as Roxio Easy Media Creator (http://www.roxio.com) or Nero (http://www.nero.com).

NOTE: To create the highest quality audio files possible, some audio purists prefer a two-step conversion method as opposed to converting audio tracks directly into MP3 files. First they copy the CD's songs to their hard drive as WAV files. Then they convert the WAV files into MP3 files with a separate MP3 encoding program, such as Exact Audio Copy (http://www.exactaudiocopy.de), LAME (http://lame.sourceforge.net), or CDex (http://cdexos.sourceforge.net), or iTunes (http://www.apple.com).

MP3Pro

Type of file: Lossy compression
Usual contents: Individual songs
Copy protection: No
Official website: http://www.mp3prozone.com
Programs used: Some MP3 players also play MP3Pro files

Intended by the RCA company as a replacement for MP3 in the early 1990s, MP3Pro hasn't earned much respect, despite creating files half the size of MP3 that are backwards compatible with MP3 players. One major drawback to MP3Pro is that when the files are played on a standard MP3 player, MP3Pro files can sound worse than ordinary MP3 files, but when played on an MP3Pro player, MP3Pro files sound as good or better than MP3 files at half the size.

Unfortunately, few portable MP3 players support the MP3Pro format, but many software players support it, such as these:

Musicmatch Jukebox	http://www.musicmatch.com
Winamp with a plug-in	http://www.winamp.com
Nero	http://www.nero.com

Admirably, MP3Pro's creators left out copy protection, knowing it would immediately kill the fledgling format. But because it doesn't offer drastically better performance than the older MP3 standard, MP3Pro remains one of many MP3 competitors that haven't quite found their footing.

AAC, M4A, and M4P

Type of file: Lossy compression
Usual contents: Individual songs
Copy protection: No
Official website: http://www.aac-audio.com
Programs used: Some MP3 players also play AAC files

Apple Computer gave AAC (Advanced Audio Coding) a huge boost by choosing it as the main format for its iTunes online record store and iPod, as well as its QuickTime video player. As an open source codec (compressor/decompressor) from Dolby, AAC lacks copy protection, although Apple slaps its own

FairPlay Digital Rights Management system onto files purchased from iTunes. But because Apple's the only major company to embrace AAC—and the format only works on Apple's iPod portable music player—AAC isn't a major contender in the digital music format arena, especially among people engaged in file sharing across the Internet.

FairPlay prevents people from swapping AAC files, but it can be beaten fairly easily. Users simply copy their AAC files to a CD, then rip the audio tracks off this CD as either MP3 or WAV files.

NOTE: *AAC files may sometimes appear with the .m4a file extension, and copy-protected versions may appear with the .m4p file extension.*

Ogg Vorbis

Type of file: Lossy compression
Usual contents: Individual songs
Copy protection: No
Official website: http://www.vorbis.com
Programs used: Winamp (http://www.winamp.com) and several other MP3 players

Whereas most audio compression schemes are created by large corporations as money-making ventures, the Ogg Vorbis format takes the open source approach; it's free and created by a community of developers. Ogg Vorbis creates digital music files with the same or better compression and quality as MP3 and competing formats, but the format remains completely free, open, and unpatented. Anybody can use the format in any program, whether freeware, shareware, or commercial software, without paying any royalty fees.

Despite the format's high quality, its lack of a large marketing budget has kept it from moving far in the audio format wars. It's currently supported by Winamp and a few other players, but the list is steadily growing. Given its open source nature and royalty-free use, it's a file format that's likely to become more popular as time goes on.

WMA

Type of file: Lossy or lossless (on Windows XP only) compression
Usual contents: Individual songs
Copy protection: Yes
Official website: http://www.microsoft.com/windows/windowsmedia
Programs used: Microsoft Windows and some MP3 players

Rather than adopt MP3, Microsoft came up with its own compression format, Windows Media Audio (WMA). While it is supported by a fairly wide number of players, it's still nowhere near as popular as MP3, mostly because of its built-in copy protection. Windows Media Player creates copy-protected WMA files by default, preventing users from playing them on other devices.

To keep Media Player from adding copy protection, click the Tools menu and select Options. In the Options dialog box, click the Copy Music tab, and then clear the check mark from the Copy Protect Music check box, as shown in Figure 8-4.

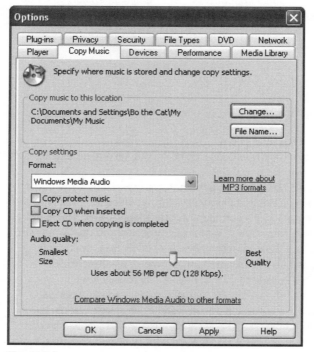

Figure 8-4
Remove the check mark from the Copy Protect Music check box to keep Windows Media Player from adding copy protection to your ripped CDs.

ASF

Type of file: Streaming audio or video
Usual contents: Music or video
Copy protection: Yes

Official website: http://www.microsoft.com/windows/windowsmedia
Programs used: Microsoft Windows Media Player

Microsoft patented the Advanced Systems Format (ASF) to broadcast streaming audio and video over the Internet. Unlike ordinary audio or video files that you must download completely before you can play them, you can play a streaming file as you receive it, which can be especially useful when download-ing large video files over the Internet.

ASF files are usually created by first storing audio or video in a WAV, MP3, or AVI file and then converting that file into an ASF file. Because ASF files are meant to be viewed or heard as you download them, most file traders aren't likely to store music or video in ASF.

LOSSLESS COMPRESSION MUSIC FORMATS

Because lossy compression degrades audio quality, many people prefer storing music in lossless file formats, which preserve all the sound fidelity of the original audio CD at the sacrifice of compressing the file size very little, or sometimes not at all. Because lossless files can be huge (a four-minute song, saved as a WAV file, can take up to 40MB of storage space while that same four-minute song, saved as an MP3 file, might only take up 4MB), few people trade files in lossless formats. When trading lossless files, many people prefer doing so through FTP sites, newsgroups, or special file sharing networks designed for handling large files, such as BitTorrent.

Because lossless files preserve the fidelity of the original recording, some music lovers store their favorite songs in both lossless and lossy formats. They play the lossless files on their desktop computer, which has a large enough hard disk to accommodate all the files, and then they convert their music to a lossy format (such as MP3) so they can play them on portable music players.

WAV, AIFF, and CDA

Type of file: Retail music CD tracks
Usual contents: Music
Copy protection: No
Official website: The CD-Recordable FAQ (http://www.cdrfaq.org) carries a vast amount of information about CD burning.
Programs used: Most CD burner programs

These three formats basically refer to the same thing—uncompressed digital sound files as they are sold on retail CDs. When viewed on Windows, a CD's songs appear as CDA (CD Audio Track) files. When extracted onto a computer's hard drive, Windows calls the same files WAV (waveform audio) files and Macintosh computers call them AIFF (Audio Interchange File Format) files.

Although WAV and AIFF formats both preserve the recorded music's original quality, they're much too large for most people to trade on the Internet.

ISO

Type of file: The uncompressed contents of an entire CD
Usual contents: Image of an entire disc
Copy protection: No
Official website: None
Programs used: Most CD burning programs

This format, which usually is referred to as an *ISO image*, refers to a single file that represents a complete CD. By using a CD burner to transfer an ISO image to a CD, traders can recreate the entire CD without loss of quality. An ISO image can contain any type of information that's stored on a CD, including music, programs, and text.

SHN

Type of file: Lossless music compression
Usual contents: Entire CDs or live performance recordings
Copy protection: No
Official website: http://wiki.etree.org
Programs used: mkwACT (http://home.att.net/~mkw/mkwact.html), and Shorten (http://www.hornig.net/shorten.html).

People wanting full-quality CDs or live recordings often trade files using SHN (Shorten) format. SHN reduces the size of files stored on a CD by up to 50 percent without removing any file quality.

FLAC

Type of file: Lossless music compression
Usual contents: Entire CDs or live performance recordings
Copy protection: No
Official website: http://flac.sourceforge.net or http://wiki.etree.org
Programs used: FLAC (http://flac.sourceforge.net), dBpowerAMP (http://www.dbpoweramp.com), and others

FLAC (Free Lossless Audio Codec), an open source project, improves on SHN files with better compression, higher-quality audio, and tag support (much like MP3 files). Like SHN, decompressed FLAC files don't lose any fidelity compared to the original CD, making them popular for trading classical music and recorded concerts.

WV

Type of file: Lossless music compression
Usual contents: Entire CDs or live performance recordings
Copy protection: No
Official website: http://www.wavpack.com
Programs used: WavPack

Another open source lossless CD compression project, WavPack lacks the momentum of SHN and FLAC, although the format turns up occasionally on newsgroups and websites.

APE

Type of file: Lossless music compression
Usual contents: Entire CDs or live performance recordings
Copy protection: No
Official website: http://www.monkeysaudio.com
Programs used: Winamp (http://www.winamp.com), Media Jukebox (http://www.musicex.com), and others

The APE audio file format is a semi–open source program that's grown nearly as popular as FLAC.

SUPPLEMENTAL MUSIC FORMATS

Although these formats don't contain music, they often appear with uploaded music to provide extra information about the music or downloaded files. Some contain reviews, or notes about the CD, while others provide ways to check the downloaded file's integrity. Still others contain playlists that play songs in a certain order, such as the order they appeared on the original CD.

SFV

Type of file: Simple File Verification (SFV) information
Usual contents: Text and numbers
Copy protection: No
Official website: None
Programs used: CheckSFV and QuickSFV (both at http://www.smr-usenet.com/software/misc.shtml)

Errors occasionally slip in as files travel through the Internet, sometimes corrupting the files. To protect against errors, people often run a "checksum" program, which calculates a number based on the specific file's contents. When sending a file, people include both the file name and its matching checksum value in a text file bearing the .sfv extension.

When someone downloads a file, they can recalculate the checksum to see if it matches the original checksum calculation. (Most people don't, but it's nice to know that this option is available to you in case you need it.) If it matches, they know they've received the file without any corruption, but if the checksums don't match, the file must have been corrupted while downloading. This difference in the checksum calculations can warn you that you need to download the file all over again.

MD5

Type of file: File verification
Usual contents: Text and numbers
Copy protection: No
Official website: http://userpages.umbc.edu/~mabzug1/cs/md5/md5.html
Programs used: Advanced CheckSum Verifier (http://www.irnis.net)

MD5 files contain a unique "digital signature" of a file, such as a video, based on that file's contents. By checking the MD5 value of a downloaded file, you can verify whether you downloaded the file without any errors.

M3U and PLS

Type of file: Playlist
Usual contents: List of song locations and play order
Copy protection: No
Official website: http://www.braindonors.net/specs/m3u.asp
Programs used: Winamp (http://www.winamp.com), Windows Media Player, and many others

An M3U file is often uploaded along with a complete CD of songs. It specifies a playlist that lets people play all the songs in a certain order—usually the order in which the songs originally appeared on the commercial audio CD.

NFO

Type of file: Information
Usual contents: Text describing details of a file upload
Copy protection: No

Official website: http://go.to/postassistant
Programs used: PostAssistant (http://go.to/postassistant)

Thoughtful uploaders include an informational file describing their music upload, including details such as its creation date, artist name, source (CD, vinyl, or tape), MP3 conversion program used, posting date, and list of tracks. Before uploading songs, many people run the PostAssistant program to create NFO, SFV, and M3U files for their songs. That makes it easy to include all three of those files with the post.

MIDI and MOD

Neither the MIDI nor MOD formats store music ripped from CDs. Instead of containing sound, a MIDI file includes a set of instructions that tells a synthesizer, such as a keyboard, how to recreate a particular sound. The sound quality depends entirely on the quality of the synthesizer, but it never sounds like a CD—it can't recreate vocals, for instance. MIDI files are mostly traded among musicians.

MOD files contain musical samples joined together, often resembling a video game soundtrack. They're limited to a small fan base and are essentially obsolete.

FILE COMPRESSION FORMATS

File compression formats typically pack one or more files into a single file that's smaller than the sum of all the parts. The most popular file compression formats work on several operating systems but some file compression formats are only used on specific operating systems, such Linux or Mac OS X, which limits their file sharing opportunities.

NOTE: *Although file compression formats can squash multiple files into a single file, they don't always work on certain types of files that are already compressed, such as certain movie, photo, and music file formats. Trying to compress MP3 or JPEG files with a file compression program can actually increase the total size of the file.*

Here's a look at the most common compression formats traded on the Internet, the type of information they usually contain, and the programs used to create or open them.

ZIP

Type of file: Lossless compression
Usual contents: Any type of file
Copy protection: Optional password protection
Official website: None
Programs used: PKZIP (http://www.pkzip.com) and WinZip (http://www.win-zip.com) for Windows; ZipIt (http://www.maczipit.com) and StuffIt (http://www.stuffit.com) for Macintosh

Zip is one of the oldest lossless compression formats around, and it combines several files by compressing them all into a single file. Retrieving all of the files is as simple as "unzipping" the single zipped file.

Although other formats are more efficient at compressing files, Zip works on nearly every type of computer, making it useful for compressing files that nearly anybody can download and unzip. For optional protection, you can password-protect a Zip file.

RAR

Type of file: Lossless compression
Usual contents: Large files like movies or entire albums
Copy protection: Optional password protection
Official website: http://www.rarlabs.com
Programs used: WinRAR for Windows and RAR for most other operating systems (http://www.rarlabs.com)

The RAR compression standard can compress files up to 15 percent smaller than Zip. Available for Windows, Macintosh, Linux, Pocket PC, FreeBSD, Unix, and many other operating systems, the RAR and WinRAR (for Windows) programs can not only compress and uncompress RAR files, but Zip files and several other file compression formats as well.

PAR AND PAR2

Type of file: Recovery
Usual contents: Recreates missing RAR files
Copy protection: No
Official website: http://parchive.sourceforge.net
Programs used: QuickPar (http://www.quickpar.org.uk)

Few things are more frustrating than downloading 105 RAR segments of a movie only to find that four of the pieces are missing or corrupt, leaving gaps. If you can't find those pieces anywhere, there's still a chance you can recreate them using PAR files.

PAR's popularity is being overtaken by a newer, better way of reconstructing missing PAR files, called PAR2. The PAR2 specification supports both PAR and the newer, more efficient PAR2 files.

YENC

Type of file: Lossless compression
Usual contents: Music or video files, usually posted on newsgroups
Copy protection: No
Official website: http://www.yenc.org
Programs used: Almost all dedicated newsreader programs
Because newsgroups only accept text, people can only trade songs and movies over newsgroups by first converting (encoding) these files into text, which can then be converted (decoded) back into the original format. One of the more popular file compression programs for trading files over newsgroups is the yEnc public domain encoding method.

ELECTRONIC BOOK FORMATS

File swappers post e-books in a wide variety of formats to accommodate different reading styles and mechanical devices. Because book files are relatively small compared to songs and movies, many people offer the same book in several different formats to ensure compatibility. The eBookMall (http://www.ebookmall.com/choose-format) contains a good description of competing e-book formats and the devices they use. Here's a look at the e-book formats most often traded on the Internet.

CHM

Type of file: Book
Usual contents: Text, graphics, and hyperlinks
Copy protection: No
Official website: http://msdn.microsoft.com/library
Programs used: Microsoft HTML Help
CHM (compiled HTML) files are often used for creating help files in Windows applications, but have also grown popular for distributing e-books as well. Unlike ordinary text files, CHM files can be searched, compressed, and organized into topics for easy browsing while displaying graphics embedded within text.

TXT OR ASCII

Type of file: Book
Usual contents: Book in unformatted text
Copy protection: No
Official website: None
Programs used: Any word processor or text editor

TXT or ASCII is plain, unformatted text, and this is by far the most versatile format and the choice of many. Although this format won't display artwork and formatting, like boldface and italics, text files can be viewed on any computer or converted into many different file formats.

RTF

Type of file: Formatted text
Usual contents: Book
Copy protection: No
Official website: http://msdn.microsoft.com/library/en-us/dnrtfspec/html/rtfspec.asp
Programs used: Microsoft Word (http://www.microsoft.com/word) and other word processors

One step up from plain text, Microsoft's Rich Text Format (RTF) mixes plain text with formatting codes that can be read by many word processors. RTF files can be converted into other formats or can be viewed by most word processors, including those that run on other operating systems such as Linux or Mac OS (OpenOffice.org or Word for Macintosh, for example).

HTML

Type of file: Formatted text
Usual contents: Book
Copy protection: No
Official website: http://www.w3.org/markup
Programs used: Any Web browser; some word processors

Any device that can browse websites can read the Hypertext Markup Language (HTML) format, as the book is simply stored as a large web page. HTML preserves formatting and graphics, but doesn't compress files, leading to awkward sizes for large documents. Its portability and formatting make it a popular choice for books with embedded pictures.

LIT

Type of file: Formatted text
Usual contents: Book
Copy protection: Yes
Official website: http://www.microsoft.com/reader
Programs used: Microsoft Reader

Microsoft Reader's LIT format presents books in a neatly formatted package, including the book's cover, if desired. Readers can easily jump from one page to another, look up words in the built-in dictionary, change the font size for easy reading, draw notes in the margin, highlight and attach comments to passages, and add bookmarks. Microsoft Reader also includes a built-in library that manages book collections. Books can be copy-protected or not. Reader files are fairly easy to create with a plug-in for Microsoft Reader. Best yet, the program is free.

The format's biggest problem is that once a book's been converted into LIT, it can't be converted back into plain text. That makes it difficult to correct the misspellings often found in scanned-in e-books, or to view the text on an incompatible device. Because Microsoft Reader only runs on Windows or Microsoft's PocketPCs, users of Mac OS, Linux, and other operating systems can't read LIT files.

Frustrated when the LIT format's copy protection prevented him from reading his Microsoft Reader books on his older PDA, programmer Dan Jackson wrote Convert LIT to crack the encryption on copy-protected LIT files. Once cracked, the LIT files can be converted to other formats and read on other devices. The Convert LIT program is illegal in many countries, including the United States under the Digital Millennium Copyright Act (DMCA), and it is currently hosted on a server in Poland (http://www.convertlit.com).

DOC

Type of file: Formatted text
Usual contents: Book
Copy protection: Optional
Official website: http://www.microsoft.com/word
Programs used: Microsoft Word (http://www.microsoft.com/word) and other word processors

Many traders swap books in Microsoft Word format, since Word is the most popular word processor around. Once opened in Word, a DOC file can be printed, spell-checked, edited, reformatted, or saved in other formats. (Some documents that are just straight ASCII text may also use a .doc extension.)

PDB AND PRC

Type of file: Formatted text
Usual contents: Book
Copy protection: Optional
Official website: http://www.palmdigitalmedia.com
Programs used: Palm Reader (http://www.palmdigitalmedia.com/help/palmreader/guide)

The PDB (Palm Database) format belongs to Palm Reader, which started as the Peanut Reader, distributed by PeanutPress. Although the format began primarily for PalmPilot owners to read e-books, it's also available for Windows, Macintosh, and PocketPC formats, as well as for any device using the Palm OS. The reader program is free, but some of the e-books use copy protection.

PDF

Type of file: Formatted text
Usual contents: Book
Copy protection: Optional
Official website: http://www.adobe.com/products/acrobat
Programs used: Adobe Acrobat Reader

Portable Document Format (PDF) files can only be viewed using Adobe's free Acrobat Reader software, available for most operating systems including handheld devices. Although some books have copy protection, many don't, allowing users to save the book into other formats and to print pages.

Although PDF files tend to be large, they preserve the "look and feel" of the book's printed page, including all fonts and graphics. The latest version of Acrobat Reader also plays embedded sounds and video. PDF remains a popular format for manuals, textbooks, and other books with lots of graphics.

As with Microsoft's Reader program, Adobe's copy protection has been cracked. The Advanced PDF Password Recovery program (http://www.elcomsoft.com/apdfpr.html) is hosted on a Russian site to avoid the reach of the United States' DMCA laws. If you want to convert a non–copy-protected PDF file into a Word document, you can use the Solid Converter PDF program (http://www.solidpdf.com) or PDF Converter (http://www.caere.com).

MOVIE FORMATS

Unlike songs, which are usually found as MP3 files, movies are stored in a wide variety of file formats. Because video files can be huge, most people compress videos in the RAR format, which was discussed earlier in this chapter. To add to the confusion, movies draw from a wide variety of *codecs*—compression mechanisms for packing the video into a certain file format. This means that even if your video player supports a particular video format, it may not support the codec used to compress the video, a problem covered in Chapter 14, in the "Finding Pornography on Newsgroups" section.

Here are some common formats and codecs used for trading movies.

DIVX

Usual contents: Video
Copy protection: No
Official website: http://www.divx.com
Programs used: DivX Player (http://www.divx.com) or any video player with the proper DivX codec installed

Created by DivXNetworks, the DivX codec compresses full-length movies into much smaller sizes. A full-length DVD, for instance, is normally about 6GB when extracted onto a hard drive. Using DivX, users can compress a movie to 600MB, which conveniently fits on a single CD. (DivX bears no relation to DIVX, Circuit City's failed DVD rental system that involved disposable DVDs.)

MPEG

Usual contents: Video
Copy protection: No
Official website: http://www.chiariglione.org/mpeg or http://www.mpeg.org
Programs used: Nearly any video player

MPEG (Moving Picture Experts Group) is an international standard for storing sound and video in a digital format. The MPEG-1 standard produces video quality roughly equal to VHS videotape at a resolution of 352 by 240 pixels. MPEG-1 is most often used to store video on CDs and VCDs (video CDs).

MPEG-2 is the standard for DVDs, and it offers better compression than MPEG-1 with a resolution of 720 by 480 pixels. The latest standard, MPEG-4, can scale pictures to play on different devices, such as cell phones and hand-held computers.

Nearly every video player can handle MPEG-1 files, making it a popular method of trading movies, although for better file compression and video quality, many files may be stored using the MPEG-2 standard instead.

AVI

Usual contents: Video
Copy protection: No
Official website: None

Programs used: Most video-playing and editing programs

Microsoft created the popular Audio Video Interleave (AVI) format, only to abandon it when they wanted to include Digital Rights Management. Many digital camcorders create this format when dumping raw footage onto a hard drive, and it's one of the more popular formats for movie trading.

MOV

Usual contents: Video, sometimes music
Copy protection: Optional
Official website: http://www.apple.com/quicktime
Programs used: QuickTime player

Apple's QuickTime media format is the current darling of the film trailer industry, and these files mostly contain video, but sometimes have just music. Launched in 1991, the QuickTime format is a Web standard for clips that can be played on many types of computers.

VCD AND SVCD

Usual contents: Video for a CD
Copy protection: None
Official website: http://www.chiariglione.org/mpeg or http://www.mpeg.org
Programs used: Most DVD playing software such as TMPGEnc (http://www.tmpgenc.net)

Short for Video Compact Disc, VCD emerged in 1993 as a way to store video on CDs for playing on computers. Embraced mainly in Asia, the format never took off in the United States or Europe, probably because of piracy concerns and picture quality. (Its early MPEG-1 encoding creates videos about the quality of VHS that fill a quarter of a TV screen.) Most stand-alone DVD players and nearly all computer DVD drives can play the format, and it has enjoyed a renaissance for storing ripped DVD footage. Super Video Compact Disc (SVCD) uses improved compression to store full-screen videos.

PHOTOGRAPH FORMATS

Many people trade photos on the Internet, whether they are porn, celebrity photos, art, or any other static visual medium. Unlike other media, photos and clip art usually come stored in one of three widely accepted formats: JPEG, GIF, or PNG. The JPEG format uses lossy compression, which means it physically removes data to reduce the file size. The GIF and PNG formats use lossless compression, which means they don't remove data to compress a file's size.

JPEG

Usual contents: Photos, art
Copy protection: None
Official website: http://www.jpeg.org
Programs used: Nearly every graphics program and web browser

Developed in the early 1980s by the Joint Photographic Experts Group (JPEG) as a lossy way for compressing photographs, JPEG is the most common method of storing photographs on the Internet. Although the JPEG format was created as a license-free compression method, a company called Forgent announced in 2002 that it held the patents and would charge licensing fees. The JPEG group soon announced JPEG 2000, a replacement technology, but JPEG remains widely used, and this is likely to remain the case until the patent case is settled in court.

GIF

Usual contents: Clip art, line drawings
Copy protection: None
Official website: None
Programs used: Nearly every graphics program and web browser

Introduced by CompuServe in the late 1980s, GIF files usually contain clip art and any type of images that aren't photographs. Although the GIF format is limited to 256 colors, it does offer the ability to create simple animation. Unisys claimed ownership of the format and began charging royalties in the 1990s, leading to the creation of the PNG format. Unisys's patents have since expired in the United States and will expire shortly worldwide.

PNG

Usual contents: Clip art, line drawings
Copy protection: None
Official website: http://www.libpng.org/pub/png
Programs used: Most graphics programs and Web browsers

The PNG (Portable Network Graphics) format was created as an open source, patent-free alternative to GIF, and it has attracted growing support. It has yet to reach the popularity of the more ingrained JPEG and GIF formats, however, and with Unisys's patents on the GIF image format expiring, it's unlikely that the PNG format will ever replace the GIF format.

WHERE TO GO FROM HERE

While so many different file formats might seem overwhelming, relax. Once you start searching and downloading files on your own, you'll find that most people stick to just a handful of common file formats, such as MP3 for music, JPEG (or JPG) for photographs, AVI for video, and DOC or PDF for books.

Rather than trying to learn all the different file formats you're likely to find on the Internet, just start out learning the file formats you're likely to find while trading your favorite types of files, such as music or video files. Once you learn the common formats for storing your favorite types of files, you'll soon learn the common formats used for storing other types of data, and before you know it, you'll be able to identify the contents of most files just by peeking at the file extension. If you're stumped by a file format that you're not familiar with, visit one of the following two sites:

FILExt	http://www.filext.com
Every File Format in the World	http://whatis.techtarget.com/fileFormatA

9

SHARING MUSIC

Music files are very widely traded over the Internet, and it's easy to see why. Everybody loves music, digital music files are usually small and easy to swap, and generations have grown up making copies of albums and tapes for friends. A quick glance at the FastTrack file sharing network lists nearly 3 million users swapping from a pool of over 501 million music files. And FastTrack is just one of many file sharing networks where you can swap music files. (Many of those 501 million files are probably duplicate files with different names—but still, that's a lot of files.)

To stop this widespread thievery, the RIAA periodically issues well-publicized lawsuits against file sharers across the United States. While some people stop sharing music files at home for fear of lawsuits, many others have simply started downloading files at work, shifting the blame to their employer's computer networks.

In short, trading music has become a way of life for many people, and it seems that the music industry can do little or nothing to stop it.

There is nothing stable in the world; uproar's your only music.

—John Keats

COPYING CDS

One of the easiest and most common ways for people to increase their music collections is also the most anonymous: borrow a CD from a friend and copy it on your computer. Because most computers come with CD burners, and nearly every office-supply store sells blank CDs, empty CD cases, and precut blank CD cover labels, all you need to do is use a popular CD burner such as Easy Media Creator (http://www.roxio.com) or Nero (http://www.nero.com). Making a copy of a CD has never been easier.

Of course, no matter how many friends you may have, you probably don't have access to all the CDs you want to copy. Many people turn to another music source: the public library. Besides offering books and magazines, many libraries also offer records, CDs, and videotapes. For example, the Phoenix Public Library's online card catalog (http://www.phoenixpubliclibrary.org) lists several thousand CDs available for checkout, including some of the latest music, such as Outkast's 2004 Grammy winner, *Speakerboxxx/The Love Below* (see Figure 9-1).

Figure 9-1
The libraries in most large cities allow you to check out popular music CDs.

Most libraries in large cities allow CDs to be reserved online, or to be shipped from one branch to another, effectively letting users borrow any CD from any library in the city. Today's libraries not only carry classics of jazz, opera, and classical music, but are surprisingly well stocked with popular music, as well.

Of course, borrowing and copying CDs does take time and patience. Many libraries don't acquire a CD until it's several months old, and sometimes you have to wait until someone else returns the CD you want. Despite these obstacles, borrowing from libraries is one of the most anonymous and risk-safe ways for people to increase their CD collections, although not without violating copyright in most cases.

NOTE: Libraries rarely used to keep records of their patrons' loans, but the USA Patriot Act changed all that in 2001 (http://www.libraryprivacy.org); library records of their patrons' borrowing habits are now open to the FBI upon request. After seeing the FBI's warnings on DVDs for many years (and on CDs more recently), many people are understandably nervous.

FINDING MUSIC ON THE INTERNET

Never mind the libraries or borrowing from friends—most of today's music-file finding is happening online on file sharing networks, newsgroups, websites, or FTP sites. Each source offers varying degrees of convenience, speed, quality, and anonymity.

DOWNLOADING MUSIC FROM FILE SHARING NETWORKS

File sharing networks are the most convenient Internet music source because you simply enter the name of a recording artist, song title, or album name, and your search will return a list of relevant, available files.

The biggest problem, though, with file sharing networks is that the selection of available songs varies greatly. If you search for music by older recording artists, such as Jimi Hendrix, file sharing networks will likely only offer the hit songs from that recording artist. While this can be useful for creating your own "Greatest Hits" collection for a particular artist, it does restrict you to a limited selection of files. In comparison, if you search for songs by newer recording artists, such as Ashlee Simpson, you can often find every song available from that recording artist's latest album (see Figure 9-2).

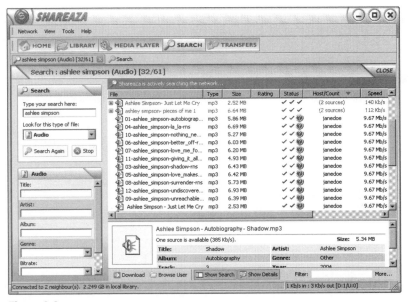

Figure 9-2

You can find every song from Ashlee Simpson's *Autobiography* album on most file sharing networks, but you may not find all the songs from albums by older recording artists.

Another problem with file sharing networks is that while they may be quick to find a particular song on the network, your success in downloading that particular file to your computer may vary widely. Sometimes the download is very fast; other times it's unbearably slow or it never completes at all. Often a popular file may have several people trying to download it at once, which means you have to wait until someone else finishes downloading it before you can start downloading it too. Sometimes the wait is only a few minutes, and at other times it could be hours. Also, if the computer hosting the file you want suddenly disconnects from the network, you won't get the file at all until you download it from another computer.

Sometimes a file sharing network may overwhelm you with too many irrelevant files, so to limit this problem, you can often define the types of files you want to find, such as audio, video, or program files. When searching for files, enter as much of the song, recording artist, or album title as possible to avoid having the file sharing network bombard you with music files that aren't even close to what you want.

For example, search for the band Air on a file sharing network and you'll find songs from Air along with irrelevant files such as Phil Collins' song "In the Air Tonight," Will Smith's song "The Fresh Prince of Bel Air," and Joe Satriani's song "Hands in the Air," as shown in Figure 9-3.

Figure 9-3

Searching with an inexact name will turn up lots of irrelevant files on a file sharing network.

*NOTE: Sometimes while searching for a song, you may find a similar one that you may not be aware of. For example, a search for **Christmas** on a file sharing network will return a variety of different Christmas songs, many of which you may not have considered searching for but which would be fun as part of a music mix.*

Once you find a specific file, the file sharing program will also identify the nickname of the person hosting your chosen file along with the type of Internet connection they have, such as T1, cable, DSL, or modem. For maximum reliability and speed, choose files hosted on computers that use broadband connections (T1, cable, or DSL). While many people offer perfectly acceptable files over an ordinary dial-up modem connection, transferring several megabytes of files through dial-up modems will take much more time. When given a choice between identical files hosted on a broadband and a dial-up connection, choose the broadband connection every time.

DOWNLOADING MUSIC FROM NEWSGROUPS

Although you can find individual songs on newsgroups, you're more likely to find complete albums instead, including rare bootleg live recordings. For example, a quick search in the alt.binaries.sounds.mp3.rock.full-album newsgroup reveals the complete Beatles album *Let It Be* (see Figure 9-4).

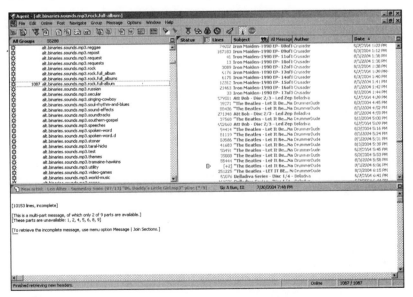

Figure 9-4
Searching for a recording artist in a newsgroup can often uncover an entire album.

Downloading files from newsgroups isn't hard, but it's not as intuitive as using a file sharing network, so plan on asking for help from a friend or going through a lot of frustrating trial and error. Unlike file sharing networks that let you search for a particular file, newsgroups are more suited for browsing and downloading whatever files happen to be available at the moment. And if you don't visit various newsgroups regularly, a song or album could appear and disappear from it before you have a chance to download it.

Hundreds of different newsgroups cater to the most esoteric of interests, but few newsgroup servers carry them all, so you'll need to find a server that carries the ones you're interested in. Also, while files in the OGG and WMA file formats each have their own newsgroup (alt.binaries.sounds.ogg and alt.binaries.sounds.wma), MP3 files tend to appear in hundreds of different newsgroups organized by categories (see Figure 9-5).

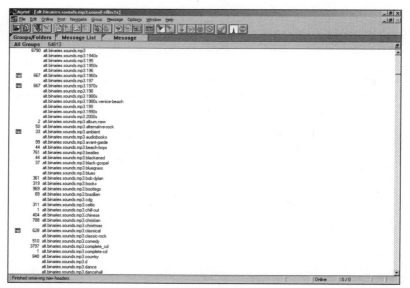

Figure 9-5
Some newsgroup servers carry hundreds of MP3 newsgroups sorted by music category.

Here's a look at the most popular music trading newsgroups carried by most servers:

alt.binaries.sounds.lossless This newsgroups hosts lossless file formats like SHN, FLAC, and WavPack. These are large files that, when burned to CD, sound as good as the original CD versions. Many people trade copies of live recordings, sometimes perfect copies of the soundboard recording. Two subgroups, alt.binaries.sounds.lossless.jazz and alt.binaries.sounds.lossless.classical, carry lossless jazz and classical music. If a jazz or classical music recording has already scrolled off the high-traffic lossless group, check the lower-traffic subgroups, where the posts last longer. Just be aware that it can take a very long time to download large, lossless files, especially if you use a dial-up connection.

alt.binaries.sounds.78rpm-era   Any recorded music dating to the end of the vinyl "78" era ends up here. This newsgroup contains a mishmash of bawdy jazz and blues tunes, old-world music, historical recordings, and anything else recorded for early radio and the crank-'em-up phonographs, captured in various audio file formats such as MP3.

alt.binaries.sounds.mp3   Nearly every MP3 file posted eventually shows up here, as well as in subgroups that further classify the posted music, such as alt.binaries.sounds.mp3.complete_cd (the most popular subgroup here). The most popular subgroups sort the music by the decade they were recorded or issued (1940s, 1950s, 1960s, 1970s, 1980s, 1990s, and 2000s).

alt.binaries.sounds.mp3.beatles   Although songs from The Beatles' retail CDs cycle through here periodically, most uploads are recording session outtakes, bootlegs, alternative cuts, limited-edition releases, cover tunes, and other "unofficial" recordings by either The Beatles or their members.

alt.binaries.sounds.mp3.bobdylan   Like the Beatles newsgroup, this contains mostly Dylan's unofficial releases and bootleg recordings as well as some retail CDs.

alt.binaries.sounds.mp3.bootlegs   This contains the latest trendy bootleg recordings, as well as classic bootlegs recorded over the years. It's not uncommon for bootleg recordings to appear here less than 24 hours after a concert.

alt.binaries.sounds.mp3.christian   Although filled mostly with inspirational music, sermons occasionally appear here, as well. (Gospel music appears in alt.binaries.sounds.mp3.black-gospel.)

alt.binaries.sounds.mp3.comedy   Anything that's supposed to be funny goes here, from novelty songs to recordings of stand-up comedians.

alt.binaries.sounds.mp3.country   True to country music's renegade roots, this official country music newsgroup doesn't receive as many posts as the *unofficial* newsgroup, alt.binaries.sounds.country.mp3.

alt.binaries.sounds.mp3.jazz   Classic jazz albums from the '50s and '60s turn up here more frequently than the newer jazz. This is a drop-off for *real* jazz, not the "soft" jazz you hear on many radio stations today. Don't visit here for Kenny G.

NOTE: *Many of these newsgroups contain recordings made by individual artists trying to get exposure for their work. However, the bulk of the audio files are generally copyrighted works, so be careful what you download.*

If you stumble upon a song you like, downloading is fairly easy, as described in Chapter 3. Unlike downloading from a file sharing network, the speed of file transfers depends on your own Internet connection and not on somebody else's. Newsreader programs, covered in Chapter 3, allow files to be queued and downloaded in the background as you work. And leech all you want. Newsgroup veterans prefer leechers to people who upload without knowing what they're doing. If too many people upload files without knowing what they're doing, the higher quality files that others have posted will get shoved off the newsgroup much faster to make room for newer files.

      The official FAQ for alt.binaries.sounds.mp3 actually tries to discourage people from posting until they've become familiar with the structure, users, and expected quality levels of files posted in newsgroups:

```
With all newsgroups it is a common and recommended practice to "lurk and
learn". This means that you follow the newsgroup, watching and learning,
before you begin posting. Posting is NOT required. There is no "ratio" or
required "trading" in the a.b.s.mp3 newsgroups. Leeching is completely
acceptable.
```

DOWNLOADING MUSIC FROM WEBSITES

Websites provide another source of music, although like file sharing networks, most websites only post the most popular songs of a recording artist, and only the most recent ones (see Figure 9-6). If a particular recording artist is no longer popular, such as now-obscure bands like Foghat or 10cc, you may not find any websites offering their songs at all.

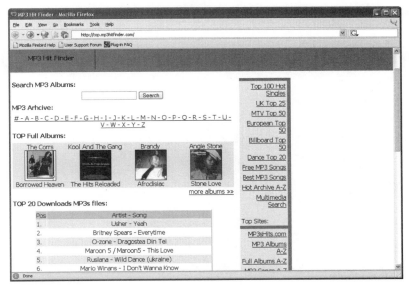

Figure 9-6

Many music websites only offer the latest songs or older songs from the most popular recording artists.

Finding a website that offers downloadable music is as easy as visiting your favorite search engine and typing in the name of a recording artist followed by MP3, such as **Eminem MP3**. Such a search will likely turn up a handful of sites that offer MP3 files of everything from individual songs to complete albums (see Figure 9-7).

To skirt the legalities of posting copyrighted music on a website, many website administrators don't provide the files themselves. Instead, they provide links to music files stored on other websites, usually the free ones that offer completely anonymous hosting, such as GeoCities (http://geocities.yahoo.com). Because they are only providing links, the authorities can't legally shut them down—the files are on the free, anonymous websites. The authorities can shut down the free websites hosting the actual music files, but when they do this, the sites are just put up at other addresses and the cycle begins all over again. (However, the resulting dead links often spell frustration for anyone trying to download music from these websites.)

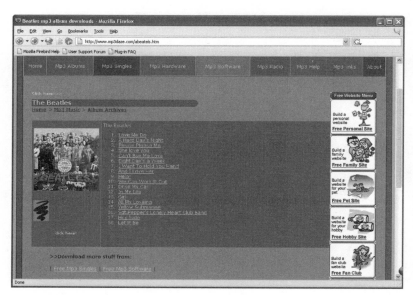

Figure 9-7
This website offers just a handful of Beatles songs stored in MP3 format.

NOTE: Be wary of "free" MP3 websites because many of them are designed to do nothing but display pop-up ads or secretly install spyware on your computer.

DOWNLOADING MUSIC FROM FTP SITES

The biggest challenge in finding music on an FTP site is finding an FTP site that offers music in the first place. FTP search engines (such as http://www.ftpsearchengines.com) are one way people find FTP sites with music; enter the name of the recording artist or album you want to find into a search engine like OTH2.net (http://www.oth2.net) and see what you find.

Like newsgroups, FTP sites tend to offer entire albums rather than just a handful of selected songs from different albums. The biggest drawback you are likely to find with downloading music from FTP sites is the difficulty in finding a site that contains the songs you want. Also, few FTP sites offer music for free, so you may have to trade some music files with the FTP administrator before you'll get permission to download any files from the FTP site. Once you gain such coveted access to a music FTP site, downloading a particular file can be fast and easy, just as long as you learn the minor intricacies of navigating and downloading files using an FTP program.

FINDING THE BEST AUDIO FILES

For most novices, the fastest way to find and download music is to join one of the many file sharing networks. Unfortunately, the quality of music on the various file sharing networks can range from excellent to downright dreadful, and it's often impossible to know the audio quality of a file until it has been downloaded. Some file sharing programs, such as LimeWire, grade the quality of a file with zero to four stars, as shown in Figure 9-8. With such a rating system to guide you, it's generally best to download only files with four-star ratings.

Figure 9-8
LimeWire rates the quality of a file from zero to four stars so you can determine the quality of a file before downloading it.

Many novices convert songs from an audio CD to an MP3 file without really understanding technical details like *bit rate*. The bit rate determines the audio quality of a song by defining how much audio data gets sent from the storage medium (such as an MP3 file) to your decoder (which is a program that translates the audio file into actual sound) per second. The higher the bit rate, the higher the audio quality of the file and the larger the file. The most common bit rate for MP3 files is 128, although 192, 256, and 320 bit rates are used to increase audio fidelity. Because many novices use a low bit rate, many songs on the file-sharing networks are of dubious quality. Once someone grabs a copy of a poorly recorded song and makes it available for sharing, more people are likely to download and spread that same copy, contaminating the entire file sharing network with mediocre recordings.

One final challenge comes from the recording industry itself, which hires companies to pollute a file sharing network with bogus music files of poor quality. Such companies flood a file sharing network seven days a week, 24 hours a day. While people often identify and delete such bogus files, they still appear often enough to annoy users.

Newsgroups tend to offer the highest-quality songs because most newsgroup users are not only technically savvy enough to understand how to navigate and post files to a newsgroup in the first place, but they're conscientious enough to post the best quality files possible. Many people who post files in newsgroups even include NFO files that describe each song's bit rate, the MP3 encoder used, the program used to process the file, and occasionally a short review describing why they posted the release. Some newsgroup files also come with scans of the CD case covers, including any booklets and track listings.

Both FTP and websites also offer consistently high-quality music files. FTP site administrators offer only high-quality audio files because doing so attracts more people to their site who will subsequently upload files to expand the site's music collection. Websites also want to attract people because the more people they attract, the more people they can bombard with advertisement-laden pop-up ads or spyware, thus earning the website administrator some extra cash.

Downloading music from IRC channels will usually snare you high-quality audio files, but it all depends on the person setting up the file server bot. Most people knowledgeable enough to set up a file server bot in an IRC channel will likely offer you the best audio files they have, but unlike web or FTP sites that offer quality files to attract people who will later upload audio files of equal quality, IRC users can possibly feed you poor quality files or bogus files. Most IRC file server bots can be trusted, but be careful anyway.

As a general rule, if you want point-and-click convenience along with the ability to search for specific songs, stick with file sharing networks. If you want to find rare songs from popular artists or bootleg live recordings, browse through newsgroups and IRC chat rooms. If file sharing networks frighten you off with the recording industry's threat of surveillance and lawsuits, visit web and FTP sites to find your favorite songs. No matter which method you choose, you'll be able to find practically any song that's ever been recorded if you just look on the Internet long and hard enough.

THE PROBLEM WITH FILE NAMES

There's no set way for naming music files, and many people have their own preference. As a result, you may run across several files with different names that could all contain the same song, like these:

```
Steve Winwood - Dear Mr Fantasy.mp3
Dear Mr Fantasy.mp3
05 Steve Winwood Dear Mr Fantasy.mp3
```

Even more troublesome is when people misspell song titles or artist names or even make up their own name for a song when they don't know the real song title.

To provide some standard, most music files include an ID3 tag that contains information about the song, such as title, artist, album, release year, genre, and track number. When you play back songs that have all or part of their ID3 tags filled out, your audio player should display this information on the screen.

However, most CD burners don't fill out the ID3 tags automatically, and many people don't bother entering this information, so many music files will have incomplete or empty ID3 tags. Unfortunately, portable music players like the iPod and Creative Nomad sort and display the songs by their ID3 tags, not their file names. If the tags are wrong or missing, the players may not find and play the song you just downloaded.

Because bad tags cause so many problems, many audio players, such as iTunes, let you edit a song's ID3 tag, as shown in Figure 9-9. If your audio player won't let you edit ID3 tags, you can use a special utility program instead, some of which can identify songs and fill out their tags automatically as long as you're connected to the Internet. Others let you enter the tag information manually.

Once you've filled out the tags, most tag programs will then rename the files using whatever naming scheme you like. Here are some of the more popular ID3 tag utilities:

ID3-TagIT	http://www.id3-tagit.de
MediaMonkey	http://www.mediamonkey.com
Mp3 Tag Tools	http://www.georgedillon.com/web/freeware/mp3tagtools.shtml
Tag&Rename	http://www.softpointer.com
TagScanner	http://xdev.narod.ru/index_e.htm

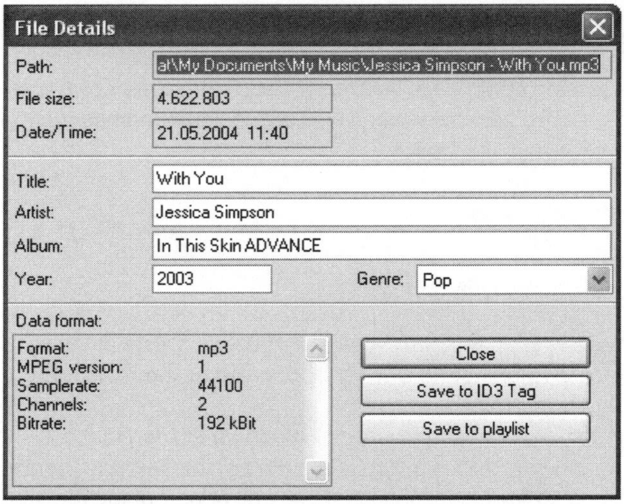

```
File Details                                        [×]
 Path:       at\My Documents\My Music\Jessica Simpson - With You.mp3
 File size:   4.622.803
 Date/Time:   21.05.2004  11:40

 Title:      With You
 Artist:     Jessica Simpson
 Album:      In This Skin ADVANCE
 Year:       2003              Genre:  Pop          [v]

 Data format:
 Format:        mp3          ^      [      Close       ]
 MPEG version:  1
 Samplerate:    44100              [   Save to ID3 Tag  ]
 Channels:      2
 Bitrate:       192 kBit            [  Save to playlist  ]
                             v
```

Figure 9-9
Many audio players let you edit the ID3 tag of a music file.

ID3 tags are designed strictly for popular music, which can cause problems for traders of operas and classical music. For instance, if you list Puccini as the art-ist and Tosca as the opera, there's no place to add the conductor or any of the singers. Without the artist, singers, or symphony, there's little way to differentiate between several recordings of the same piece. The solution? There isn't one. However, ID3 tags contain an area reserved for comments, which can be useful for storing this additional information.

WHO'S STEALING FROM WHOM?

The recording industry blames the drastic plunge in CD sales on people swap-ping songs over file sharing networks. However, even that basic assumption isn't a fact but rather one of many hypotheses for why CD sales have dropped in recent years. The fact is that book sales have dropped dramatically too, as have sales of many other items, and not all of these losses can be directly linked to file sharing networks.

THE PRICE OF CDS

Curiously, while the cost of manufacturing a CD (once the recording has been mastered) is much less than the cost of manufacturing a vinyl record or even a tape cassette, the price of CDs has increased an average of 12.53 percent, from $13.01 to $14.64, between the years 1991 and 2001. The attorney generals of 43 states and territories even accused the major music companies (Sony Music Entertainment, EMI Music Distribution, Warner-Elektra-Atlantic Corp., Universal Music Group, and Bertelsmann Music Group, as well as retailers Tower Records, Musicland Stores, and Trans World Entertainment) of conspiring to fix CD prices.

The music industry eventually agreed to a $143 million settlement, without admitting any wrongdoing. Anyone who signed on to the music lawsuit wound up collecting $12.60 for their share in buying overpriced CDs all those years. An additional part of the settlement stipulated that schools and libraries receive $75.7 million worth of CDs, although many schools and libraries are complaining that the music industry is only giving them CDs that they couldn't sell anyway. One library wound up with 57 copies of *Three Mo' Tenors*, 48 copies of Mark Willis's *Loving Every Minute*, and 47 copies of *Corridos de Primera Plana* by Los Tucanes di Tijuana.

"This is a landmark settlement to address years of illegal price-fixing," New York Attorney General Eliot Spitzer said. Former FTC chairman Robert Pitofsky added that consumers had been overcharged by $480 million for CDs since 1997.

Although the music industry's alleged price gouging has convinced many that pirating music can be justified as a way to get back their money, it's no more justified than stealing a book to get back at a bookstore. While music piracy isn't the answer to price gouging, it's definitely part of the backlash the music industry is facing these days.

COMPETITION FROM OTHER FORMS OF ENTERTAINMENT

High CD prices aren't necessarily to blame for causing people to forego buying CDs. The problem is that given 20 bucks to spend, there's a whole range of new alternatives for people to spend their money on, from video games and DVDs to interactive role-playing games on the Internet and cell phone services. So the reason why people are buying fewer CDs may not be because they're stealing music. They could just be buying fewer CDs because they'd rather spend the money on another source of entertainment.

Even if people want music, they don't necessarily want it on a CD. Lugging around a portable CD player is nice, but if you want to listen to 50 of your favorite songs, you may be forced to carry dozens of CDs and swap them in and out of your portable CD player just to hear the songs you want. Portable digital music players, such as Apple's iPod, have proven popular because they allow you to store and listen to more songs (10,000 songs on a 40GB iPod) without lugging around a briefcase full of CDs. This desire for portability could explain the wild popularity of Apple's iTunes online music store, which has sold over

100 million songs. People are still willing to pay for music just as long as they can take it with them anywhere they go.

So even if people want to buy more music, few of them want to buy music trapped on the archaic CD format, especially if the music companies include cumbersome copy-protection mechanisms that not only prevent people from copying a CD, but also prevent them from playing that same CD in a computer or car stereo. (Chapter 17 discusses various copy-protection mechanisms that the recording industry has used to copy protect both CDs and individual audio files.)

FILE SHARING AFFECTS MUSIC SALES

The basic assumption is that file sharing causes people to buy fewer CDs, but the reverse may actually be true. Given the high cost of CDs, many people aren't willing to buy a new CD just to see if they might like a particular album. Instead, people prefer to buy CDs that contain songs they already want to hear.

Strangely enough, file sharing networks may increase an artist's exposure and generate more interest in that recording artist. Daniel Bedingfield recently had the top-three song "Gotta Get Thru This." However, most of his music wasn't available through any of the file sharing networks. His album lasted on the Billboard Top 200 for less than a month, even though the single had been on radio playlists all over the country for several months.

In contrast, one of the most downloaded albums of all time was *The Eminem Show*, by Eminem. Toward the end of 2002, *The Eminem Show* became the best-selling album of the year, which lends support to the theory that file sharing exposes more people to music that they wouldn't normally buy otherwise. Once they enjoy a particular recording artist, they're more likely to buy albums by that same artist, although they may not buy a CD, preferring to buy their music electronically for their iPod through Apple's iTunes online music store.

WHO'S REALLY LOSING MONEY

The music industry often claims that stealing music deprives artists of royalties from their albums. Yet many recording artists claim that the recording industry is actually responsible for depriving artists of their royalties.

For example, when the Dixie Chicks' two albums *Wide Open Spaces* and *Fly* sold over 19 million copies, the trio complained that Sony had engaged in "systematic thievery" by underpaying them $4 million they were due in royalties. The Dixie Chicks claimed that Sony's contract virtually enslaved its talent by "obligating its artists to continue to record for Sony no matter how repeatedly and blatantly Sony breaches its payment obligations."

150

Prince had a similar legal dispute with Warner Bros. and resorted to changing his name to a symbol to escape the legal clauses of his contract and to appearing in public with the word "slave" printed across his cheek.

Prince and the Dixie Chicks aren't alone in their complaints about the recording industry's unfairly structured contracts. Don Henley, Billy Joel, Sheryl Crow, and Beck have even raised money for the fledgling musician lobbying group called the Recording Artists Coalition (http://www.recordingartistscoalition.com).

These are some of the issues that recording artists face:

— Recording contracts that require seven albums, with no end date. The music companies claim this keeps popular artists with a recording label that initially invested in that artist, but musicians claim it turns the recording artist into an indentured servant of the music company.

— The record label's right to reject an entire album and then extend the contract by one more album. Record labels don't want to promote something they don't believe will sell, but artists feel they have no control over what a record label may declare as "commercially or artistically unacceptable."

— Recording contracts include an initial advance, but the cost of recording the album along with producing videos and other promotional material gets charged against the artist's royalties. While record companies risk the initial investment in supporting artists who may never earn enough to recoup the recording costs, successful artists wind up paying for much of their own recording and promotional costs while trusting that the recording company is fairly charging expenses. (The publisher of this book would love to adopt a model like this; he thinks he'd be very rich and driving a real car rather than an antique.)

— Contracts that give the bulk of royalties to the recording companies. Given that the five major companies release over 90 percent of commercial music, artists must sign standard agreements or give up their recording careers altogether. If artists wish to audit their royalties, their contracts stipulate that they must go to court in order to get the full amount due and pay the cost of the audit just to get what they were rightfully due anyway. As a result, they often settle for some amount less than the total amount due.

— "Packaging" or "container" deductions in a contract can reduce an artist's royalties by 15 to 25 percent. This cost once paid for brown paper sleeves to hold a vinyl record, along with an actual cover with artwork, to package the record. Now with compact discs costing less than $1 to manufacture, and assuming a $15 suggested retail price with a 15 percent deduction, the artist is charged $2.25 to manufacture a CD that costs $1 to make, providing the record company with an additional source of income taken from the artist's royalties.

– Royalty contracts that reward songwriters, not performers. When Madonna announced her 2004 tour, many people speculated that she needed the money since she received very little from her previously recorded albums, because she didn't write most of her older songs.

– Contracts that essentially "own" a recording artist's songs. If a record company stops selling an album, the recording artist can't rerecord the songs on another album for a different record company.

The real threat of file sharing isn't stealing royalties from recording artists; it's about stealing royalties from the recording industry. While some of the record labels will undoubtedly refuse to adapt and wind up dying, the smarter ones will take advantage of the new opportunities that file sharing networks provide.

Warner Bros., Disney, and Atlantic Records hire the services of BigChampagne (http://www.bigchampagne.com), which keeps track of the most popular songs traded over file sharing networks, along with the IP addresses of the people sharing them. Instead of using this information to file more lawsuits, these companies are using the statistics compiled by BigChampagne to determine which songs are most popular in different geographical areas, so they can target their advertising campaigns to promote certain recording artists in different parts of the world.

If the recording industry refuses to adapt, newer companies will likely step into the void and pursue opportunities that file sharing offers. Apple turned itself around from a strictly computer and software company to an online music store with iTunes, and a leader of portable digital music players with its iPod. Sales of the iPod actually help subsidize the cost of iTunes, so while Apple makes little money selling music online, it makes the bulk of its profits by selling iPods.

Another company, Mercora (http://www.mercora.com), offers a unique twist on the file sharing market. Instead of letting people swap music files, Mercora lets people connect to each other's computers and stream music to each other. That way people can listen to music files stored on other computers, but they can't copy and store that same music on their own computer. Thus, you get to share music without infringing copyright, which file trading entails.

Will the music industry be smart enough to adapt to change? Or will it follow the path of the slide rule, buggy whip, and turntable manufacturers into the dustbins of history? The way things are going, you can pretty much bet that the next leaders of the music industry won't be any of the names that people had heard about a few years ago.

10

FINDING MOVIES (OR TV SHOWS)

Soon after people began downloading music, the movie industry saw itself as the next logical target. Yet it felt secure, because movies were too large for most people to trade online easily, and most personal computers didn't have the hard disk space or processing power to store or view an entire movie file anyway. These technological limitations fell in quick succession in the mid-'90s with the combination of cheaper and larger hard disks that offered several gigabytes of storage; faster processors that could play video files; and most importantly, the widespread adoption of broadband connections that allowed massive movie files to be transferred quickly across the Internet.

Ironically, the switch from storing movies on video cassette (VHS) to DVD marked the final step for Internet movie piracy. Ripping a video off a DVD is much faster and more convenient than ripping that same video off a cassette tape, because you don't have to scroll through the entire length of a cassette tape to do it.

Initially, the movie industry felt itself secure because when it created the DVD standard, it included something called the Content Scramble System (CSS) to restrict copying and force manufacturers of DVD players to pay royalties to the DVD Copy Control Association (http://www.dvdcca.org). Before anyone can manufacture and sell a DVD player, they must pay for the right to use a special decryption key, which allows their DVD players to play DVDs encrypted with CSS.

Well, many hackers didn't like that. In late 1999, a hacker group named MoRE (Masters of Reverse Engineering) created a program called DeCSS, which stripped away the CSS encryption from DVDs. Without the CSS protection, not only could DVDs be played on devices that hadn't paid the required royalty fee, such as computers running Linux, but such DVDs could also be copied as well.

To get your hands on a copy of the DeCSS program or its source code, visit the Free DVD site (http://www.free-dvd.org.lu).

Never hesitate to steal a good idea.

—Al Neuharth

The movie industry promptly sued websites that published the DeCSS code, but programmers struck back. To keep the cracking code well distributed, crafty programmers began hiding the code in works of "illegal art," including haiku poems, photographs, T-shirt prints, movies, dramatic readings, and other works on display at the Gallery of CSS Descramblers (http://www-2.cs.cmu.edu/~dst/DeCSS/Gallery). The ASCII art in Figure 10-1, for example, contains the source code for cracking a DVD's encryption.

```
                                DVDlogo.c

/*     efdtt.c     Author:  Charles M. Hannum <root@ihack.net>        */
/*                                                                    */
/*     Thanks to Phil Carmody <fatphil@asdf.org> for additional tweaks. */
/*                                                                    */
/*     DVD-logo shaped version by Alex Bowley <alex@hyperspeed.org>   */
/*                                                                    */
/*     Usage is:  cat title-key scrambled.vob | efdtt >clear.vob      */

#define m(i)(x[i]^s[i+84])<<

          unsigned char x[5]      ,y,s[2048];main(
          n){for( read(0,x,5      );read(0,s ,n=2048
                 ); write(1  ,s,n)        )if(s
          [y=s     [13]%8+20]  /1614  ==1    )(int
          i=m(     1)17  ^256 +m(0)    8,k    =m(2)
          0,j=     m(4)    17^ m(3)    9^k*    2-k%8
          ^8,a     =0,c    =26;for    (s[y]    -=16;
          --c;j    %=2)a=      a*2^i&    1,i=i /2^j&1
          <<24;for(j=        127;      ++j<n;c=c>
                              y)
                              c

               +=y=i^i/8^i>>4^i>>12,
          i=i>>8^y<<17,a^=a>>14,y=a^a*8^a<<6,a=a
       >>8^y<<9,k=s[j],k            ="7%o-'G_\216"[k
       &7]+2^"cr3sfw6v;*k+>/n."[k>>4]*2^k*257/
             8,s[j]=k^(k&k*2&34)*6^c+~y
                        ;)}
```

Figure 10-1
This ASCII art lists the source code for cracking a DVD's encryption.

A few years later, the movie industry accidentally let the code out of the bag by including the cracked code's full text in a public legal filing. Once made public, the code spread worldwide, eventually becoming so commonplace that the industry dropped its suit in 2004. Not that it mattered much. Today, most movies appear on the Internet *before* they've been distributed on a DVD or even before their theatrical release. Once a copy leaks onto the Internet, it quickly spreads worldwide.

COPYING A MOVIE

The movie industry can't completely stop video piracy; but it can limit it as much as possible. Perhaps the simplest way for people to steal movies is by copying them using a process known as *back-to-back copying*. Anyone can simply connect one VCR or DVD player to another VCR or DVD recorder and play a legitimately purchased movie in one while copying it onto a blank cassette or DVD in the other.

However, the process is slow, and it limits the video pirate to copying only those movies already available on videotape or DVD. Also, if the movie is converted from DVD to videotape, it's not a perfect digital copy, but since it's free, many people don't mind the minor imperfections in the copy.

As a result, back-to-back copying can never be stopped, so it remains a nagging thorn in the movie industry's side.

NOTE: *Because most people want the latest releases, many pirated videos come from recently released DVDs of popular TV shows, such as an entire season of* The Sopranos.

PIRATING MOVIES WITH A CAMCORDER

Despite the ease of back-to-back copying, the highest profit margins come from the latest movies, so video pirates often rely on two additional ways to steal movies: camcorders and screeners. Anyone can sneak into a movie theater with a video camcorder and record the entire movie. Once you've captured a movie with a video camcorder, you can store it on videotape or DVD and then make as many copies as you want from that single master copy.

To protect the latest movies from camcorder piracy, many theaters now force patrons to walk through metal detectors, and they arm security guards with night-vision goggles so they can peer into a darkened theater and spot anyone aiming a video camcorder at the screen. Warner Bros. went so far as to provide military-style night-vision goggles to British theaters along with the movie *Harry Potter and the Prisoner of Azkaban* to catch any cinema pirates. The studio considered the price of the goggles to be small compared to the loss of revenue caused when bootleg copies of the first two Harry Potter films ended up on the Internet.

Unfortunately for the movie industry, video camcorders keep getting smaller and lighter. Some handheld computers even have an attachment that can record up to 122 minutes of video, enough for a whole movie in many cases. Imagine running that attachment from your handheld out from under your shirt, and you can see why the movie industry is concerned.

As you might imagine, capturing an entire movie with a camcorder isn't easy. To avoid a shaky picture, camcorders need a tripod or a stable mount. They also need a clear line of sight to the screen to avoid capturing the back of people's heads or silhouettes of people standing up and going to the bathroom. As a result, the video and audio quality of videos captured through a camcorder varies in quality from acceptable to poor.

That may be changing, though, as video pirates get smarter. Within hours of the initial release of *Shrek 2*, a group calling itself MPT (Movie Premier Team) had captured the entire film through a video camcorder and released it over the Internet (see Figure 10-2). To improve the audio quality, MPT apparently plugged a camcorder into a headphone jack built into the armrest, a feature that many movie theaters provide for the hard of hearing.

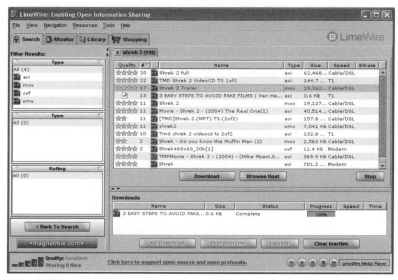

Figure 10-2

Within hours of its official release, video pirates captured and distributed *Shrek 2* over the Internet.

While the movie industry isn't likely to demand that theaters eliminate these headphone jacks, it is taking measures to degrade the visual quality of a pirated video.

For example, Cinea (http://www.cinea.com), which created an encryption system for DVDs, and Sarnoff (http://www.sarnoff.com), a technology research firm, have jointly developed a system that flickers the light cast on a movie screen. To the naked eye, this rapid flickering isn't perceptible, but that constant flickering makes the video captured by a video recorder unwatchable.

PIRATING MOVIES FROM THE INSIDE

The video quality captured by camcorders can range from abysmal to acceptable, but it will never be as crisp as a copy of the original. That's why the biggest threat to the movie industry comes from within the industry itself. Many video pirates simply hire a projectionist to set up a tripod and record a movie from within the safety and anonymity of the projection booth.

A 2003 study by Lorrie Cranor (http://lorrie.cranor.org) involved examining nearly 300 popular movies circulating on the Internet, and she found that 77 percent appeared to have been leaked by industry insiders, because only 5 percent of them had been released on DVD (thus eliminating DVD copying as the source). Additionally, the movies' high video and audio quality ruled out camcorders.

When a copy of *The Hulk* appeared on the Internet several weeks before its theater release, the uploaded copy was eventually traced to a Kerry Gonzalez. Gonzalez reportedly obtained a videotape of a prerelease "work print" of the movie from a friend, who had in turn received it from an employee of a Manhattan print advertising firm that was promoting the movie, according to an investigation by the FBI's Computer Hacking and Intellectual Property Squad.

In another widely publicized case, actor and Academy member Carmine Caridi received copies of movies as "screeners"—preview copies—to be viewed before voting for the 76th Academy Awards. Identifying watermarks on the movies show that Caridi gave his copies to his friend, Russell Sprague, who subsequently posted them on the Internet, according to allegations in a complaint filed by Warner Bros. Entertainment.

Six former employees at the Fox Cable Networks even used the company's own computer servers to pirate and distribute software (worth more than $121,000), computer games, and several movies, including Fox's *Daredevil* and *X2: X-Men United,* as well as *The Matrix Reloaded* from Warner Bros. and *Daddy Day Care* from Revolution Studios.

If the movie industry has this much trouble policing its own workers, how can it ever hope to reign in piracy by individuals or organized crime rings? They probably can't.

TYPES OF VIDEO PIRACY

Internet piracy is just one part of the overall piracy problem faced by the movie industry. Movie studios are concerned about three general types of piracy:

Hard goods piracy   Sale of illegally copied videos at swap meets and through online auction sites and email

Circumvention devices   Tools used to break the copy protection on legal DVDs, making it possible to copy a film

Internet piracy   Distribution of movies over the Internet

PIRATING HARD GOODS (VIDEOTAPES AND DVDS)

Internet piracy accounts for an estimated $3 billion in lost revenue yearly. But the real piracy threat is from fake VHS and DVD copies of films, which account for an estimated $30 billion of lost revenue yearly. Counterfeit movies are often sold through swap meets, by mail order, via online auction sites, and by street hustlers.

To lure unsuspecting people into buying pirated films, many video pirates repackage movies as sequels to popular movies. For example, if you were to pick up a copy of "Gladiator 2," you might actually see a movie called *Titus*; "American Beauty 2" might really be *Strike*; and "Gone in 60 Seconds 2" might actually be a movie called *RPM*.

While most people expect pirated films to have shoddy video quality and amateurish packaging, some video pirates create such high-quality duplicates that only a trained eye can spot the forgery—the packaging is nearly perfect. For example, in 2002, the police raided a series of warehouses in Attleborough, Norfolk (England), and discovered 712 video recorders and 700,000 blank video cassettes that had been used to duplicate that year's biggest blockbusters, including *The Matrix, Gladiator*, and *Saving Private Ryan*. The videos confiscated were of such high quality that many had been bought by unsuspecting legal distributors and sold throughout Europe.

Li Yixin, of China's State Pornography and Illegality Crackdown Office, estimates that pirated videos make up 95 percent of China's video market. Across the border, Nadezhda Nazina, Russia's chief trade inspector and department head at the Economic Development and Trade Ministry, estimates that 83 percent of all videos sold in Russia today are fakes.

While video piracy thrives in China and Russia, few people realize that Italy has the highest rate of piracy in the Western world. In Italy, pirated videos account for almost 30 percent of the total market. Not only do Italian authorities have to worry about finding and arresting video pirates, but they have another problem that their Russian and Chinese counterparts don't have. Aurelio De Laurentiis of Italy's national producers' union said he had been warned against pursuing video pirates. "I got a phone call from two judges who told me I'd probably be killed by the Mafia."

To keep up with the latest news about video piracy around the world, visit the following websites:

Report Piracy
http://www.reportpiracy.co.uk

Motion Picture Association of America
http://www.mpaa.org/anti-piracy

International Intellectual Property Alliance
http://www.iipa.com

RIPPING DVDS

Because CSS doesn't stop people from copying DVDs and playing them on authorized DVD players, DeCSS wasn't really as much of a threat to the movie studios as DVD copying software, known as *rippers*. DVD ripping software, like 321 Studios' DVD X Copy program, could copy entire CSS-encrypted DVDs. (After losing several appeals, 321 Studios eventually replaced their original program with a modified version, called DVD X Treme, which did not allow copying of CSS-encrypted DVDs. When the cost of lawsuits overwhelmed them, 321 Studios soon went out of business.)

Despite this setback for 321 Studios and the apparent victory for the movie studios, the DVD ripper market is still alive and thriving. Instead of selling their products, rival programmers simply give away their DVD ripper programs for free. DVDs can be ripped into a wide variety of other video compression formats, including the commonly used AVI and DivX formats (two popular file formats for compressing video), and the VCD and SVCD formats (two popular formats for storing video on ordinary CDs). Figure 10-3 shows one such DVD ripper program.

Figure 10-3
DVDx, like most DVD rippers, can copy a DVD to the hard
drive or to another DVD.

Unlike Internet music pirates, who have settled on the MP3 file format by default, Internet video pirates have yet to settle on a single video file format. As a result, DVD rippers can often save videos in different file formats. Some people prefer watching movies in AVI format, while others prefer DivX format. For those who don't have rewritable DVD drives, DVD rippers often include the ability to store videos in VCD or Super VCD formats so you can save and play the video on an ordinary CD.

To find a DVD ripper, visit your favorite search engine and search for **DVD ripper**, or visit one of the following sites instead:

AfterDawn.com	http://www.afterdawn.com
BurnWorld	http://burnworld.com
Digital Digest	http://digital-digest.com
DVDRHelp.com	http://www.videohelp.com

DOWNLOADING MOVIES

Because movie files are typically huge, most people break them into parts so that others can download the individual parts that they need, rather than downloading a single, massive file. Not only can small files be downloaded faster, but more people are likely to offer them, so it increases the chances that you can download the same file from multiple sources. Figure 10-4 shows an example from Kazaa.

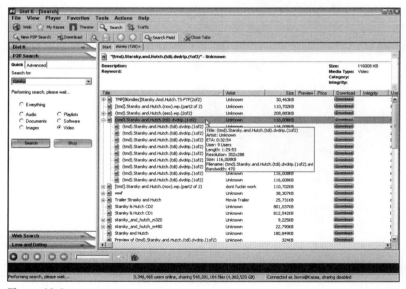

Figure 10-4

Many movies appear on file sharing networks, divided into several smaller files.

Just because you happen to find a file that contains a movie you want, it doesn't necessarily mean that the video quality will be good enough to make the movie worth watching. Besides people filling the Internet with poor quality videos, the movie studios themselves often hire companies, such as MediaForce, which purposely flood a file sharing network with bogus movie files that contain nothing but static in an attempt to discourage video piracy.

When people download and view a video file that's fake or of poor quality, they often erase it right away rather than post it on a file sharing network for other people to waste their time downloading and viewing. As a result, you can find the highest quality files by reviewing the sizes of all available files to determine which file size appears most often. For example, if you want to download the second part of the movie *Spider-Man 2*, you may see a dozen files listing the file size as 116,458KB but just one similar file with a size of 125,795KB. Chances are good that the 116,458KB file will be the best copy, which is why so many people have and distribute it.

To save time when you are looking for a particular file, try using a search engine like FileDonkey (http://www.filedonkey.com) or Sigster (http://www.sigster.com). As shown in Figure 10-5, these tools can search through multiple file sharing networks for the files you want.

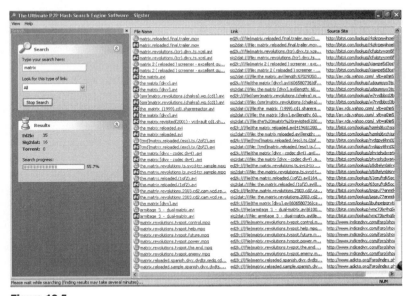

Figure 10-5

Programs like Sigster can pinpoint the location of your chosen file, no matter which file sharing network it may be found on.

While file sharing networks like Kazaa can be great for finding and download-ing MP3s, they're not ideal for finding and downloading full-length movies that gobble up several hundred megabytes of storage and take hours to download.

To download large files, many people now use BitTorrent, a file sharing program designed specifically to distribute large files. Just install BitTorrent (http://bitconjurer.org/bittorrent) or one of its variations, like BitTornado (http://bittornado.com) or BT++ (http://btplusplus.sourceforge.net), and then search in a web browser for a "torrent" that contains the files you want, or visit a hash-file link site, such as Up2dat (http://www.up2dat.com). Once you find a file you want, just double-click it, and BitTorrent will start downloading your movie.

In addition to posting movies on file sharing networks, many people also post movies in newsgroups. Unlike file sharing networks, where movies are often broken into just a few parts, newsgroups often break movies up into doz-ens, sometimes even hundreds, of files stored in the RAR file format, a popular file compression format. To learn more about RAR files, see the following "Using RAR files" section.

Downloading and collecting hundreds of separate RAR files to make up a single video may be a daunting task, but it can be even more frustrating if a handful of files are missing or corrupted. To avoid this problem, many people also include PAR and PAR2 files with RAR files. PAR and PAR2 files can help you recreate missing RAR files, as explained in the "Recovering missing RAR files with PAR and PAR2 files" section later in the chapter.

Newsgroup file sharing isn't a high-profile way of sharing video files, unlike the file sharing networks, so you're less likely to find novices and mali-cious users flooding the newsgroup with poor quality or bogus files. Breaking up a huge video file into multiple RAR files also makes newsgroups a cumber-some way to download videos. The initial complexity involved in breaking up and posting a video file to a newsgroup helps ensure that only dedicated users will actually post files, and these users tend to take pride in posting high-quality video files.

To find movies in newsgroups, head for these main newsgroup categories and see which branches your newsgroup server carries:

- alt.binaries.dvd

- alt.binaries.movies

- alt.binaries.movies.divx

- alt.binaries.multimedia

- alt.binaries.vcd

USING RAR FILES

Any video files you'll find in a newsgroup will likely be compressed in multiple RAR files. Basically, the RAR format can split massive files like movies and TV shows into smaller, consecutively numbered files, making them easier to share on newsgroups. Users post the numbered pieces over several days, thus avoiding any bandwidth limits that may be imposed by their Internet service provider. Swappers, in turn, log on over several days and download the latest pieces. Once they've downloaded all of the file parts, WinRAR or another RAR program combines the pieces into the original file.

The key to downloading videos divided into RAR files is grabbing *all* of the pieces. For example, have a look at the three parts of a *Sex and the City* episode, shown in Figure 10-6.

```
HBO - Sex and the City - An American Girl in Paris.rar (*/23)  ─── First file
HBO - Sex and the City - An American Girl in Paris.r00 (*/23)
HBO - Sex and the City - An American Girl in Paris.r01 (*/23)
HBO - Sex and the City - An American Girl in Paris.r02 (*/23)  ⟩ Middle files
HBO - Sex and the City - An American Girl in Paris.r03 (*/23)
HBO - Sex and the City - An American Girl in Paris.r04 (*/23)
HBO - Sex and the City - An American Girl in Paris.r05 (*/23)
HBO - Sex and the City - An American Girl in Paris.r06 (*/18)  ─── Last file
```

Figure 10-6
Download the initial RAR file and every consecutively numbered RAR file immediately following.

This large file has been split into two types of files.

- The *first* part is the single file that ends with the .rar extension.

- The *subsequent* parts are the consecutively numbered files with extensions such as .r03, .r04, .r05, and so on.

You must download all the parts in order to extract the entire video, as shown in Figure 10-7.

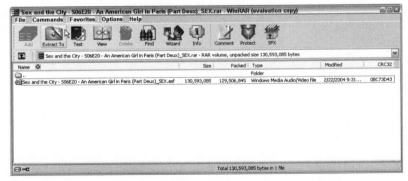

Figure 10-7
Once you've downloaded all the parts of an RAR compressed file, WinRAR can combine them
to extract the original file.

Newer versions of RAR (versions 3.0 and later) simplify the numbering format
slightly by giving all the files a .rar extension and inserting part numbers into the
file names, as shown here:

```
HBO - Sex and the City - An American Girl in Paris.part1.rar (*/23)
HBO - Sex and the City - An American Girl in Paris.part2.rar (*/23)
HBO - Sex and the City - An American Girl in Paris.part3.rar (*/23)
HBO - Sex and the City - An American Girl in Paris.part4.rar (*/23)
HBO - Sex and the City - An American Girl in Paris.part5.rar (*/23)
HBO - Sex and the City - An American Girl in Paris.part6.rar (*/23)
HBO - Sex and the City - An American Girl in Paris.part7.rar (*/23)
HBO - Sex and the City - An American Girl in Paris.part8.rar (*/18)
```

RECOVERING MISSING RAR FILES WITH PAR AND PAR2 FILES

Few things are more frustrating than downloading 105 pieces of a movie, only
to find that your news server choked on four of the pieces, leaving your movie
with several short gaps. You can leave a message, begging the uploader to
resend your missing files. But what if somebody else's news server choked
on *different* pieces of the same movie? With the newsgroup's global reach, an

uploader could spend days or weeks reposting missed pieces. The solution to this modern dilemma hails from a 1960s algorithm known as the Reed-Solomon error-correction protocol, used previously for correcting errors in data storage and satellite broadcasts. When packaged in a program called SmartPar (http://parchive.sourceforge.net/#clients), that same formula keeps uploaders from needing to constantly repost missed files.

Here's how it works: Before uploading all the pieces of their movie, uploaders run SmartPar to analyze the data. SmartPar places its analysis in a small file named "PAR." The program also grabs integral data bits from the movie and places them in several "recovery" files bearing consecutive numbers: P01, P02, P03, P04, and so on. The uploader posts all the movie's pieces, the PAR file, *and* the sequentially numbered recovery files. Yes, this requires more time and effort. But it's worthwhile, because those four PAR files can recover *any* four missing movie files.

Downloaders grab all the movie's pieces and the PAR file, then run their own copy of SmartPar. If the program discovers that the movie is missing some pieces—three, for instance—they simply download any three of the numbered PAR files. SmartPar runs its error-correcting protocol on this data, and by using its formula on the PAR files and the recovery files, it reconstructs those three missing pieces.

Here's an example. If SmartPar says your newly downloaded *Sex and the City* episode isn't missing any RAR files, ignore the PAR files. They were a safety net that you didn't need. But if SmartPar says *one* RAR file is missing or corrupt, download any *one* of the numbered PAR files to recover it. Missing *two* RAR files? Download any *two* of the numbered PAR files. But what if you're missing *four* or more RAR files, and the uploader only posted *three*? Then you're out of luck, unfortunately. You don't have enough PAR file information to recover the four missing pieces.

PAR files have been around for several years, and a new, improved version called PAR2 also has a large fan base. Which program should you use? It's probably best to use PAR2, because many programs, including QuickPar (http://parchive.sourceforge.net/#clients), support both the PAR and PAR2 formats.

PAR2 works much like PAR, but with smaller recovery files that use a different numbering scheme. For example, Figure 10-8 shows that an uploader used RAR to post a complete *Sex and the City* episode in 12 pieces (.r01, .r02, .r03, .r04, .r05, .r06, .r07, .r08, .r09, .r10, .r11, and the initial RAR file). The poster also thoughtfully included three PAR files (.par, .p01, and .p02), and seven PAR2 files (.par2, .vol00+01.par2, .vol01+02.par2, .vol03+04.par2, .vol07+08.par2, .vol15+16.par2, and .vol31+09.par2).

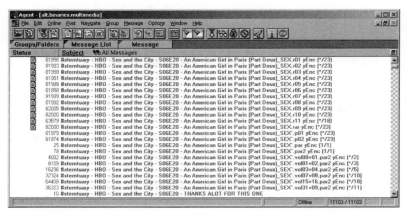

Figure 10-8

This *Sex and the City* episode is posted in RAR format, with both PAR and PAR2 files included for reconstructing a few missing, corrupt, or incomplete RAR files.

Although the PAR2 numbering scheme looks much more complex than the PAR numbering, it's actually faster and easier to use. Download all the episode's pieces and the first PAR2 file, and run QuickPar to examine your downloaded files, as shown in Figure 10-9.

Figure 10-9

Double-click the PAR2 file in QuickPar, and the program tells you how many blocks you need to recover the missing files.

If all the RAR files came through fine, you don't need to recover anything—don't bother downloading the PAR or PAR2 files. But if QuickPar finds a corrupt or missing RAR file, QuickPar tells you how many "blocks" you need to recover that file. In Figure 10-9, for instance, QuickPar found a missing file and says you need 21 blocks to recover it.

So, how many blocks are in a PAR2 file? The PAR2 file's numbering system provides the answer: The *last* number before the .par2 extension reveals the number of blocks in each file. For instance, here are the six numbered PAR2 files from Figure 10-8. (Their block numbers are in bold):

.vol00+**01**.par2

.vol01+**02**.par2

.vol03+**04**.par2

.vol07+**08**.par2

.vol15+**16**.par2

.vol31+**09**.par2

Those PAR2 files contain 1, 2, 4, 8, 16, and 9 blocks respectively—a total of 40 blocks. That's much more than 21; you could download them all to recover the missing file, or you can save time by just downloading the files with 1, 4, and 16 blocks. Those add up to exactly 21 blocks. Download those three files, and QuickPar uses their data to recover the missing piece, as shown in Figure 10-10.

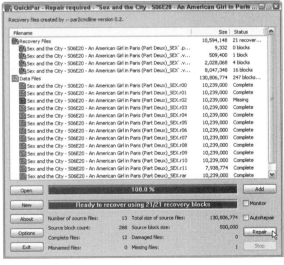

Figure 10-10

Once you've downloaded the required number of blocks in PAR2 files, QuickPar recreates the video.

THE FUTURE OF VIDEO PIRACY ON THE INTERNET

Every time a new consumer technology appears, the movie studios proclaim that it will kill off their business. When television sets first arrived, the movie studios worried that free television shows would stop people from going to movie theaters, but television wound up creating another market for movies. When VCRs and video rental stores appeared, the movie studios once again feared that nobody would go to movie theaters, but video rentals wound up creating another market for movies. Now that file sharing networks have arrived, the movie studios have started screaming that nobody will drive to the movie theaters. We'll know in a few years whether the movie industry's fears have finally come true or whether the Internet will provide yet another source of revenue for the studios.

11

SHARING BOOKS

The world of rampant copyright violation and file sharing has angered the music industry and now threatens to encroach upon the publishing industry as well, with a practice dubbed *bookwarez*. Like recording artists, book authors often differ in their views about releasing their books on the Internet's file sharing circuit. When a publisher accepted science fiction author Cory Doctorow's first novel, Doctorow decided to use the Internet to boost publicity for his book. After receiving permission from his publisher, Doctorow created a website (http://www.craphound.com) to give away the book in e-book form while simultaneously trying to sell it through bookstores.

"You can download it," Doctorow wrote, "put it on a P2P net, put it on your site, email it to a friend, and, if you're addicted to dead trees, you can even print it . . . this site is a place where you can download the whole goddamned book, completely gratis." Visitors downloaded more than a hundred thousand copies of his novel within a few months, and word-of-mouth publicity led to a sellout of the printed copy, as well. Delighted, Doctorow took the same approach with his second novel.

Longtime science fiction author Harlan Ellison, by contrast, took the opposite approach. A press release on his website (http://www.harlanellison.com) states:

> INDIVIDUALS SEEM TO THINK THAT THEY CAN ALLOW
> THE DISSEMINATION OF WRITERS' WORK ON THE
> INTERNET WITHOUT AUTHORIZATION, AND WITHOUT
> PAYMENT, UNDER THE BANNER OF "FAIR USE" OR
> THE IDIOT SLOGAN "INFORMATION MUST BE FREE."
> A WRITER'S WORK IS NOT INFORMATION: IT IS OUR
> CREATIVE PROPERTY, OUR LIVELIHOOD AND OUR
> FAMILIES' ANNUITY. WHY SHOULD ANY ARTIST, OF ANY
> KIND, CONTINUE CREATING NEW WORK, EKING OUT AN
> EXISTENCE IN PURSUIT OF A CAREER, FOLLOWING THE

I have seen men hazard their fortunes, go on long journeys halfway around the world, forge friendships, even lie, cheat and steal, all for the gain of a book.

—A.S.W. Rosenbach

MUSE, WHEN LITTLE INTERNET THIEVES, RODENTS WITHOUT ETHIC OR UNDERSTANDING, STEAL AND STEAL AND STEAL, CONVENIENCING THEMSELVES AND "SCREW THE AUTHOR"? WHAT WE'RE LOOKING AT IS THE DEATH OF THE PROFESSIONAL WRITER!

To help avoid "the death of the professional writer," Ellison went to court after finding his work posted on alt.binaries.e-book newsgroups. AOL didn't remove the work from its newsgroup servers when Ellison's attorney emailed them a removal order, so Ellison filed suit (*Ellison v. AOL, Inc.*, No. 02-55797) in April 2000. To continue his fight as the suit continues its journey through several court appeals, Ellison has requested donations to his "Kick Internet Piracy" campaign (http://www.harlanellison.com/kick). Feel like donating? Send your check, payable to the Law Office of M. Christine Valada, to this address:

> Kick Internet Piracy
> Post Office Box 55935
> Sherman Oaks, CA 91413

Ellison's big-guns approach might actually be successful in stopping the posting of his work. Since filing suit, his works rarely turn up on e-book newsgroups or file sharing networks. Of course, Ellison told the Wall Street Journal he's spent more than $300,000 during the legal struggle, most of it his own money. There's no word, though, on whether his legal battle has increased his in-store sales.

NOTE: *To learn more about book piracy (aka ePiracy), visit the Science Fiction and Fantasy Writers of America site (http://www.sfwa.org/epiracy/faq.htm).*

SCANNING A BOOK

One reason why books aren't traded as often as music or video files is that the average American only reads one book a year, so there are fewer people willing to trade, let alone steal, a book (except this one, of course). A second reason involves the amount of work needed to convert a printed book into a digital file, unless you're able to steal the digital file. (See the "Cracking an E-Book's Copy Protection" section later in the chapter.)

Believe it or not, most books that appear as bookwarez are meticulously scanned in by hand, one or two pages at a time. It's a boring, time-consuming job: automatic high-speed scanners are too costly for most file sharers. For faster scans, some people purchase a sheet feeder for their scanner, cut the book apart at the binding, and slide the sheets through one at a time.

After saving the scanned pages as graphic files, the bookwarez maker can either convert them to text using optical character recognition (OCR) software (like OmniPage), or save the graphic files as a PDF (Portable Document Format) file. If they convert the files into text, they can run the file through a spellchecker to correct most of the scanning problems, and then post the resulting e-book to the Internet.

The alt.binaries.e-book FAQ (http://ebook.23ae.com) offers plenty of information about creating e-books, including tips for scanning a book (see Figure 11-1), naming files, and posting them to newsgroups and IRC channels.

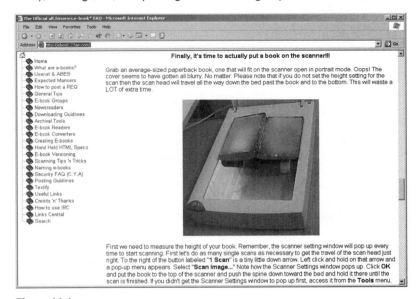

Figure 11-1
Most books are scanned in by hand, page by page.

Each newsgroup has its own rules and customs that everyone needs to follow. For example, if you're going to upload an e-book, you need to include the author's name and book title in the e-book file name such as: Orwell_George_-_Animal_Farm(v1.0(htm).zip. To provide additional information, you may also want to include a brief description of your e-book posting that includes one of the following identifiers:

[NEW]   A new e-book

[REPOST]   An e-book that had been previously posted but has been posted again due to popular demand

[TECHNICAL]   An e-book that contains technical information, such as computer manuals

[SCRIPT]   A film or play displayed in script format

[FICTION]   A novel or short story e-book

[NONFICTION]   A nonfiction e-book

For example, you might name a file like this: [REPOST] Orwell_George_-_Animal_Farm(v1.0(htm).zip.

To provide e-books that people can view on practically any type of computer, e-book newsgroups prefer that people supply e-books in open formats, such as plain ASCII text, HTML, Rich Text Format (RTF), or Adobe's Portable Document Format (PDF). Of course, nobody will complain too much if you supply an interesting e-book trapped in a proprietary format, such as Microsoft's Reader (LIT) format, but you should always strive to make any posted e-books accessible to everyone.

Newly posted books often show errors, such as hyphens in the middle of a word in the middle of a line. Some downloaders will actually proofread e-books, correct any errors, and repost the book as a new version. A book title ending in v1.0 usually means the book is newly scanned and fairly clean of formatting errors. The same book ending with v2.0 has been proofread and corrected, almost always by a third party. Once an e-book reaches v3.0, you can safely assume that it's free of most spelling and formatting errors.

Instead of scanning a book page by page, some people just take the much simpler route of copying books from book services, such as Safari Books Online (http://www.safaribooksonline.com) and Books24x7 (http://www.books24x7.com), which offer subscribers access to hundreds of technical books that they can browse, copy, and save. Because these services have taken the trouble of digitizing popular technical books already, subscribers can simply save the digitized books they want and "share" those book files through newsgroups or file sharing networks.

WHAT TYPES OF BOOKS ARE STOLEN?

The most common e-books found on the Internet are advanced computer books from O'Reilly, Que, Sams, Microsoft Press, New Riders, and Peachpit (see Figure 11-2).

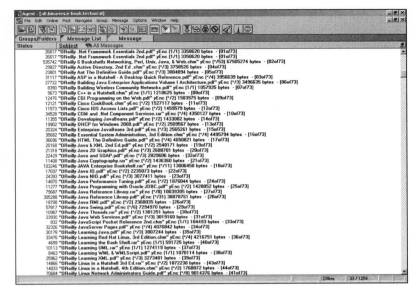

Figure 11-2

E-books from O'Reilly appear frequently on newsgroups and file sharing networks.

The latest bestsellers also often appear on the Internet. J.K. Rowling's *Harry Potter and the Order of the Phoenix* appeared as an e-book on file sharing networks and newsgroups just hours after going on sale. And practically every book and short story written by Isaac Asimov, Ursula Le Guin, and Roger Zelazny can be found on newsgroups or file sharing networks along with horror stories by Stephen King (see Figure 11-3).

Other popular e-books are ones that cover taboo subjects, like lock picking, erotica, creating fake IDs, building your own handguns, password cracking, brainwashing, hacking, cable and satellite TV descrambling, and the usual penis-enlargement techniques.

For many downloaders, the thrill comes from finding and downloading books, not from actually reading them. Stuffing thousands of e-books onto their computers gives bookwarez traders the modern-day thrill of owning something akin to a huge mahogany-shelved library. The point is often just to show themselves (and others) that they own them.

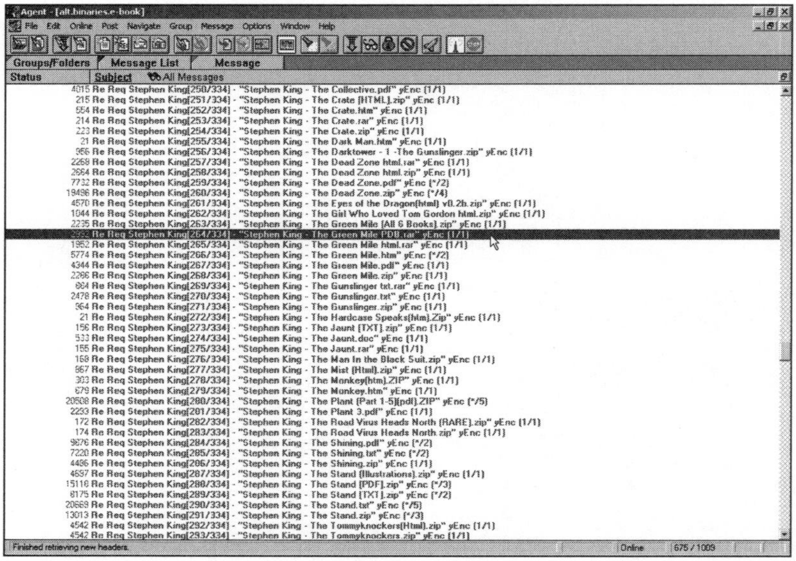

Figure 11-3

Over 300 postings in the alt.binaries.e-book newsgroup contain nearly all of Stephen King's
books, with most books being posted in several different formats for the reader's convenience.

CRACKING AN E-BOOK'S COPY PROTECTION

Traditional paper and hardbound books can be cumbersome to copy, but electronic books can be copied as easily as MP3 files. To protect their electronic books, publishers have come up with copy-protection methods designed to discourage widespread illegal copying and encourage legitimate purchasing.

That's the fantasy anyway. The reality is that no one has settled on a standard e-book file format that every computer can use. Even if it's possible to grab a copy of your favorite best-seller as an e-book, you might not be able to read it on your computer or operating system. Some publishers even hope that copy protection will force people into buying separate versions of the same e-book if they wish to read the e-book on different computers. But forcing people to buy different versions of the same e-book is like forcing people to buy two different copies of the same CD just so they can play one CD in their car stereo and the other in their home stereo.

Incompatible portable e-book readers, copy protection, and the lack of a standard file format are just some of the problems that discourage widespread e-book adoption. But perhaps the biggest obstacle to e-books' acceptance is the price. Publishers often try to sell e-books for the same price as the printed copy, and because buyers don't pay for paper, binding, or printing, they expect e-books to cost much less than the paper version. Just as people release a continuous stream of MP3 files of their favorite albums to protest the high cost of CDs, so do many people crack the e-book copy-protection methods to protest the high cost of e-books.

While copy-protection frustrates legitimate users, it does little to foil the real thieves. Many people have developed tools for removing the copy-protection from e-books, ostensibly to allow others to make backups of their files and to read them on different computers. Naturally, these same tools can be used to circumvent the copy protection and spread the unprotected version of the e-book all over the Internet.

It isn't very surprising that these copy-protection schemes can be cracked, but it is surprising how easily they can be cracked. Rather than use proven encryption algorithms, most companies develop their own copy-protection schemes that just wind up annoying legitimate users who can't copy their e-books or read them where they want. Hackers spot the flaws in an e-book's weak copy-protection scheme and, within hours, post notices of these copy-protection flaws to other thieves across the Internet.

In most cases, copy protection simply hurts consumers and gives Internet thieves another target to crack for fun or profit.

CRACKING ADOBE'S E-BOOK PROTECTION

A small Russian company called ElcomSoft (http://www.elcomsoft.com) drew the wrath of Adobe when it released Advanced eBook Processor, a Windows program that could remove both password encryption and usage restrictions from Adobe's secure e-book file format and turn the files into ordinary Acrobat PDF files. Invoking the controversial Digital Millennium Copyright Act (DMCA), Adobe originally brought the Advanced eBook Processor's potential violation of the DMCA to the attention of the FBI, which later arrested ElcomSoft's 27-year-old Russian programmer, Dmitry Sklyarov, at DEFCON, an annual hacker convention in Las Vegas.

While ElcomSoft didn't dispute the potential for its Advanced eBook Processor program to remove usage restrictions on e-book files, it did claim that removing such usage restrictions allowed people to read their legally purchased e-books on different computers, which is considered "fair use" under the law.

After intense public pressure, especially from the programmer community, Adobe backed off. During cross-examination, Adobe even admitted that it had hired two companies to search the Internet, but neither company could find a single stolen e-book that had been cracked with ElcomSoft's program. A jury eventually acquitted ElcomSoft and Dmitry Sklyarov of all charges, but not before Dmitry had spent three weeks in a U.S. jail.

When asked to comment on the Advanced eBook Processor, Sklyarov replied, "It has legal applications; it could be used for many legal things, for good things. A weapon could be used for killing and for protecting myself, but in [the] United States [a] weapon is legal."

Perhaps most embarrassing for Adobe wasn't that the Advanced eBook Processor had cracked the copy-protection scheme, but that it had exposed how weak the copy-protection scheme had been in the first place. "If somebody produces bad stuff," Sklyarov said, "and someone proves that this stuff is real bad, nobody will like it."

Sklyarov's case highlighted the central problem with the DMCA. If someone creates poor copy protection and another person exposes its flaws, is the person who reveals the faulty copy protection actually a criminal? The Electronic Frontier Foundation (http://www.eff.org) believes the answer is no and that "U.S. copyright law is flawed because it outlaws technologies instead of actions."

To learn more about the ElcomSoft case, visit the Free Dmitry Sklyarov site (http://www.freesklyarov.org) or read criticism about the DMCA from the Anti-DMCA site (http://www.anti-dmca.org).

CRACKING MICROSOFT'S READER PROTECTION

Following closely upon the heels of Sklyarov's exposure of Adobe's weak copy-protection method, independent programmer Dan Jackson soon attacked Microsoft's Reader format with a program called Convert LIT (http://www. convertlit.com).

Like the Advanced eBook Processor, Convert LIT can strip away any usage restrictions on any e-book trapped in the Microsoft Reader format, allowing the reader to make backup copies or read the e-book on different operating systems and computers.

If you are interested in peeking into the guts of the program, the Convert LIT site also provides full C source code so you can modify the program or just study how it strips away copy protection from Microsoft Reader files.

FINDING ILLEGAL E-BOOKS

Some people steal books for fun. Others steal books to avoid paying for them. But no matter what the motive, you'll find that the Internet may be the biggest library in the world, with books available from eBay, newsgroups, and all the popular file sharing networks.

BUYING COPIED BOOKS ON EBAY

More than 20 million items are bought and sold on eBay at any given time. Just as bootleg DVDs and CDs often sneak into swap meets, copied books (as well as movies, music, and software) turn up regularly on eBay. It's surprisingly easy for somebody to sell a CD stuffed with hundreds of bootleg computer books (as shown in Figure 11-4).

Figure 11-4
Many people download books from the Internet and then resell them on CDs through auction sites like eBay.

When a CD with nearly 100 books sells for as little as $15, it's obvious that somebody's selling copies without permission from the authors or publishers. Some sellers avoid postage costs by simply emailing copied e-books to the winning bidder. The buyers apparently don't know that they can download the books for free just as easily as the seller did.

Obviously, eBay prohibits selling illegally copied goods, so it regularly follows up on removal requests and searches for keywords that signal possible copyright violations. But when a complaint stops an illegal auction, the seller simply signs up for a new account under a different name and sells the same goods with a slightly different description to avoid detection. No matter how hard eBay tries to police its auctions, it can't catch everybody breaking the law.

STEALING BOOKS FROM NEWSGROUPS

The most popular e-books on newsgroups generally cover technology, fantasy, science fiction, and mechanics. Files posted on newsgroups often consist of properly spelled names sorted by subject with details on the book's format.
Here are the most popular newsgroups for finding e-books:

alt.binaries.ebook   This is not widely used, but it occasionally receives a misplaced post.

alt.binaries.e-book   The main repository for e-books, this newsgroup receives a constant flow of new and older e-books. Everything from best-selling fiction to older classics to complete collections of science fiction authors is posted. (It was a post in this newsgroup of Harlan Ellison's short stories that brought about Ellison's suit against America Online.)

alt.binaries.flood   Many people collect works by certain authors, and the flood newsgroup is for people who "flood" a newsgroup with hundreds of books by a certain author or dealing with a certain subject. The flood inevitably pushes everything else off the newsgroup, so books posted here don't last very long before another flood replaces them.

alt.binaries.mathmad   Books on math and physics show up here, although they're usually crossposted to alt.binaries.ebook, as well.

alt.binaries.palm   Books formatted specifically for the Palm's small screen appear here, usually in PDB format for the Palm's popular eReader program (http://www.palmdigitalmedia.com).

alt.binaries.rpg   Fans of role-playing games post books and games in this active group. Back issues of Dragon Magazine are popular, as well.

alt.binaries.technical   This huge repository is usually stuffed with computer books, but technical material of any kind shows up: repair manuals for Briggs & Stratton small engines, laser printers, and cameras; military field guides; certification exam study guides; and other bits of technical viscera. College textbooks occasionally turn up here, as well.

alt.binaries.sounds.mp3.audiobooks   Books on tape appear here as MP3 files. The resulting files are quite large and are broken up into a long string of posts. Most downloaders rely on PAR and PAR2 files (covered in Chapter 10) to retrieve any posts they miss.

STEALING BOOKS FROM FILE SHARING NETWORKS

Although most people use file sharing networks for stealing music, e-books can be readily found just by typing in the name of an author or the title of a particular book, as shown in Figure 11-5. These are ten of the most popular authors, whose works you can find on many file sharing networks:

1. Stephen King *(Misery, The Shining)*
2. J.K. Rowling (the Harry Potter series)
3. Terry Pratchett *(The Colour of Magic, Wyrd Sisters)*
4. Tom Clancy *(Red Storm Rising, Patriot Games)*
5. Douglas Adams *(The Hitchhiker's Guide to the Galaxy)*
6. J.R.R. Tolkien *(The Lord of the Rings)*
7. John Grisham *(The Client, A Time to Kill)*
8. Iain M. Banks *(Complicity, Inversions)*
9. Irvine Welsh *(Trainspotting)*
10. Douglas Coupland *(Generation X, Microserfs)*

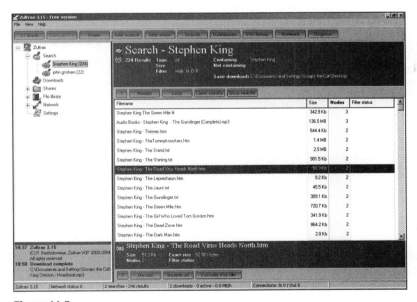

Figure 11-5

The works of popular authors, such as Stephen King, can be found on practically any file sharing network.

Besides searching for author names or book titles, you can often find e-books on a file sharing network just by searching for terms such as **e**, **ebooks**, or **pdf**, as shown in Figure 11-6.

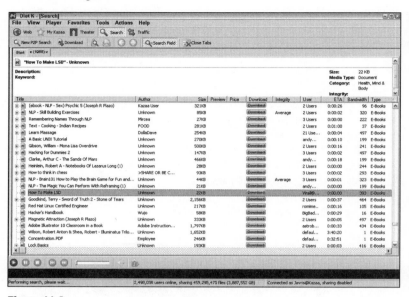

Figure 11-6
A search on Kazaa turned up nearly 2,000 books that cover a wide variety of topics.

Some additional terms to use for searching include topics, such as **Java programming**, or the name of specific publishers, such as **No Starch Press** or **O'Reilly**. When searching for e-books, many file sharing programs give you the option of restricting your search to specific types of files, such as audio, video, or text, as shown in Figure 11-7. By narrowing your search to text files, you can just search for e-books without the distraction of seeing video or audio files.

THE FUTURE OF E-BOOKS

Publishers want to restrict copying while readers want the freedom to read their e-books in any form without artificial limitations. Compounding the problem of copy protection, e-books also face an uphill battle for widespread acceptance, since no single file format has emerged as a standard. To fix this problem, several companies have banded together to form the Open eBook Forum (http://www.openebook.org), but more time has been spent squabbling over Digital Rights Management and copy protection, so don't expect its members to find a solution to e-book piracy any time soon.

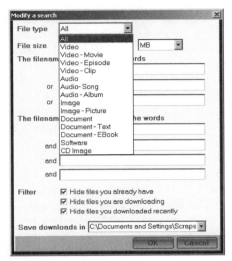

Figure 11-7
File sharing programs can limit a search to a specific
file type, such as video or text.

Unlike the music industry, where corporations spend millions of dollars buying the rights to songs only to see their investments get swapped across the
Internet for free, book publishers are in a slightly more favorable position. For
book publishers, the greatest expense comes from printing and distributing their
products, which is exactly what e-books eliminate.

After people cracked the copy protection on Stephen King's e-book
Riding the Bullet, critics spoke about the problems of piracy, but others saw
the hack as a unique marketing opportunity to attract additional publicity for
the e-book. "In book publishing, a little bit of piracy may be good marketing,"
says Chris MacAskill, former CEO of the once-independent online electronic
publishing sites Fatbrain.com and MightyWords.com in Santa Clara, California.
Eliminate the bulk of your expenses (printing and distributing) through e-
books, and Internet piracy can just be part of the cost of doing business, much
like factoring in the inevitable cost of shoplifting when calculating profits for a
printed book.

Unlike songs that sound the same whether they play from a CD or as an
MP3 file, e-books and physical books differ because an e-book may be convenient to carry, but it's not as convenient to read on a bulky and tiny e-book
reader, such as a handheld computer. Despite the threat of blatant copying,
e-books can actually reach more people who might never have known about
the e-book's existence and entice them to buy a physical copy later. "The more
people who see the books, the better, especially if the book is good," says

Bill Pollock, founder of No Starch Press. "And if the book is bad, this is a great way to sort that out before spending your hard-earned dough on something that isn't worth the paper it's printed on." E-books could complement printed books and possibly expose people to a wider variety of books to read.

That's part of the plan for TeleRead (http://www.teleread.org), a proposed national digital library for storing e-books and distributing them to schools and libraries across the country. By providing a national library that anyone can use, TeleRead hopes that e-books can finally give everyone equal access to information regardless of their physical location or economic status.

China has already started a similar project dubbed the China Digital Library Project (http://www.china.com.cn/english/PP-e/32407.htm). So far, this Chinese national digital library has collected over 23 million books, making it the largest book collection in Asia. The Digital South Asia Library (http://dsal. uchicago.edu) also plans to store reference and scholarly works about Asia in digital format. Although copy protection may be necessary to protect the rights of copyright holders, projects like TeleRead, Digital South Asia Library, and the China Digital Library Project can't let copy protection interfere with the public's legitimate need to read that same information.

THE FUTURE OF E-BOOKS AND PIRACY

No matter how effective copy protection may be, it still can't prevent the simplest form of book stealing: scanning a book page by page. In Japan, bookstores are wrestling with a new problem called *digital shoplifting*, where people use cameras in their cell phones to take pictures of books and magazines instead of buying them.

Perhaps the real future of e-books lies with e-paper, dubbed Gyricon (http://www.gyriconmedia.com) by its Xerox PARC creators. Gyricon consists of a thin layer of transparent plastic filled with millions of small black and white or red and white beads in an oil-filled cavity. When voltage is applied, the beads rotate to present a colored side to the viewer, mimicking the appearance of a printed page, complete with text and graphics. Gyricon can be reused, it is brighter than today's reflective displays, and it consumes minimal power.

If Gyricon becomes popular, trading e-books may become as common as trading MP3 files, and then the debate can start all over again about whether technology and legislation can ever regulate human behavior in lieu of ethics and honesty. And then book publishers will simply need to find a way to profit from this new form of distribution.

12

PIRATING SOFTWARE (WAREZ)

Given the astronomical costs of some programs, such as Adobe Photoshop, Microsoft Office, or Quark XPress, many people justify stealing software by arguing that software companies overcharge for their products in the first place. In some parts of the world, a single word processor can cost more than most people make in a month, so it's no surprise that software piracy is so rampant.

Software piracy isn't new. Even as early as 1976, during the fledgling days of the personal computer, software piracy threatened to halt innovation in the software business. Recognize this guy?

AN OPEN LETTER TO HOBBYISTS
By William Henry Gates III
February 3, 1976
An Open Letter to Hobbyists

To me, the most critical thing in the hobby market right now is the lack of good software courses, books and software itself. Without good software and an owner who understands programming, a hobby computer is wasted. Will quality software be written for the hobby market?

Almost a year ago, Paul Allen and myself, expecting the hobby market to expand, hired Monte Davidoff and developed Altair BASIC. Though the initial work took only two months, the three of us have spent most of the last year documenting, improving and adding features to BASIC. Now we have 4K, 8K, EXTENDED, ROM and DISK BASIC. The value of the computer time we have used exceeds $40,000.

The feedback we have gotten from the hundreds of people who say they are using BASIC has all been positive. Two surprising things are apparent, however, 1) Most of these

It is certain that stealing nourishes courage, strength, skill, tact, in a word, all the virtues useful to a republican system and consequently to our own.

—Marquis de Sade

"users" never bought BASIC (less than 10% of all Altair owners have bought BASIC), and 2) The amount of royalties we
have received from sales to hobbyists makes the time spent
on Altair BASIC worth less than $2 an hour.

Why is this? As the majority of hobbyists must be aware, most
of you steal your software. Hardware must be paid for, but
software is something to share. Who cares if the people who
worked on it get paid?

Is this fair? One thing you don't do by stealing software is
get back at MITS for some problem you may have had. MITS
doesn't make money selling software. The royalty paid to us,
the manual, the tape and the overhead make it a break-even
operation. One thing you do do is prevent good software from
being written. Who can afford to do professional work for
nothing? What hobbyist can put 3-man years into programming, finding all bugs, documenting his product and distribute
for free? The fact is, no one besides us has invested a lot of
money in hobby software. We have written 6800 BASIC, and
are writing 8080 APL and 6800 APL, but there is very little
incentive to make this software available to hobbyists. Most
directly, the thing you do is theft.

What about the guys who re-sell Altair BASIC, aren't they
making money on hobby software? Yes, but those who have
been reported to us may lose in the end. They are the ones
who give hobbyists a bad name, and should be kicked out of
any club meeting they show up at.

I would appreciate letters from any one who wants to pay
up, or has a suggestion or comment. Just write to me at
1180 Alvarado SE, #114, Albuquerque, New Mexico, 87108.
Nothing would please me more than being able to hire ten
programmers and deluge the hobby market with good software.

Bill Gates
General Partner, Micro-Soft

Thirty years later, Bill Gates and Microsoft are still fighting software piracy, and
the problem hasn't improved. (Though, of course, many thousands of programmers have shown that it is possible to develop great software and give it away
for free—witness the open source movement.)

People are still stealing software, and companies are still claiming that they're losing billions of dollars as a result. The problem isn't just that software costs too much or that companies lose money when people pirate their software. The real problem is that copying and sharing software is easy, and anything that's easy and profitable is also likely to be rampant and uncontrollable.

THE WAREZ UNDERGROUND

When people pirate software such as games, operating systems, utilities, and applications, they call those pirated copies *warez*. While organizations such as the Business Software Alliance (the BSA, at http://www.bsa.org) claim that software piracy causes publishers to lose $13 billion in revenue every year, that figure can be impossible to verify.

For instance, many people pirate software for nothing more than the thrill of finding the latest copy of a popular program so they can earn bragging rights among their friends; they may never even use the program. Others enjoy toying with pirated programs but never use them for an extended period of time. Despite the fact that some programs are copied and pirated by thousands of people, not everyone who pirates software does so to avoid buying it.

In some countries, certain programs are simply unavailable or are so outrageously expensive that few people can afford to buy a legitimate copy. In those cases, people may pirate programs to get access to software they wouldn't normally be able to afford or can't obtain legally.

Some people argue that piracy may actually help software publishers in the long run. College students, with their limited budgets, often pirate software to save their money for buying more important items (like beer). Yet once students get familiar with a particular program, they may end up purchasing a legitimate copy of a later version simply because they've grown accustomed to the pirated program. Eliminate the pirated copy, and these same students might eventually purchase a different program altogether.

HOW WAREZ TRADING WORKS

Anyone can trade warez, and many, many people do every day, without much forethought. Ever ask a friend or coworker to make a copy of a program for you? However, while this small-scale trading is illegal, it isn't nearly as disturbing to the software industry as the large-scale, organized warez trading that occurs among amateurs and professionals.

Many hackers organize themselves into warez trading groups and simply pirate software for the fun of it. To them, pirating software is a game where the object is to be the first to offer a popular commercial program. Of course, offering a pirated copy of Curious George Learns Phonics isn't nearly as impressive as being the first warez group to offer a full working copy of the latest version of Microsoft Windows or Office, which is why children's software turns out to be hard to find on the file sharing networks. It's the cool factor at work.

If a warez group can offer pirated software on the same day as the official release (known as *0-day warez*), their status shoots up considerably. And if they can offer a pirated copy before the official release date (known as *negative-day warez* or *pre-release warez*), their status skyrockets exponentially.

To get a copy of a major program before it's released, warez groups rely on someone who either works for the company developing the program, or who is involved in the shipping, duplicating, or packaging of a program. Corporate insiders can slip out a copy of the program and pass it along to a warez group simply for the thrill of doing so.

Once a warez group gets their hands on a program, they enlist the help of a cracker, who specializes in removing any copy protection embedded in the software. Crackers use disassembler programs such as IDA Pro (http://www.datarescue.com) or hex editors such as Hex Workshop (http://www.bpsoft.com) to disable any product-activation features (used in programs such as Windows XP), to strip away any copy-protection mechanisms, or to insert the warez group's name in the program's splash screen as a mark that they were the ones responsible for cracking that particular program.

Once the program has either been stripped of any copy-protection schemes or branded with the warez group's name and logo, the warez group contacts others by email, instant messaging, or chat rooms to trade for warez cracked by other warez groups. Eventually every warez group winds up with the latest copies of almost every commercial program available.

Most warez groups post their warez on web or FTP sites for anyone to download (see Figure 12-1). Warez FTP sites are often accessible by invitation only to members who get access by first uploading a pirated program that the FTP site administrator doesn't have; this ensures that the site will continue to grow.

Setting up a warez FTP site can be risky, because the site can be easily traced back to its physical location. To avoid this problem, some warez traders find space on another computer at work, at a university, or on a hacked computer anywhere in the world, and they secretly set up an FTP site on that computer stocked full of warez. (It's not illegal to link to pirated programs, but it is illegal to store those pirated files on your own site.) The warez trader can then publicize the existence of this secret FTP site, often called a *drop site*, so others can access the pirated programs. Such drop sites can run for days or longer until the system administrator notices that something is gobbling up both disk space and bandwidth. Of course, should the authorities eventually trace the location of this latest warez FTP site, they'll only find an innocent and likely puzzled system administrator instead of the real warez pirate.

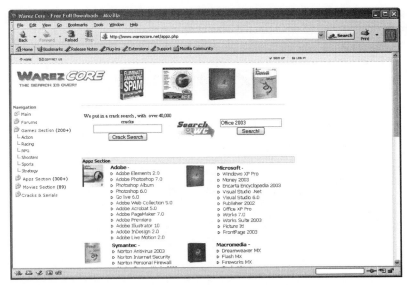

Figure 12-1
Many warez websites list an incredible variety of commercial software available for downloading.

To protect themselves, warez groups may also provide links to warez files stored on free web hosting sites created on GeoCities (http://geocities.yahoo.com) or FortuneCity (http://www.fortunecity.com). Such free web hosting services allow anyone to create a website anonymously, thereby protecting the warez group. If you ever find a warez website and can't seem to download a copy of a pirated program because the links are broken, you can pretty well guess that the free web hosting sites containing the illegally copied programs were shut down.

Chat rooms and newsgroups are another rich source for warez trading. Warez trading newsgroups, such as alt.binaries.cd.image, alt.binaries.mac, alt.binaries.mac.cd.images, alt.cracks, alt.binaries.cd.image.games, and alt.binaries.games are usually flooded with pirated software, web or FTP sites where a particular pirated program can be found, or serial numbers to activate pirated programs. Wade through the mostly meaningless responses, and you'll eventually find a message that contains a pirated program or a list of serial numbers needed to run that program (see Figure 12-2).

Because anything posted over the Internet can be traced, some warez traders avoid the Internet altogether and rely on direct dial-up electronic bulletin board systems (abbreviated as BBSs). A BBS is simply an ordinary computer accessible through a phone line. To access a warez BBS, you must know both the phone number to call and the correct password to get in. While warez BBSs can be nearly impossible for authorities to find, once the phone number is discovered (usually through spying on warez chat rooms and newsgroups), the person who owns that number is a sitting duck.

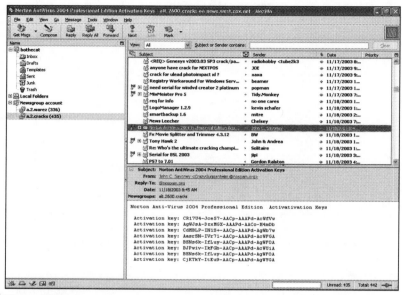

Figure 12-2
Through newsgroups, you can find plenty of warez and serial numbers needed to run pirated programs.

TRADING WAREZ FOR PROFIT

While many warez groups trade simply for the fun and challenge, some use pirated software to lure people to their websites for financial gain. Once people visit their sites, they may suddenly find themselves bombarded by porn pop-up ads that sprout faster than you can shut them down. The porn companies pay websites each time their ad pops up in somebody's browser, so warez groups earn extra money every time they lure another unsuspecting person into a barrage of pop-ups that won't go away (and also never seem to give access to the warez files in the first place).

PROFESSIONAL WAREZ PIRACY

Although warez groups provide stolen copies of programs to others, they rarely profit directly from their activities. The bigger problem for software publishers comes from professionals who specialize in mass producing counterfeit CDs (including music, video, and software).

For less than a few thousand dollars, these professionals can purchase CD and DVD duplicating machines to mass-produce copies of popular programs such as Norton Utilities or Macromedia Flash. Toss in a few scanned images of program logos wrapped in a CD case, and many counterfeit programs can look like legitimate copies, and they can be sold through flea markets, swap meets, eBay, or to unsuspecting (or equally guilty) domestic and overseas merchants.

Professional pirates rarely rely on warez trading, because the quality can be doubtful and availability unreliable. Instead, most buy one legitimate copy of the program and then make thousands of copies of it. The profits they make from selling illegal copies more than cover the cost of buying the legitimate copy of the program and their duplicating equipment.

HOW COMPANIES FIGHT BACK

While no one knows exactly how much piracy hurts software publishers, piracy undoubtedly translates into significant lost sales, especially when people buy counterfeit goods while thinking they're getting a legitimate copy at a greatly reduced price. With millions of dollars at stake, software companies fight back against the pirates using a variety of tactics.

SERIAL NUMBERS: THE KEY TO INSTALLING SOFTWARE

To prevent people from copying their programs and handing them out to every-one, many programs won't run on your computer until you enter a serial number, which is usually a series of seemingly random letters and numbers. Of course, any legitimate buyer of a program can simply pass out the serial number along with the pirated copy of the program. Because the serial number was valid to begin with, it will work on any number of pirated copies of that same program. In fact, many warez websites, such as MSCracks.com (http://www.mscracks.com), shown in Figure 12-3, contain nothing but lists of valid serial numbers for popular programs, and people can just match the version of their pirated program with the correct serial number and start using the pirated copy right away.

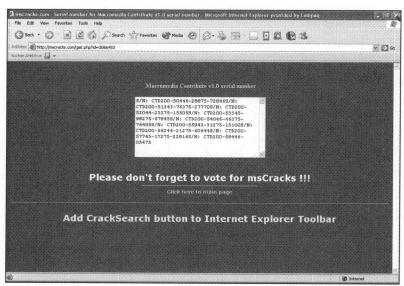

Figure 12-3

Many warez websites let you click a program name to view a list of valid serial numbers.

It's even possible to download a database program, such as Serials2000 (http://www.serialz.to), that contains nothing but valid serial numbers for the latest programs. By running these programs and searching for the name of a pirated program, such as Photoshop or CorelDRAW, pirates can find a valid serial number (see Figure 12-4).

One problem with using a serial number found on a website or posted on a newsgroup is that other people will likely use that same serial number, and the software makers can use that against the thieves. For example, when Microsoft discovered a batch of stolen serial numbers used to register Windows XP, it fought back by reprogramming its Windows Update service to stop patching any copy of Windows XP that used one of these serial numbers.

For those who can't find a valid serial number or who don't want to risk using a serial number that dozens of others may be using, there is the serial number generator. Although serial numbers appear to consist of randomly jumbled letters and numbers, they're actually generated by an algorithm, and the program just applies that algorithm to typed-in serial numbers to determine whether they're valid. Serial number generators mimic a program's algorithm to generate a list of serial numbers that the program mindlessly accepts as valid, as shown in Figure 12-5.

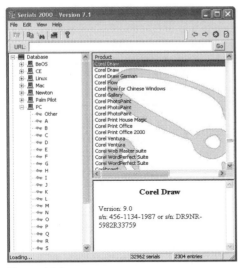

Figure 12-4

A serial number database program, such as Serials2000, lists valid (though stolen) serial numbers for use in different versions of pirated programs.

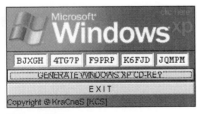

Figure 12-5

This serial number generator creates serial numbers to use in pirated copies of Microsoft Windows XP.

COPY PROTECTION: LOCKING THE GATES

Because serial numbers alone will never keep people from pirating software, some software publishers also try to prevent pirates from copying their programs. Many specialized programs, such as AutoCAD, cost several thousand dollars because they have a limited market and are highly technical. Few warez traders need the computer-aided design features of a program like AutoCAD, but companies may try to save money by buying one copy and pirating additional copies for the rest of the company. To prevent dishonest businesses from pirating software, many companies copy-protect their programs.

The two most popular methods for copy-protecting software involve software and hardware implementations. Software-based copy-protection schemes work in two ways: they prevent someone from copying a program, and they stop people from removing the program's copy-protection method altogether.

At the simplest level, a software copy-protection scheme might require shipping an additional file with your program. Before the program runs, it checks for this file, typically a DLL (dynamic link library) or OCX (OLE custom control). If this file doesn't exist, the program assumes that it's an illegal copy and either refuses to run or runs in limited demo mode. Naturally, it's possible to just copy this missing DLL or OCX file and pass it along with a pirated copy, and lo and behold, the program will still work.

Some software publishers copy-protect their installation CDs by including a hidden file on the disc. If someone tries to copy the CD, their computer will likely miss the hidden file, so when they try to install the program from a copy of the CD, it won't work.

Once again, this problem can be overcome by copying a CD in Raw mode. Instead of copying the files from a CD and storing them on a duplicate copy, Raw mode captures an exact image of the CD, snaring any hidden files in the process and duplicating them exactly on the copy of the CD. Some CD burning programs that offer Raw copying mode include Alcohol 120% (http://www.alcohol-soft.com), Raw CD Copy (http://www.mpegx.com), and BlindWrite (http://www.vso-software.fr).

Any type of software copy protection can eventually be overcome with enough patience, because crackers can keep probing a program until they find a way to break the copy-protection method. That's why many software publishers prefer hardware copy-protection schemes that require users to attach a device, called a *dongle*, to the parallel or USB port of the computer.

With hardware-based copy protection, it doesn't matter if people copy the program or not—the program won't run unless it detects the presence of the dongle attached to the computer. Because you can't duplicate dongles and pass them around as easily as you can duplicate CDs, hardware copy-protection schemes tend to offer more security, but at greater inconvenience to legitimate users. If you lose the dongle, you can't use the program, even though you paid for it. Too, sometimes the mere presence of the dongle can interfere with other devices.

Although dongles can't be easily duplicated, they can be mimicked. The whole copy-protection scheme revolves around the program periodically checking for the presence of the dongle, but if you emulate the existence of the dongle without the dongle itself, the program won't know the difference.

For example, there are two companies that can create software to mimic dongles: Virtual Dongles (http://www.endlessvisions.com) and Soft-Key Solutions (http://www.software-key.org). For a price, these companies will sell you a program to mimic the dongle protecting a program so you can copy it, along with your dongle program, to any other computer you want.

PRODUCT ACTIVATION: TYING SOFTWARE TO ONE COMPUTER

One problem with ordinary copy protection is that you can install dozens of copies of a program using the exact same serial number for each of them. To prevent this, the latest copy-protection method involves product activation, where a program creates a unique key based on the installed components of a computer, such as the following:

- Display adapter
- SCSI adapter (if available)
- IDE adapter
- Network adapter MAC address (if available)
- RAM amount
- Processor type
- Processor serial number
- Hard drive
- Hard drive volume serial number
- CD-ROM, CD-RW, or DVD-ROM drive

This unique key is tied in with a serial number and sent to the software publisher. Then, if somebody tries to reuse that serial number, the product activation feature notices that the program has been installed on a different computer and stops the program from working. That's the theory, anyway. The reality is that product activation can sometimes cause more problems for legitimate users.

For example, when Intuit added product activation to its TurboTax tax-preparation program, customers immediately complained that the product activation slowed down or crashed their computers and prevented them from installing the same copy of the program on both a desktop and a laptop computer, essentially forcing them to buy multiple copies of the same program to run on different computers. Intuit eventually dropped product activation after enough customers howled, which showed that product activation can sometimes hurt legitimate users just as much as it might discourage software piracy.

Symantec ran across similar product-activation glitches when it added product activation to their Norton AntiVirus program. A small percentage of users soon found that the program kept asking to be reactivated every day, eventually stopping altogether. Symantec soon released a patch to fix this problem, but not before angering some customers for the unnecessary nuisance.

Naturally, crackers have found ways to fool product activation. Some have developed programs that trick the product activation feature into believing that it's already been activated, or into thinking that the user hasn't used the program past its initial time limit.

Because product activation ties a specific serial number to your computer hardware, you may find that you can't use software activated in this way when you upgrade your computer. While product activation may allow you to change a handful of devices, such as swapping out a video card or plugging in a new sound card, a radical upgrade may trigger the product activation anti-piracy feature and stop the program from working.

Product activation by itself can't stop piracy, but it can slow it down and discourage casual piracy among friends. Although product activation may currently be limited to a handful of high-profile software publishers like Microsoft, Symantec, Quark, Adobe, and Macromedia, expect more programs to include product activation in the near future.

INFILTRATION AND LEGAL ACTION

All the copy-protection methods in the world are nothing more than locks designed to slow down a determined cracker, but they do nothing to catch the people breaking the law in the first place. To find software pirates, government agencies and a handful of major software companies have hired hackers to infiltrate warez trading groups.

By masquerading as traders (who trade pirated software), couriers (who deliver fresh versions of software to crack), crackers (who remove copy protection), and collectors (who try to store as many programs as possible), these hired guns can learn who's involved, how they find and transfer files, and where they save them. Once they collect enough evidence to track a major warez trading ring, they attempt to identify everyone involved so they can be prosecuted.

Through massive sweeps and high-profile arrests, government authorities and software publishers hope to punish the larger and more prominent warez group members while sending a message to others that warez trading will not be tolerated. Still, for every warez cracker who gets busted, more pop up to replace them, so it's a never-ending battle. Catching warez traders can temporarily slow down the process of warez distribution but can never stop it completely. Nevertheless, the threat of prosecution and the fear of infiltration keeps warez groups cautious about attracting too much attention.

WHERE THE WAREZ ARE

Finding warez can be tricky. Although any search engine, such as Yahoo! or Google, will turn up lists of warez websites, few of those sites will provide actual working copies of anything. The reason is simple. After taking all the time and risk of snaring a pirated copy of a major program, why would anyone blatantly advertise their law-breaking activities and offer to give away the fruits of their crime for free? To profit from their warez, many sites will force you to download spyware or display a barrage of pop-up ads that you will likely need to click through before you can (presumably) access their warez. (These pop-ups may contain nothing more than fake links which, when you click them, make money for the site owner.) Finding a warez website isn't easy, but it's still possible.

WEBSITES

While most warez websites offer enticing lists of programs like Photoshop, Dreamweaver, or Microsoft Windows, they're more often designed to lure people into seeing pornography instead. If you want to find warez, be prepared to invest hours wading through misleading sites until you find what you want. And if you do spend the time, your chances of finding a minor program, such as a CD burning utility or an antivirus program, is much greater than finding the latest version of a major program, such as Microsoft Office or Quark XPress.

The best way to find warez is to ignore the standard search engines and visit a specialized warez search engine instead, like the one shown in Figure 12-6. Rather than scan thousands of irrelevant sites for a match, a warez search engine scans a limited list of known warez sites. (Whether those warez sites have more to offer than pornography, though, is another matter.)

Astalavista (http://www.astalavista.com) is one of the more popular warez search engines, but you may also want to visit some of these other warez search engines as well:

ZoneFree	http://www.zonefree.de
AppzWorld	http://www.appzworld.com
EasyWarez	http://www.easywarez.com

Warez.com	http://search.warez.com
KatzWarez	http://www.katzwarez.com

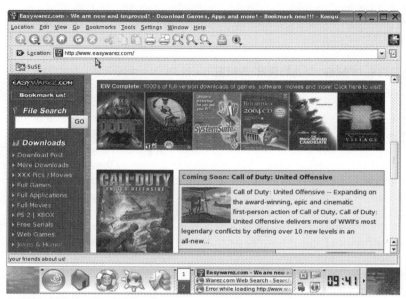

Figure 12-6
A warez search engine can help you track down a pirated version of a popular program hidden somewhere on the Internet.

FTP SITES

FTP sites are much more reliable sources for warez, but again there's a catch. Most warez FTP sites (along with BBSs) are private, which means that unless you know the exact address or telephone number to access the FTP site or BBS and have the right password to get in, you won't be able to download anything. Keeping a warez FTP site or BBS secret prevents authorities from discovering the site, shutting it down, and prosecuting the people responsible. So until you can gain the confidence and trust of a private warez trading group, finding a warez FTP site or BBS will likely not be an option for most people.

If you're feeling lucky, you can use an ordinary search engine and look for the strings **ftp** and **warez** to find a list of warez FTP sites that may or may not let you in. Warez FTP sites tend to appear and disappear with distressing regularity, so you might want to try some of these websites to help you find FTP warez sites:

OthNet	http://www.oth.net
Warez FTP Search Engine	http://www.dinkerland.com/warez.html
Warez Search Engine	http://www.duthie.com/warezsearch.htm

NEWSGROUPS

Many people trade warez through newsgroups. By using a fake email address and anonymous surfing to mask their real IP address, software pirates can post warez for anyone to download. Just ask for a particular program, and if someone reading your message feels generous, they might be willing to send you a copy or post your desired warez in the newsgroup for everyone to download.

Although warez files can be huge, people often post them to newsgroups. Some particularly trusting souls may even provide a password and IP address or telephone number to their own warez FTP site or BBS, although like most warez trading, you'll be expected to offer something in return. Some of the more popular warez newsgroups belong to the alt.binaries hierarchy (such as alt.binaries.cd.image, alt.binaries.mac, alt.binaries.mac.cd.images, alt.cracks, alt.binaries.cd.image.games, and alt.binaries.games).

Unfortunately, some ISPs may block access to warez newsgroups for both the illegal nature of the activity and for the technical reason that heavy warez trading tends to clog a network's bandwidth. If your ISP won't allow you access to a warez newsgroup or restricts the amount you can download in a day, you may want to subscribe to a special newsgroup service. Not only will these services give you a chance to access any newsgroups you want, but they may offer a generous download limit that far exceeds the trivial download restrictions that most ISPs may impose. Supernews (http://www.supernews.com) offers a free 30-day trial, but you may also want to investigate some of these other popular newsgroup servers too:

AllTheNewsgroups	http://www.allthenewsgroups.com
EasyNews	http://www.easynews.com
Giganews	http://www.giganews.com
Grablt Newsservice	http://www.shemes.com
Meganetnews.com	http://www.meganetnews.com
NewsHosting	http://www.newshosting.com

IRC CHANNELS

When warez traders crack the latest program, they often post it in an IRC channel to publicize their achievement. Besides offering the latest programs, IRC channels often harbor high-profile warez like cracked copies of Microsoft Windows XP or the latest video game.

When trading files in an IRC warez channel, be especially alert for virus-infected files, Trojan horses, and denial-of-service attacks (a classic hacking attack designed to paralyze your computer by bombarding it with a barrage of legitimate requests that overwhelm your computer and essentially shut it down). Wandering unprepared into an IRC warez channel is like walking into the middle of a saloon in a bad part of town crowded with veteran gunslingers. Say or do something stupid or annoying, and you're likely to get attacked or tricked into downloading a booby-trapped file that will release a virus or Trojan horse that allows others to infiltrate your computer.

Still, IRC can be a useful resource for downloading files or finding warez sites. To find a warez channel, visit an IRC channel search engine, such as IRC Search Engine (http://irc.netsplit.de/channels) or SearchIRC (http://searchirc. com), and type **warez**, as shown in Figure 12-7.

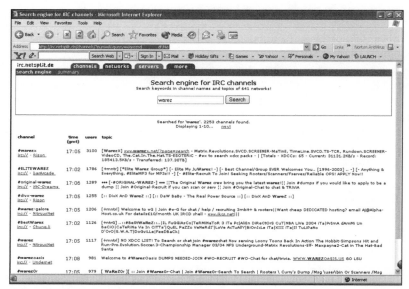

Figure 12-7

An IRC channel search engine can help you find a warez channel where you can chat with warez traders and software pirates to find copies of the latest programs.

FILE SHARING NETWORKS

Nearly every file sharing network allows you to trade any type of file, whether it's a music, video, or program file, as shown in Figure 12-8. To look for a program, just type its name or the strings **cracks**, **serial**, or **warez** into your favorite file sharing program. (To narrow your search to avoid irrelevant results, look for a way to tell your file sharing program that you only want to search for program files as opposed to MP3 or video files.)

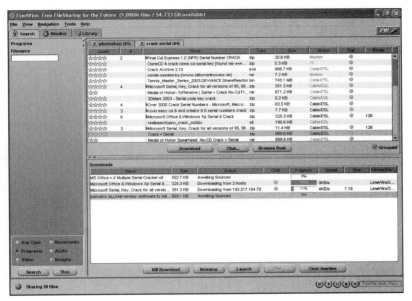

Figure 12-8
Practically every file sharing network is loaded with warez files, cracking programs, and serial number generators.

Because most major programs, like Microsoft Office or Macromedia FreeHand, can be huge, pirated copies are prevalent but they are tricky for file sharers to download successfully. Downloading a massive file can take time, and if the person with the file disconnects from the file sharing network, the download fails.

File sharers who are patient and persistent can find almost any file they want, though they may need to find a crack to run the program or a list of serial numbers to activate the program. For the average person, warez trading can be cumbersome and tedious, but for a warez trader, these minor nuisances are just obstacles to overcome, which makes getting the final warez program working on their own computer all the more worthwhile.

13

SHARING VIDEO GAMES

Nobody really buys a computer to balance their budget. Most people buy a computer to access the Internet or play video games. And while the music industry suffers from declining sales, the video-game industry continues to enjoy record-breaking sales. The European Entertainment and Leisure Software Publishers Association (ELSPA) (http://www.elspa.com) even claimed that video-game sales in 2003 hit $18.5 billion and forecast continuing growth of up to 10 percent every year. That's a heck of a lot of dough.

Games lubricate the body and the mind.

—Benjamin Franklin

Naturally, with so many people playing games, there will always be a minority who want to steal them. To keep that minority as small as possible, video-game manufacturers employ a wide variety of tricks. Some try traditional copy-protection mechanisms, and others use colored ink to print secret codes that users must enter whenever they want to play the game. (The colored ink keeps the codes visible to the human eye but renders them invisible when photocopied.) Not surprisingly, the anti-piracy schemes don't slow down the dedicated pirate.

In one of the latest examples, Ubisoft (http://www.ubi.com), publishers of Tom Clancy's Rainbow Six 3: Raven Shield, used a copy-protection scheme from MacroVision (http://www.macrovision.com) dubbed SafeDisc 2. This copy protection mysteriously prevents a video game from running if it detects any of the following three programs running on a computer:

Daemon Tools	http://www.daemon-tools.cc
Alcohol 120%	http://www.alcohol-soft.com
Clonecd	http://www.clonecd.net

Not only can these three programs copy a copy-protected CD or DVD, but they can also store the disc's contents as a virtual drive on your hard disk. A virtual drive basically saves the contents of a CD or DVD as a file on your hard disk, but it tricks your computer into thinking that the file is an actual CD or DVD drive. So instead of playing the game directly from a CD or DVD, your computer plays the game directly from the virtual drive, which makes your games run much faster.

Once people copy and save all of their game CDs and DVDs onto their hard drives as separate virtual drives, they can store or loan their original CDs and DVDs to others. As an alternative, many people simply share their virtual drive files instead. You can run that virtual drive on any computer that has the same program that created the original virtual drive. To learn more about a commercial tool that can store and run copy-protected game CDs and DVDs as virtual drives on your hard disk, visit FarStone (http://www.farstone.com).

Making your legitimately purchased games run faster by storing them as virtual drives is completely legal. However, the game industry fears people will illegally give away copies of the virtual drive files containing copies of copyrighted video games, and they're probably right.

Besides SafeDisc 2, some additional copy-protection mechanisms designed to defeat virtual drive programs include SecuROM (http://www.securom.com), CD-Cops (http://www.linkdata.com), and LaserLock (http://www.laserlock.com). Still, despite the prevalence of so many different copy-protection schemes, programmers keep updating the software that allows people to duplicate copy-protected CDs or to run copy-protected CDs as virtual drives.

Besides relying on copy protection, video-game publishers are using lawsuits to thwart video-game piracy. Atari, Electronic Arts, and Vivendi Universal Games recently teamed up to file a lawsuit against 321 Studios, which marketed Games X Copy, a program that could duplicate copy-protected CD and DVD games. In the lawsuit, the game companies claimed that "321 Studios' actions directly violate the Digital Millennium Copyright Act ("DMCA") . . . which prohibits trafficking in products or services that circumvent technological protection measures designed to prevent unauthorized access to and copying of copyrighted materials." 321 Studios eventually went out of business.

While legal action may prevent companies from selling programs that can copy game CDs, there will always be programs available that can copy CDs and run copy-protected games on virtual drives. To find programs that can duplicate copy-protected CDs and DVDs, visit BurnWorld (http://www.burnworld.com) or use your favorite search engine to look for the phrase **CD copying** or **DVD copying**. Many individuals create CD and DVD burning tools and give them away for free, while many companies incorporate in other countries and sell their products over the Internet, thereby circumventing U.S. copyright laws. By using programs that can copy and run copy-protected CDs and DVDs as virtual drives, you can stay one step ahead of the latest copy-protection mechanisms that may be stopping you from playing the games you own legally (or illegally).

VIDEO GAMES AS WAREZ

In the world of the computer underground, *warez* is a slang term for any software illegally traded online. While some people who trade warez, known as *warez traders*, specialize in collecting popular applications like Adobe Photoshop or Microsoft Office, most warez traders focus on video games. (See Chapter 12 for more on how people download warez from the Internet.)

Newsgroups offer a rich source of video-game warez, because they give warez traders the chance to offer a popular program on a specific date. Warez traders always strive to offer warez the same day or a few days before the official release date of a popular program, and newsgroups give such traders a forum to date-stamp and post their files for everyone to verify. To find Windows games, visit alt.binaries.cd.image.games and alt.binaries.games. To find Macintosh games, visit alt.mac.games. For ROM images of games for the Sony PlayStation 2 or Microsoft Xbox, visit alt.binaries.cd.image.xbox and alt.binaries.cd.image.playstation2.

While newsgroups are great for finding the latest video games, constantly searching different newsgroups to find a particular game can be tedious. As an alternative, many people also use file sharing networks to track down video games, particularly older, but still popular, games that are less likely to appear in newsgroups simply because they've been around for so many years. Poke around a file sharing network for specific game titles, such as Sim City or Zoo Tycoon, and you'll see that the latest video games aren't at all hard to find (see Figure 13-1).

Figure 13-1
Many file sharing networks offer complete video games for downloading.

To find a website that offers video games, visit your favorite search engine and search for **warez games** and visit one of the many sites that pop up, such as the warez files site shown in Figure 13-2.

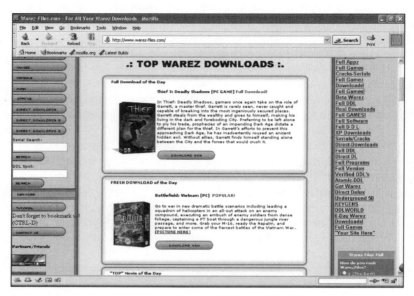

Figure 13-2

Video games are one of the most popular types of pirated programs you can find offered on warez websites.

One site, GameCopyWorld (http://www.gamecopyworld.com), lists servers around the world that provide cracks that allow you to install and play a duplicate of a copy-protected game CD. They provide the "crack" that normally allows a user to play a copied game CD (thereby avoiding the copy protection involved in ISO copies of games). These cracks normally are an executable file that replaces the one that is installed (the modification usually removes the copy-protection check so that the program will not detect a copied CD).

Besides stealing commercial video games, pirates have found another way to steal games: steal the source code. The source code contains the actual instructions that tell a computer what to do. Getting access to a video game's source code is like getting the recipe to McDonald's special sauce—once you know how something works, you can duplicate it and sell it yourself, albeit not legally.

VIDEO GAMES AS EMULATION

While many people pirate the latest computer video games, many others seek out video games from their youth. Such video games may have originally appeared in coin-operated arcade machines or specialized home video-game consoles that have long since been discontinued. Arcade machines and game consoles basically consist of a dedicated computer and a video game stored in a ROM (read-only memory) chip. Video-game consoles allowed people to play different games by plugging in different game cartridges that held different games burned into their ROM chips. The problem is that unless you have the actual hardware to run a particular video game and the ROM chip that holds the game, you can't play the video game.

To overcome both problems, game enthusiasts have developed ways to burn the contents of a ROM chip to a digital file, known as a ROM image, and they have created emulation programs that allow a Windows, Macintosh, or Linux computer to emulate the actual hardware that the original game ran on. So if you want to run old video games on your computer, you just need to find the ROM image of the video game and an emulator program that can run that particular ROM image on your specific computer. Figure 13-3 shows a Nintendo Game Boy emulator running on Windows XP.

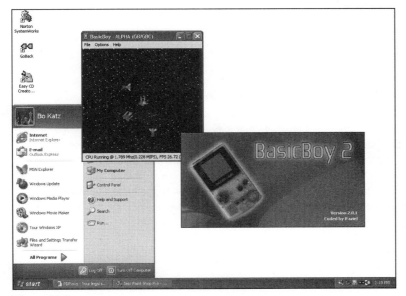

Figure 13-3

With the BasicBoy emulator, you can play Nintendo Game Boy games under Microsoft Windows.

NOTE: Most people create emulators for the sheer joy of playing a favorite video game on their personal computer. Because emulating another machine can be tricky, emulators range in quality from excellent to buggy. Unlike most programs that you can install and run, installing and running most emulators is not particularly easy. Be sure to read any documentation that comes with an emulator so you can install and run it correctly without any problems.

FINDING AN EMULATOR

Basically, there are three types of emulators: single-machine, multi-machine, and personal computer emulators. A single-machine emulator only mimics one type of machine, usually an obsolete home video-game console, such as an Atari 2600 or ColecoVision. Once you have a single-machine emulator running on your computer, you can run all of the video games that were designed for that video-game console. To find an emulator for a specific machine, visit one of the following sites, as shown in Figure 13-4:

ClassicGaming	http://www.classicgaming.com
emulation.net	http://www.emulation.net
Emulators Unlimited	http://www.emuunlim.com
Game Revolution	http://www.game-revolution.com/ download/emulator/emulator.htm
MorphGear	http://www.pocketgb.com

Multi-machine emulators typically mimic coin-operated arcade machines rather than home video-game consoles. One of the most popular multi-machine arcade emulators is MAME (Multiple Arcade Machine Emulator), as shown in Figure 13-5. To grab a Windows or MS-DOS version of MAME, visit the official MAME site (http://www.mame.net). To find a Macintosh version of MAME, visit MacMAME (http://www.macmame.org).

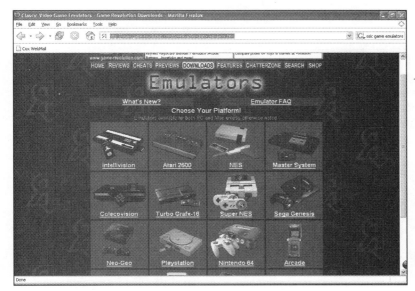

Figure 13-4

Many people have created programs to emulate once-popular home video-game consoles, such as Sega Genesis, Turbo Grafx-16, and Nintendo 64.

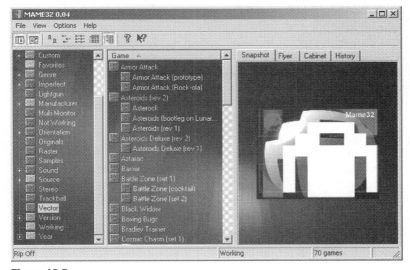

Figure 13-5

The MAME emulator lets you play classic arcade video games on a personal computer.

Besides programs that can emulate video-game consoles or arcade machines, there is also a handful of programs that can let your computer emulate another personal computer. So if you want to play an old video game designed for the Macintosh or Atari ST, you can always turn your PC into a Macintosh or Atari 400/800/ST clone by visiting Emulators, Inc. (http://www.emulators.com). If you have an old MS-DOS or Windows game that you want to play, grab a copy of Virtual PC (http://www.microsoft.com), which runs on Windows and Macintosh, or VMware (http://www.vmware.com), which runs on Windows and Linux. Figure 13-6 shows Virtual PC running the classic MS-DOS video game, Doom.

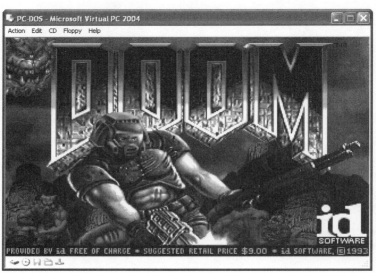

Figure 13-6
Virtual PC lets you play MS-DOS games on a Windows or Macintosh computer.

GETTING ROM IMAGES

Once you have an emulator installed on your computer, the next step is to get a game. Video-console games were often sold on ROM chips packaged as cartridges, while arcade machines often had their games burned into ROM chips soldiered directly into the machine. Because you can't plug a PlayStation cartridge or arcade machine ROM chip directly into your computer, video-game pirates copy the instructions stored in a ROM chip to a digital file known as a ROM image. With a copy of a ROM image of a game, you can play that game through an emulator on your computer. ROM images of games often take up less than 1MB of storage space, so the copying and distribution of ROM images is rampant on the Internet.

NOTE: *If you're using a computer emulator program, such as Virtual PC, you don't need ROM images. You just need a copy of the video game and whatever operating system that game needs to run on. You can often find old video games through file sharing networks or on websites.*

To find a website that offers ROM images, just visit your favorite search engine and search for **ROM images**. Some video-game pirates even sell CDs stuffed with ROM images over the Internet and through online auction sites, as shown in Figure 13-7.

You can buy legitimate ROM images of different video games from StarROMs (http://www.starroms.com). For ROM images of public domain games, visit PDROMS (http://www.pdroms.de).

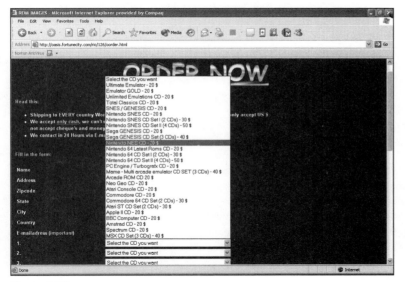

Figure 13-7
Many websites sell CDs full of illegally copied video-game ROM images.

To find ROM images or to get help installing and running an emulator program for your computer, visit one of the following newsgroups:

- alt.binaries.emulators.mame

- alt.binaries.emulators.misc

- alt.binaries.emulators.arcade

- alt.binaries.emulators.neogeo

THE LEGALITIES OF ROM IMAGES

Emulation programs themselves are not illegal, but it is illegal to copy and distribute the ROM images they run. Still, the legalities blur when one considers that U.S. copyright laws allow people to make backup copies of computer programs for archival purposes. So if you create a ROM image of a video game that you already own, you're within the boundaries of the law, but if you download a ROM image of a game that you already own, you're breaking the law, because you aren't allowed to transfer copyrighted information over the Internet unless you either own the copyright or have permission from the copyright holder.

Many video-game ROMs are of games produced by companies that are no longer in business. As such, ROM traders assume that the copyrights are no longer valid. However, according to U.S. copyright law, copyrights remain valid for 75 years from the date of publication. And a game doesn't enter the public domain simply because the company that produced it went bankrupt or because the game is no longer sold. Remember, that game could now be owned by another company. For example, Atari video games have been around for years, yet at different times the Atari copyrights have been owned by Time Warner, WMS Gaming, and Hasbro.

NOTE: *For more information about video-game copyrights, visit the Entertainment Software Association site (http://www.theesa.com).*

Despite copyright infringements, the video-gaming industry is taking a more cautious approach toward the problem of people sharing video-game ROM images over the Internet. "We are very aware that there is a strong community of classic game players online," said Dana Henry, spokeswoman for Hasbro Interactive. "We certainly don't want to alienate that base of fans."

Perhaps the music and movie industries could learn from the approach of the video-game industry and address the issue of piracy while balancing the concerns of their customers. Such a move might, in fact, more effectively limit piracy than an endless string of lawsuits.

14

SHARING PORNOGRAPHY

Probably one of the few facts the media gets right about the Internet is that despite the promise of online libraries, workgroup collaboration, and shopping from your computer, one of the most common uses for the Internet is looking at pornography, and you don't have to look very far to find it. Once one of the most heavily trafficked newsgroups on the Internet, alt.sex was where people routinely swapped graphic sexual images to cater to all types of sexual fetishes. Nowadays, alt.sex has been flooded mostly with spam and many other sex-related newsgroups suffer from this problem as well.

Because of the popularity of pornography on the Internet, the porn industry became one of the first industries to face file sharing problems when people started scanning pictures and centerfolds from magazines and sharing the images over the Internet.

Because the porn industry knew they wouldn't get much sympathy from Congress, they embraced the enemy and fought back by creating their own websites that charged admission. Many people even credit the porn industry for driving the creation of several Internet innovations, including streaming audio/video content, online payment systems, interactive webcams, and Digital Rights Management (as well as spam, cookies, and pop-up ads).

Today, pornography is so pervasive on the Internet that most people don't want to steal it as much as they want to get rid of it. Porn sites hijack our web browsers, and unwanted ads for pornography often clog our email accounts. Despite the apparently free nature of pornography, stolen images still cost the porn industry lost revenue, but unlike the music and movie industries, the porn industry just counts their losses as part of doing business over the Internet, and they work to offer a superior alternative that actually makes money.

> I've looked on a lot of women with lust. I've committed adultery in my heart many times. This is something that God recognizes I will do—and I have done it—and God forgives me for it.
>
> —Jimmy Carter

FINDING PORNOGRAPHY

Perhaps in a backhanded attempt to shut down file sharing networks, several U.S. government officials have focused on the fact that file sharing networks can be used to distribute pornography (as if cable TV, printed magazines, and the government's own post office can't also be used to distribute pornography).

U.S. Rep. Joe Pitts (R-PA) actually introduced the Protecting Children from Peer-to-Peer Pornography Act (HR 2885) in 2003 to keep pornography off file sharing networks. But before trying to slap government controls on legally evasive file sharing networks, Pitts might want to start by legislating search engines, webcams, and websites, all of which offer free porn to anyone who can find it.

FINDING PORNOGRAPHY WITH SEARCH ENGINES

Perhaps the simplest way to find pornographic pictures on the Internet is to ask for them using an image search engine, such as Google's image search (http://www.images.google.com). By searching for the word **porn** with Google's filter turned off (click Advanced Image Search and choose the No Filtering option under SafeSearch), you can find hundreds of pornographic images (see Figure 14-1). Add your own words after **porn** to fine-tune your search to your own fetish. Although Google can't serve up sound or video, it's fast, free, and accurate.

Figure 14-1
Google turns up plenty of free pornographic images if you turn on its No Filtering option.

To find more pornographic images for free, visit AltaVista Image Search (http://www.altavista.com/image), Excite Image Search (http://www.excite.co.uk/

search/image), or Lycos Multimedia Search (http://multimedia.lycos.com) and turn off their parental controls so you can access pornographic images.

Visit any search engine, such as Yahoo!, and type in words like **sex**, **xxx**, or **porn**, and you'll find plenty of adult-oriented websites to satisfy your carnal desire. Most adult websites offer free samples, but if you want access to a variety of pictures, you'll have to sign up with a credit card.

For voyeurs, type in the words **upskirting**, **downblousing**, or **voyeur** in your favorite search engine to find websites that offer pictures taken from underneath a woman's skirt, down a woman's blouse, or in shower rooms in public gyms. (With cameras shrinking in size and even embedded in cell phones, it's easy for strangers to sneak pictures of unsuspecting men and women in public places and then post the compromising images on a website.)

In case you prefer video to static images, type **adult webcams** in your favorite search engine, and browse through the list of adult-oriented webcam sites that offer continuous, unedited video of naked people posing in front of a webcam. (If you have a webcam attached to your own computer, you can often share your own captured video of yourself with others.)

Perhaps video and static images don't excite your libido as much as your own imagination. In that case, type in the phrase **cybersex chat rooms** and browse through the list of adult-oriented chat rooms where you can chat about any particular sexual fetish you might desire. (Just remember that cybersex chatting can lose its appeal real fast if you're a slow typist prone to frequent misspellings.)

Type the phrase **naked celebrities** into a search engine, and you can browse through websites that offer real (and faked) video and photographs of celebrities having sex, including video of Pamela Anderson having sex with Tommy Lee, Paris Hilton having sex with her boyfriend, and early photographs of Dr. Laura Schlessinger posing nude.

With so much free pornography available, how does the porn industry avoid the piracy that's rampant with music and videos? Basically, they don't, but instead of suing individuals who trade copyrighted porn pictures and videos, the porn companies sue the pirates who make *money* copying and reselling the porn industry's products.

To make money from individuals, the porn industry takes advantage of the fact that horny people don't have much patience. As a result, people are willing to pay for reliability, something rarely found when scrounging the Internet for free porn. If you search the file sharing networks and find a porn video called *Sex Bomb*, you could download the whole thing before realizing that its video quality is shoddy, or that it's actually a completely different movie than what you expected.

Successful porn sites combine quality and reliability with convenience so customers know exactly what they're getting. Click a few buttons on an inexpensive pay porn site and you can look for anything ranging from blonde cheerleader pictures, gay black male videos, or interactive webcam sessions with a Russian amputee.

"Free is very anarchistic and hard to deal with," one successful pornography entrepreneur told the *New York Times*. "You don't know what you're getting. Cheap is more convenient." Their strategy seems to be working. Nielsen/NetRatings says about 35 million people visited porn sites in December 2003.

Other porn publishers use file sharing networks as a promotional tool. When award-winning porn publisher Jules Jordan saw yet another of his DVDs ripped and swapped on the Internet, he began placing his website's name (JulesJordan.com) in the screen's bottom corner, as shown in Figure 14-2, similar to the way television stations add their call signs to advertise themselves.

Figure 14-2
To profit from piracy, porn publisher Jules Jordan watermarked the
Flesh Hunter 4 DVD with his website's name in the lower right corner.

"The main thing is to deter pirates that are ripping off images from the DVD and using it on the Internet," Jordan told AVN (http://www.avn.com), a porn industry news site. "If these pirates still want to rip off my shit, essentially, I'm going to use them for promotion."

FINDING PORNOGRAPHY ON FILE SHARING NETWORKS

Pornography is the weak link in the file sharing networks. Sure, you can type phrases such as **Traci Lords** or **pornography** and have a file sharing network overwhelm you with more pornographic pictures and videos that you could ever watch in a lifetime. The problem is that government officials, under prodding from the recording industry, have blamed file sharing networks for spreading pornographic material to minors and for distributing child pornography.

When debating the problems of pornography on file sharing networks, Orrin Hatch (R-UT) even asked law enforcement officials, "Do you suggest we put out of business the networks that allow this to occur?"

Wendy Seltzer, an attorney with the Electronic Frontier Foundation (http://www.eff.org), claimed that cracking down on child pornography was just a pretext to targeting the file sharing networks in general. "We don't have hearings calling the photo industry to task when their film is used to create child porn," Seltzer said.

Until the government succeeds in using the threat of child pornography to shut down your favorite file sharing network, you can still find your favorite pornographic videos and pictures by typing in the titles of pornographic movies (**Deep Throat** or **Debbie Does Dallas**), the names of famous porn stars or celebrities (**Ron Jeremy** or **Cameron Diaz**), descriptions of different centerfolds (**Playboy playmate** or **Penthouse pet**), or words often associated with adult entertainment (**fetish** or **lesbian**). Figure 14-3 shows the typical pornographic files you can find on a file sharing network, such as Kazaa.

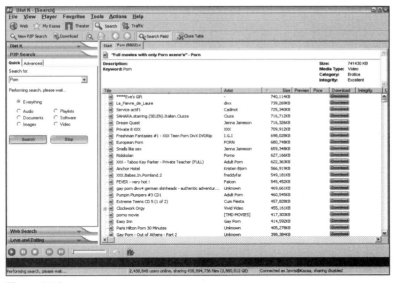

Figure 14-3

You can find both pornographic video and photographs on file sharing networks like Kazaa.

Trading copyrighted pornographic images may be a crime, but you probably won't get sued by the porn industry. However, if you start swapping child pornography, you could get caught in a government dragnet designed to catch child pornographers. When police asked one child pornographer why he used the file sharing networks, he simply replied, "Because the cops are in the chat rooms."

FINDING PORNOGRAPHY ON NEWSGROUPS

If you visit any adult-oriented newsgroups, you'll find them flooded with pornography. (Many ISPs block access to adult-oriented newsgroups, so if you want to see them, you may need to subscribe to a separate newsgroup server, as discussed in Chapter 3.) In fact, pornography fills 28 of the top-29 most trafficked binary newsgroups, according to NewsAdmin (http://www.newsadmin. com/top100reads.htm).

Unfortunately, pornography is so popular that many virus writers launch their work by disguising their latest virus creations with misleading headers, such as "Christina Aguilera Nude," "Britney Spears hot sexy nude 3034," "Hillery_Duff.scr Nude," or "Halle_berry.scr Nude." Perhaps the one advantage for the porn industry is that with so many viruses and Trojan horses masquerading as free pornography, many people are flocking to fee-based porn sites as a way to *avoid* catching viruses.

Still, if you want to take the risk of catching a virus when looking for free porn, you'll find more than 100 newsgroups devoted to nearly every fetish, as shown in Figure 14-4. And those are just the newsgroups devoted to photos.

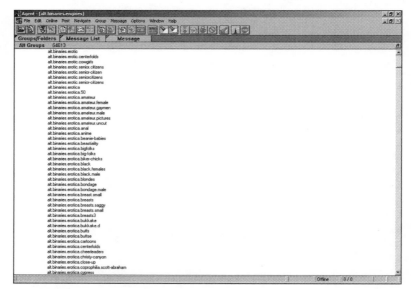

Figure 14-4
You can find more than 100 different newsgroups catering to different types of porn.

The videos live on alt.binaries.multimedia.erotica (ABME), with each fetish separated into its own newsgroup. Most contain DVD rips of popular erotic videos, although rips of "classic" VHS tapes and even old 1920s movies turn up occasionally.

Because video takes some time to download, most posters include "previews" containing several screenshots from the video. A look at the subject header on the porn video in Figure 14-5, for instance, shows the name of the star (Dina Jewel), the movie clip's length (nine minutes and 17 seconds), and that it includes ten JPEG screenshots. By downloading the screenshots, you can find out exactly what you should expect if you take the time to download the entire clip.

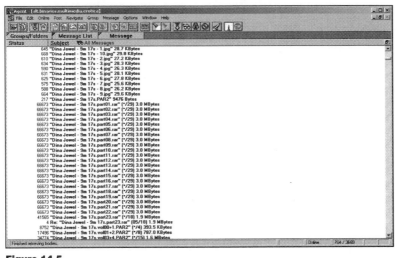

Figure 14-5

The headers of this porn video clip indicate that it includes ten JPEG screenshots of the video, which will let you know at a glance whether you should download the entire clip.

Although some uploaders simply use Windows' PRTSCR key to take screenshots, and then post the JPEGs as individual files, others prefer creating "contact sheets" of the video, each full of thumbnail shots. Here are some of the most popular programs for creating and viewing previews of images:

ACDSee	http://www.acdsystems.com
Graphic Workshop Pro	http://www.mindworkshop.com
IrfanView	http://www.irfanview.com
LView Pro	http://www.lview.com
VirtualDub	http://www.virtualdub.org
ImageMagick	http://imagemagick.sourceforge.net

The ABME FAQ (http://abmefaq.net) is one of the longest, most current, and best researched tutorials on newsgroups and computer video anywhere, which is a strong testament to the seriousness of its fans. Some unrelated newsgroups forward new users to the ABME FAQ to find answers to questions about Internet video. The FAQ comes in especially handy when explaining *codecs*—the algorithms used to compress video into easily transmitted computer files.

Often you may download a video file only to find that your computer won't play it because it lacks the right codec. Most porn videos use DivX (http://www.divx.com) for compression, but some use other, less mainstream codecs. When you try to play such a video back, Windows Media Player displays an error message, as shown in Figure 14-6.

Figure 14-6
Windows Media Player displays an error message when you try to play a video that uses an unfamiliar codec.

The solution is to figure out what codec you're missing, and then download and install it. Sometimes an NFO file that accompanies the video file will contain information on the exact codex needed to play the video, but otherwise you might need to visit the Codec Corner site (http://www.codeccorner.com). This site can test which codecs are installed on your computer and, if necessary, download and install the ones you're missing. Although it is maintained by the adult video enthusiasts, the page comes in handy when your computer is missing a decoder for nearly any downloaded video.

PORNOGRAPHY: A REFLECTION OF SOCIETY

Nothing incites heated emotions faster than the topic of pornography. Whether you find it in bookstores, magazines, cable TV programs, or on the Internet, pornography has evaded all attempts at both definition and regulation. Comedian Bill Hicks once commented, "The Supreme Court has defined pornography as anything without artistic merit that causes sexual thought. Hmm. Sounds like every commercial on television, doesn't it?"

Some people say that pornography is free speech. Others say that pornography is evil, although what's pornographic in one culture is just considered normal behavior in another. Janet Jackson caused an uproar when she inadvertently flashed her breast during a half-time Super Bowl presentation, yet women in many European and Latin American countries routinely walk around topless on public beaches.

Too often, government authorities have used pornography as a smoke-screen to mask their true intentions, whether it's to justify regulation of the radio and television airwaves or to shut down file sharing networks on the Internet.

As distasteful as it might appear, pornography stands at the front line in the debate over free speech and freedom of the press. To question the definition of pornography, Larry Flynt, publisher of *Hustler* magazine, once printed photographs showing atrocities from the Vietnam War with the heading, "This is the REAL pornography."

15

MISCELLANEOUS THIEVERY

When kids began swapping music, they certainly weren't doing anything new. Another generation had already been swapping for years. Many needlework enthusiasts, often older women and grandmothers, had saved money by copying and sharing "counted cross stitch" needlework patterns: grid-filled pieces of paper with instructions for stitching ornate designs on pillows and wall hangings. At first, the women simply made a few copies on the copy machine, passing them along to friends.

When computers and scanners became popular, women could scan the patterns and email them to friends much more easily. For example, Carla Conry, profiled in an August 2000 *Los Angeles Times* article, created an Internet ring on Yahoo! called "Pattern Piggies Unite" where hundreds of avid traders met to swap scanned patterns. To weed out any industry snoops, the women demanded that new members upload copyrighted patterns before being allowed to join. In several months, members posted more than 10,000 messages, with many bearing attachments of copyrighted patterns.

When pattern-publisher Jim Hedgpeth of Pegasus Originals (http://www.pegasusor.com) saw his revenue stream drop by 40 percent, he gathered others in the industry. Some industry members snuck into the groups, observed the trading, and asked the members to stop infringing on copyrighted material. But when the trading continued, the pattern publishers began suing under the DMCA, effectively shutting down the websites.

Women still trade patterns today, but not as openly as before. Instead, they've embraced the same technology used by music traders: file-sharing networks and newsgroups. They still trade needlework patterns, trademarked embroidery patterns (such as Winnie the Pooh, Mickey Mouse, and other popular cartoon characters), and patterns for computerized sewing machines. Today, copyrighted and trademarked patterns appear regularly on Usenet's alt.binaries.crafts.pictures and alt.binaries.patterns.plastic-canvas newsgroups.

Although a few websites allow downloads of cross-stitch patterns, most are based outside the United States, like the Russian site shown in Figure 15-1.

The heart is deceitful above all things, and desperately wicked. Who can know it?

—Jeremiah 17:9

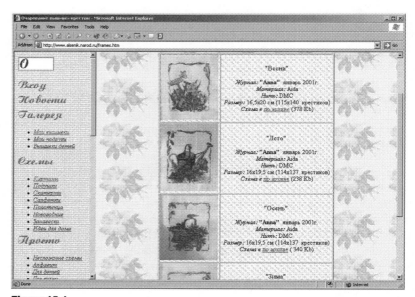

Figure 15-1

This Russian site offers free downloads of copyrighted needlework patterns.

While the media focuses on people stealing music, movies, TV shows, books, programs, and computer games online, few people realize that every type of copyrighted information can be stolen and traded when stored digitally. The threat of stealing copyrighted information goes beyond the entertainment industry and into the world of patient health records and DNA sequences for genetically modified plants. The general rule is that if it can be scanned, copied, or saved as a digital file, it can eventually be stolen and distributed illegally.

STEALING SOUNDS

Although the music industry bemoans music swapping by its customers, many musicians are also swapping different types of music files. For example, a wide variety of computerized music programs, like Sony's ACID and Sound Forge lines (http://mediasoftware.sonypictures.com) let musicians create songs on a computer by mixing loops of presampled sounds. Other samples, like those from Spectrasonics (http://www.spectrasonics.net) are created directly for a musician's keyboard or synthesizer, letting players create and record orchestras of exotic sounds. The prices of many samples, like Quantum Leap's "Voices of the Apocalypse" for $499 (http://www.soundsonline.com), exceeds the budget of most musicians.

That makes the alt.binaries.sounds.samples and alt.binaries.sounds.samples.music newsgroups popular stops for musicians who are eager to try out the latest samples, stay on the technological edge, and simultaneously stick to their budget.

STEALING GUITAR CHORD CHARTS

Very few musicians make money from their music, and fewer still would be called wealthy. Many aspiring guitarists who can't afford lessons or songbooks, but who still want to learn the latest Steve Vai licks, drop by the alt.binaries.guitar.tab newsgroup. This newsgroup contains scanned-in tablature showing chords, guitar leads, bass tracks, and other music for specific songs and bands. Blues legend Robert Johnson's work, for instance, appears in Figure 15-2.

Figure 15-2
Guitar players scan in tablature from popular songs and swap them on Usenet's alt.binaries.guitar.tab forum.

Once copied and stored on a computer, these music charts are easy to print out and carry in a guitar case or give away to friends during jams. Most importantly to starving musicians, such charts are free.

STEALING HDTV SHOWS

Thought downloading a DVD took a long time? Try downloading a High-Definition TV (HDTV) show from the alt.binaries.hdtv newsgroup, created in early 2004. An HDTV post of the movie *Shrek* consumed 4.159GB, a post so large that people spent several 24-hour days downloading it with their broadband modems.

The newsgroup's posts are so large that some newsgroup veterans fear that newsgroup servers won't be able to handle the increased load. Of course, people have been heralding the demise of newsgroups since file sharing first began, but to be safe, visit the newsgroup while the looting's available.

STEALING BANDWIDTH

Bandwidth theft, also known as *hot linking*, is similar to plugging an extension cord into the neighbor's house and using it to power your electric heater so you get all the benefits while someone else pays all the bills.

Similarly, some people don't bother storing images on their own website's server. Instead, they'll just link to an image being displayed on somebody else's website. Although their website's page still looks the same to a visitor, the other person's web server does all the work of sending the image. That makes the host's web server work harder, sometimes resulting in higher charges or even "bandwidth exceeded" problems for the host server, but not for the site hot linking to the files.

Bandwidth theft is fairly common on the Internet, whether through malice or ignorance. However, it's easy for a victim to detect pilferage from their website. Their server keeps a record of every file being dished up, as well as the website that requested it. When somebody sees another site draining one particular image, they not only know that they've become the latest bandwidth theft victim, but they also know the culprit. A quick visit to the offending site can confirm the problem.

People avoid this problem in several ways. Some quickly rename their own site's hot-linked image to something else—image2.jpg, for instance—and then copy a porn file onto their server and give it the same name as their old image. The result is that when somebody visits the thief's site, they no longer see the expected image—they see the embarrassing porn picture.

NOTE: *If somebody's hijacking an image on your website, and you want to fight back, replace one of your images with one of the many from the arsenal of offensive images available on the alt.binaries.pictures.tasteless newsgroup or from rotten.com (http://www.rotten.com), dedicated to collecting images that "present the viewer with a truly unpleasant experience." Be forewarned.*

STEALING WEBSITES

Some people don't just steal a few images from a neighboring website. They steal the *entire* website. It's much easier to change a few words on an existing site than to create one from scratch or hire a web designer. So, after changing a few links, the pirates post the copied site onto their own server under their own domain name. This saves them the time and expense of creating their own websites from scratch while mimicking a more established company's website that can trick people into buying products from the thief's website rather than the original website that the thief copied.

The Internet's open nature makes stealing a website fairly easy. Just choose Source from a browser's View menu, and a text editor quickly lists the web page's programming. There are even specialized programs, like SurfOffline (http://www.surfoffline.com), that will download up to 100 files simultaneously, copying a website as fast as your Internet connection allows.

Once you've copied and saved the website's entire source code, it's easy to pick through it for useful tidbits. Some people steal logos, alter them a little bit, and call them their own. Others steal buttons, graphics, and other attractive, custom-made design elements.

The Pirated Sites website (http://www.pirated-sites.com), shown in Figure 15-3, showcases side-by-side comparisons of sites "suspected of borrowing, copying or stealing copyright-protected content, design or code."

Figure 15-3
The Pirated Sites website showcases side-by-side comparisons of websites suspected of copying from each other.

For instance, the BidBay (http://www.bidbay.com) site in Figure 15-4 once bore a striking resemblance to eBay (http://www.ebay.com). The resemblance was so close that eBay eventually sued for trademark infringement, forcing the site to drop the design elements that mimicked eBay.

Figure 15-4
The eBay auction site sued BidBay for trademark infringement when the site mimicked eBay's own name and design.

When one person found out his website had been stolen, he turned the tables by changing his own site to link to the images and content on the thief's site. Suddenly, everyone trying to access the thief's and the victim's sites were directed to the thief's site, essentially creating a simple denial-of-service attack by overloading the thief's servers, which couldn't handle the sudden increase in traffic.

To protect your website from theft, try a program like one of these:

WebLock Pro	http://webpageprotect.com
HTML Protector	http://www.antssoft.com
HTML Guard	http://www.aw-soft.com

These programs prevent people from viewing (and copying) the HTML source code for your site, while still allowing browsers to display the web page correctly.

STEALING PHOTOGRAPHS AND IMAGES

Anytime you view a photo or image on the Internet, your browser automatically stores it on your computer in your browser's *cache*, which is a folder for temporarily storing images. This way, the next time you visit a previously viewed web page, the browser loads the web page's images from your computer rather than from the Internet, making the web page load faster. Of course, any image saved in your cache can also be shared.

Naturally, this causes great concern to photographers trying to sell their work through the Internet. Few people will purchase photos that they can't preview, but any image that can be viewed online can also be saved and stolen. To keep people from stealing images, most photographers follow some or all of the following guidelines for preventing image theft:

- Don't place the image on the Internet at all. This is the safest method, but it defeats the purpose of trying to sell photographs through the Internet.

- Use visible or invisible watermarks. Whether it's the word "Copyrighted" stamped across the photo's bottom or a code hidden inside the photo's data, watermarks can prove ownership of a photo. Digimarc's (http://www.digimarc.com) MarcSpider image-tracking technology searches over 50 million Internet images each month, seeking out unauthorized use of digitally watermarked images. However, programs like StirMarc (http://www.petitcolas.net/fabien/watermarking/stirmark) can disable watermarks found in many digital photos.

- Post small, low-resolution preview photos on the Web. This won't stop visitors from copying a photo or using it on their own website, but commercial publishers, the ones most likely to purchase the photo, require high-resolution images for their work.

- Break the photo into pieces, and then reassemble it on a website as a table. When somebody right-clicks the photo and chooses Save, they'll only save one piece of the photo.

Although these techniques may delay some photos from ending up on trading sites, there's really no way to stop people from physically scanning in a printed photo and posting the resulting file to the Internet. Popular newsgroups for sharing digital photos include the following:

- alt.binaries.pictures.cd-covers

- alt.binaries.pictures.clip-art

- alt.binaries.pictures.fine-art

- alt.binaries.pictures.original

- alt.binaries.pictures.wallpaper

STEALING RECIPES

According to the U.S. Copyright Office, mere listings of recipe ingredients aren't subject to copyright protection. Add an explanation or directions for using those ingredients, however, and it's an original work, subject to copyright laws. Of course, that hasn't stopped people from sharing recipes for hundreds of years.

Today, people often post recipes on the Internet, whether they've created the concoction themselves, typed it in from a favorite cookbook or magazine, or copied and pasted it from a cooking program or recipe CD. Once posted, the recipe becomes part of the Internet's huge (and often illegal) library.

For instance, if you search Cook's Illustrated (http://www.cooksillustrated. com) for **mashed potatoes**, you'll find a pointer to a mashed potatoes recipe from January 2003. The website doesn't list the recipe, though, because the magazine charges a subscription fee for access. But chefs who don't want to put down their spatula and pull out a credit card can find the exact same recipe by searching for **mashed potatoes** and **cook's illustrated** (or **cooks illustrated**) on Google.

An even better way to find recipes is to use Google, because recipes are stored as text, not binary files. Google indexes newsgroup conversations, so a search at http://groups.google.com pulls up thousands of recipes. When looking for published recipes, search for ingredients as well as the magazine, newspaper, or cookbook that ran the original recipe. Most people mention the source of the original recipe, along with the recipe itself (although mentioning the source doesn't keep them from violating copyright law).

STEALING EVERYTHING DIGITALLY

Needlework patterns, sampled sounds, guitar chord charts, HDTV shows, websites, photos, and recipes—these are just a few things now stored digitally that once took other forms. Computers make things easy to copy, which initially caused rejoicing among many industries. But now that computers are small and inexpensive enough to enter most homes, practically every industry that deals with printed or recorded information is battling Internet piracy or will have to do so eventually.

If you're really worried about Internet piracy, become a plumber. There will always be some things that can never be digitized and stolen with a computer.

PART 3

THE FUTURE

16

THE LEGAL ALTERNATIVES

File sharing is perfectly legal in itself; it's only when you share certain types of files that you may be breaking the law. So while the recording industry tries to track down blatant file sharers and haul them to court while millions of people continue sharing files anyway, there's a third group of people who have seen the popularity of file sharing and decided to capitalize on it rather than sue it.

These new legal file sharing networks collect money through subscriptions or charges for each file downloaded, and they redistribute part of that money as royalties to the copyright holders of the files. The public is happy because they can download the files they want without the risk of getting sued, the copyright holders are happy because they get paid for their work, and the file sharing networks are happy because they get to earn money legally too.

Unlike the freewheeling file sharing networks that allow you to share anything from music and videos to books and pictures, legal file sharing networks tend to specialize in niche markets, which means that if you want to find music, you have to join one file sharing network, and if you want to download movies, you'll have to join an entirely different file sharing network.

More annoying is the lack of selection and the cumbersome legal and technical restrictions placed on each file that you download. Because each file sharing network needs to make agreements with each recording artist, record label, movie studio, or other corporate entity, you won't find nearly as many files to download as you can find on the free file sharing networks like Gnutella or FastTrack. Some of the legal file sharing networks even encrypt or modify files so they can only be played on a particular computer or can only be copied a few times—all intended to prevent widespread Internet copying.

Despite these problems, legal file sharing networks have managed to carve out a steady and growing niche market. So if you like the idea of file sharing but don't want to break the law, take a look at the many legal alternatives.

Nothing is illegal if a hundred businessmen decide to do it.

—Andrew Young

MUSIC

With so many file sharing networks offering free music, why would anyone want to pay money to download the same music from a fee-based service? The biggest problem with free file sharing networks is that you can't always download a given file when you want it, and the audio quality of any music file on a file sharing network may be questionable.

To address these problems, along with the legal issues surrounding file sharing, many companies have started their own fee-based file sharing businesses where you can download music legally. While these legal music file sharing services guarantee the audio quality of their files, their selections of files may be limited, since they need to secure permission from every record company whose music they carry. Also, they often use proprietary file formats that restrict copying and playing.

For example, Musicmatch (http://www.musicmatch.com), MusicNow (http://www.musicnow.com), BuyMusic (http://www.buymusic.com), Streamwaves (http://www.streamwaves.com), Napster (http://www.napster.com), and even Wal-Mart (http://www.walmart.com) distribute music files in the WMA (Windows Media Audio) format, which uses Microsoft's Digital Rights Management (DRM) technology to prevent people from copying the WMA file. Unfortunately, not every portable music player can play WMA files, nor can all non-Windows computers.

Anyone downloading music files from RealRhapsody (http://www.real.com) or iTunes (http://www.apple.com/itunes) will find a different file format called AAC (Advanced Audio Coding), which also restricts copying and poses compatibility problems for many portable music players. Naturally, Apple's own portable music player, the iPod, can play both MP3 and AAC files but not WMA files, although it can convert WMA files into AAC files so you can play them on your iPod.

To find music stored in the MP3 file format, visit eMusic (http://www.emusic.com) or MP3.com (http://www.mp3.com), where you can download legal music files and even submit your own music so others can hear what you may have created. For a glimpse of the possible future of downloadable music, visit CokeMusic (http://www.cokemusic.com), a site that offers MP3 music files to promote the brand name of Coca-Cola, as shown in Figure 16-1. To test the feasibility of offering a full online music service, Coca-Cola has even opened a site exclusively for British customers called MyCokeMusic (http://www.mycokemusic.com), where they can download songs for 99p (approximately $1.72 USD).

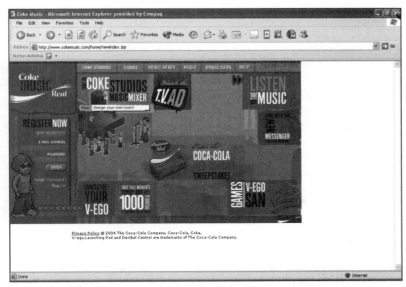

Figure 16-1
In the future, legal music downloading services may be funded by promoting another product.

With Napster orignally run by Roxio (publisher of CD burning software), iTunes by Apple (which sells iPod portable music players), and MyCokeMusic by Coca-Cola, the downloadable music business may soon become nothing more than an advertising vehicle to promote something other than the actual music.

NOTE: *Before you join any music sharing service, such as iTunes or Napster, make sure you can play the files that they offer for downloading on your particular computer or portable music player.*

Legal music file sharing services may be inexpensive, but they may never become dominant until they can match the selection and convenience of the free (but illegal) file sharing services.

NOTE: *Be careful when signing up with a seemingly legitimate music file sharing network. Many deceptive "legal" file sharing services simply trick users into purchasing software that turns out to be nothing more than a client program like Kazaa or LimeWire, which you could have downloaded for free anyway. Purchasing such a free client program still leaves you open to recording industry lawsuits, along with the insult of losing your money to a con artist.*

MOVIES

Movies can take several hours (or even days) to download, even over a fast broadband Internet connection. So while full-length movies aren't traded as easily over file sharing networks, many people are still willing to invest the time to download massive video files legally or illegally. Not surprisingly, movie studios hope to avoid the fate of the music industry by jumping into legal movie downloads before it's too late.

If you don't care for the latest Hollywood blockbusters that emphasize special effects over substance, then you might like the movie selection offered at MovieFlix (http://www.movieflix.com). MovieFlix provides old movies, commercials, and television shows from the 1950s to the present, all viewable with the RealPlayer or Windows Media Player program.

Some of the curious offerings available on MovieFlix include the science fiction movie *Rocketship X-M*, a 1954 commercial starring Betty Crocker, Betty Boop cartoons from 1948, and the 1997 documentary *About Tofu*. If you're looking for something obscure that you will probably never find in your local video store, join MovieFlix and watch movies for free or for a small charge.

For more hilariously obscure movies that you can watch for free, visit the Internet Archive (http://www.archive.org), where you can watch government films such as the Department of Defense's classic *Duck and Cover* film that teaches children how to survive a nuclear war by covering their heads with newspapers. Another, *In Our Hands, Part 3*, dramatizes how a communist-style "master plan" could affect your property and freedom. *All About Fallout* explains how to recognize and protect yourself against fallout, including life-saving tips like taking a shower after an all-out nuclear war has annihilated your city.

If you think that bizarre and campy movies only belong to the past, then join Kanakaris (http://www.kanakaris.com, shown in Figure 16-2), which offers such modern-day productions as *Cyber Sea Kittens*, *Bikini Beach Bust*, and *City of the Walking Dead*. With titles like these, you can be sure to find high-quality entertainment, and you can wonder at the poor saps who actually had to audition for roles in dead-end films like these.

To find more contemporary movies that have just been released to video, visit Flixs.net (http://www.flixs.net) or Download Free Films (http://www.downloadfreefilms.com). Unlike low-quality movies available on underground file sharing networks, these services offer DVD-quality files. If you join one of these services, you may find you no longer need to rent movies from your local video store anymore (which means yet another business is destined to fade into obscurity thanks to file sharing technology).

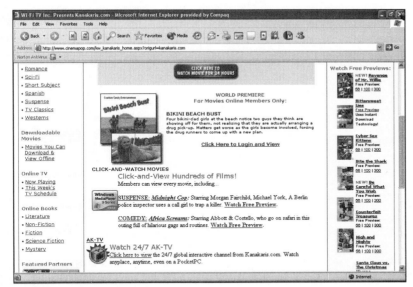

Figure 16-2

Many legal movie downloading services offer both popular and obscure movies that you may never find at your local video store.

BOOKS

Unlike software, music, or video, books aren't as easy to copy, and they lack mass public appeal, because the average American only reads one book a year (but watches nearly five hours of television a day). However, the ease of copying has changed somewhat with the introduction of both audio books and e-books, which can be swapped as easily as digital files. Despite the growing ease with which people can exchange audio and e-books over the Internet, books are probably the least popular item available on the major file sharing networks.

You can find the more popular audio and e-books over file sharing networks, but you'll find a much greater selection if you go through one of the legal audio or e-book online stores instead. Such online bookstores tend to stock everything from Bibles and cookbooks to the latest bestsellers in both fiction and non-fiction, along with classic literature and reference works, so if you need to find a little-known book, you'll probably save time going through one of the websites described in the following sections.

AUDIO BOOKS

Most stores that sell audio books only sell cassettes or CDs, although a handful now sell MP3 files of popular books. If you can't buy an MP3 version of an audio book, you'll have to convert the cassette or CD into an MP3 file yourself to play it on a portable MP3 player, such as an iPod.

These are some of the more popular online stores that sell audio books:

Audiobooks Online	http://www.audiobooksonline.com
Books on Tape	http://www.booksontape.com
Recorded Books	http://www.recordedbooks.com

One of the more unique audio websites is Audible (http://www.audible.com), which not only sells audio versions of books, but also audio versions of popular magazines and recordings of public broadcasting radio shows, such as *Car Talk* or *Fresh Air* with Terry Gross. If you want to listen to more than just books, Audible is sure to offer something else that you might be interested in hearing.

E-BOOKS

An e-book (short for *electronic book*) often appears as plain text or in a propri-etary file format, such as Adobe Acrobat's PDF (Portable Document Format) or Microsoft Reader. Proprietary formats protect the text from modification and display text with fancy fonts as if it were printed on a page.

Perhaps the biggest drawback to e-books is that you need to read them using a computer of some sort, such as a laptop or a handheld. Even the light-est handheld computer can be bulky and cumbersome to read for an extended period of time.

Despite these drawbacks, e-books can still be convenient to have when you want something to read without lugging around a handful of books in addi-tion to a computer. Many file sharing networks offer e-books, but like audio books, the selection is limited, so if you want to find an e-book on a specific topic or by a certain author, you'll probably have better luck visiting one of the follow-ing e-book stores where you can buy and download the e-book that you want.

Blackmask Online	http://www.blackmask.com
eBooks[3]	http://www.ebooks3.com
eBooks-Online	http://www.ebooks-online.com

FREE E-BOOKS

If you want to find the latest bestseller, you'll have to visit one of the many web-sites that sell e-books online. But if you want to read classic literature or browse through old reference or religious texts like the Bible, visit one of the many web-sites that distribute free public-domain e-books in the form of plain-text files.

These free e-book sites offer e-books on anything that's no longer copy-righted, such as William Shakespeare's plays or novels by H.G. Wells. Although plain-text files lack the fancy fonts and formatting that a commercial e-book may provide, they can be read on any computer, and they give you a chance to read some of the greatest literary treasures without having to pay for them. To find a free e-book, visit one of the following websites:

Bartleby	http://www.bartleby.com
Bibliomania	http://www.bibliomania.com
Books-On-Line	http://www.books-on-line.com
Children's Books Online	http://www.childrensbooksonline.org
Children's Storybooks Online	http://www.magickeys.com/books
Internet Public Library	http://www.ipl.org/div/books
netLibrary	http://www.netlibrary.com
The Online Books Page	http://digital.library.upenn.edu/books
Page By Page Books	http://www.pagebypagebooks.com
Project Gutenberg	http://www.promo.net/pg
University of Virginia's e-Book Library	http://etext.lib.virginia.edu/ebooks/ebooklist.html

SOFTWARE

How do you make money when people can copy your product for free? In the music industry, that question has generated lawsuits and litigation, but in the software industry, that question has formed the basis for a new business model that has created new jobs and businesses—writing, distributing, and selling soft-ware over the Internet.

While there are currently no legal alternatives for trading major applications over the Internet, such as Adobe Illustrator or Microsoft Word, there has long been an underground market for less popular, but sometimes equally powerful, programs known as *shareware*.

Unlike commercial software, shareware allows you to try the program on your computer, and if you like it, you can pay for it. Some shareware is fully functional, which means you can use it for as long as you want until you decide to pay for it. However, most shareware is restricted in some way to encourage people to pay for the program. Related to shareware is the category of *open source* software, which consists of programs that are available to be copied, distributed, and used without payment for as long as you care to use them.

Similar to open source is another category of software known as freeware. Unlike open source programs, which gives you the source code to study or modify if you wish, freeware programs can only be copied and shared freely; you can't peek at the source code at all. Freeware programs range from little utilities written by individual programmers to big name programs given away by corporations to encourage more people to use their products, such as Adobe Acrobat, Apple's iTunes, Macromedia Flash Player, and Microsoft PowerToys for Windows.

Despite their lower public profile, compared to software from big companies like Microsoft, Symantec, Adobe, and Macromedia, many shareware, freeware, and open source programs are nearly as good, and sometimes even better, than their commercial counterparts. Best of all, their lower price can make them an attractive alternative to the commercial programs.

MICROSOFT OFFICE ALTERNATIVES

If you need to share files created by word processor, spreadsheet, or presentation software, chances are good that you'll need Microsoft Word, Excel, or PowerPoint. While there's nothing wrong with using any of these programs, they cost way too much for the average person (who can't justify them as a business expense), and they come loaded with more features than most people will ever need in their lifetime.

If you want to save money and use a simpler word processor, spreadsheet, or presentation program without sacrificing the main features that you'll need, try some of the following Microsoft Office alternatives. These programs can save files in Microsoft Office formats (Word, Excel, and PowerPoint) so you can share data with anyone still stuck using Microsoft Office. Best of all, many of the following office suites are a fraction of the cost of Microsoft Office, which gives you Microsoft Office compatibility and ease of use without the expense or complexity of Office.

These are some popular Microsoft Office alternatives:

602PC Suite	http://www.software602.com
EasyOffice	http://www.e-press.com
ElOffice	http://www.evermoresw.com
GoBeProductive	http://www.gobe.com
OpenOffice.org	http://www.openoffice.org
SOT Office	http://www.sot.com
ThinkFree Office	http://www.thinkfree.com

ADOBE PHOTOSHOP ALTERNATIVES

Adobe Photoshop belongs on the computer of every professional graphic designer. Unfortunately, the high cost and even higher complexity keeps most people who aren't professionals from using Photoshop, even if they too would like to edit images and create designs. To meet the needs of the average computer user, Adobe (http://www.adobe.com) has released a lower-cost companion program dubbed Photoshop Elements.

Photoshop Elements may offer enough features for the average person, but if you need more advanced image-editing features without the high cost of Photoshop, take a look at the following programs:

Paint Shop Pro	http://www.jasc.com
PhotoLine	http://www.pl32.com
The GIMP	http://www.gimp.org
Turbo Photo	http://www.turbo-photo.com

INTERNET EXPLORER ALTERNATIVES

Every computer with Microsoft Windows comes with a free copy of Internet Explorer. While not a bad web browser, Internet Explorer isn't the fastest browser, nor does it offer the ability to open multiple web pages within a single Internet Explorer window. Older versions of Internet Explorer didn't even offer a pop-up ad-blocking feature to stop pop-up ads from bombarding you every time you connect to the Internet.

Because of Internet Explorer's flaws, many people prefer using alternative web browsers that run faster than Internet Explorer, offer tabbed windows (for opening multiple websites within a single window), and block pop-up ads. These are some popular alternative web browsers:

Avant Browser	http://www.avantbrowser.com
DeepNet Explorer	http://www.deepnetexplorer.com
Kopassa Browser	http://www.kopassa.com
Mozilla and Mozilla Firefox	http://www.mozilla.org
NetCaptor	http://www.netcaptor.com
Opera	http://www.opera.com
Optimal Desktop	http://www.optimalaccess.com
Slim Browser	http://www.flashpeak.com
UltraBrowser	http://www.ultrabrowser.com

SHAREWARE LIBRARIES

Browse through any shareware library, and you'll find all kinds of programs for a wide range of users, including programs for creating resumes, fixing problems on your hard disk, blocking spam from swamping your email account, and many more that you may never realize you need until you get a chance to try them first. These are some of the more popular shareware libraries for Windows, Linux, and Mac OS:

Tucows	http://www.tucows.com
CNet Download.com	http://www.download.com
Shareware.com	http://www.shareware.com
Jumbo	http://www.jumbo.com
VersionTracker	http://www.versiontracker.com

Windows software

Microsoft Windows represents the largest market, so it's no surprise that many shareware libraries focus exclusively on Windows programs. Here are some such libraries:

Any Windows Shareware	http://www.shareme.com
MajorGeeks.com	http://www.majorgeeks.com
Soft32.com	http://www.soft32.com
WinSite	http://www.winsite.com
Windows Users Group Network	http://www.wugnet.com

Macintosh software

Although the Macintosh consists of less than 10 percent of the total computer market, Macintosh users tend to be fanatically loyal and rabid about their choice of computers. So a handful of shareware libraries cater exclusively to the Macintosh crowd, such as these:

MacintoshOS.com	http://www.macintoshos.com
MacShare	http://www.macshare.com
MacOSArchives	http://www.macosarchives.com

By experimenting with different shareware programs, you can find less expensive alternatives to the more popular applications, and you just might surprise yourself by finding a useful program, such as a restaurant management program or a horse race betting program that you might never have heard about otherwise. Take a close look at your legal alternatives. You might just be surprised at how much you can find for free or at a much lower cost than you expected.

LEGAL FILE SHARING SPINOFFS

The idea behind file sharing is so simple and powerful that many people have taken the file sharing model and applied it to a variety of legal uses. Once you are finished downloading music, movies, and books from legal file sharing services, you might want to study some of the other ways file sharing technology has become a useful tool for doing more than just stealing files.

LONG-DISTANCE PHONE CALLS

File sharing networks work by shuffling data from one computer to the next until it finally arrives at its intended destination. Theoretically, you can send any type of data over a file sharing network, including pictures, movies, music, and even telephone calls.

That's the idea behind Skype (http://www.skype.com), created by Janus Friis and Niklas Zennström, who also created the popular Kazaa file sharing network. By downloading the free Skype software and using an ordinary headset and microphone, or the $54.99 Skype CyberPhone that plugs into your computer's USB port, you can make free long-distance phone calls anywhere around the world.

Skype claims that the audio quality of their phone calls rivals that of traditional land-based telephone lines. Even better, Skype encrypts every phone call, which means government authorities are going to have a hard time wiretapping anyone using Skype to make their phone calls.

Perhaps the biggest drawback to this system is that you can only make calls to other Skype users, not to any ordinary cell or landline telephone. Still, the idea of sharing computing power to transfer phone calls from one side of the planet to another for free makes Skype one of the more unusual applications for legal file sharing technology.

SHARING BUSINESS FILES

In the business world, people often need to share files with each other. While attaching files and sending them by email can be convenient, it doesn't always work when sending massive files, such as those created by desktop publishing or photo editing programs. While some technically savvy businesses simply post their files on FTP sites and allow their workers to download the files they need using an FTP client program, many businesses don't want to train their workers to use FTP at all.

As a compromise, several companies now offer software that allows you to create your own private file sharing networks. Such file sharing networks typically encrypt data to keep strangers from prying into your network, allowing complete privacy when chatting or sending files.

Two popular file sharing programs are Groove Virtual Office (http://www.groove.net), created by Ray Ozzie (the man who created the group collaboration program, Lotus Notes), and FolderShare (http://www.foldershare.com). Both Groove Networks and FolderShare let people designate which folders to share on the private file sharing network, and then any authorized users can freely tap into shared files on someone else's computer and copy the files they want.

Creo (http://www.creo.com) offers an interesting twist on the business advantages of file sharing. Instead of sharing specific folders on your computer with other people in your private file sharing network, Creo Tokens lets you send special files, called *tokens*, in an email to someone else. When someone receives a token, they can click on it to retrieve the specific file designated by that token. By sharing files in this manner, Creo Tokens lets each person decide who can retrieve which files off their computer, providing an even tighter layer of privacy and security for everyone involved.

SHARING PHOTOGRAPHS

Many people are now capturing pictures with digital cameras, and they naturally want to share their pictures with others. Sending out individual pictures by email can be clumsy, though, and posting pictures for others to view on a website can be time consuming and very public. To make picture sharing simple and easy, many companies are now offering file sharing networks for digital photographs.

Instead of sending out pictures individually, file sharing lets you designate which folders you want to share and then you can let anyone you want browse and download your digital photograph collection at any time (as long as your computer is hooked up to the Internet at the time). Here are some popular file sharing services for sharing photographs:

Electric Shoebox	http://photos.constanttime.com
OurPictures	http://www.ourpictures.com
ShareALot	http://www.sharealot.com

Just be aware that these digital photograph file sharing services may restrict the types of images you can share. The end-user license agreement for OurPictures specifically bans "content that is unlawful, harmful, threatening, harassing, defamatory, obscene, pornographic, vulgar, invasive of another's privacy or right of publicity, infringing of a third party's intellectual property rights . . . hateful, racially, ethnically, or otherwise objectionable, encouraging of conduct that could constitute a criminal offense, give rise to civil liability, or otherwise violate any applicable local, state, national or international law." In other words, you can't share anything that might get the file sharing services in trouble.

With so many different applications for file sharing, it's only a matter of time before practically everyone will use file sharing for some purpose or other, whether they know it or not. The key to using legal file sharing is accepting whatever slippery definition of "legal" your government imposes on you at the time.

17

HOW THE CORPORATIONS FIGHT BACK

Chances are good that there's an empty storefront near you that once housed a major music store. With sales of new CDs dropping every year, music companies have been shutting down shops across the country, and the few remaining stores continue to struggle. The music industry immediately identified the culprit: file sharing networks.

Although people had been trading files through newsgroups and websites for years, 1999 introduced the first major file sharing network in the form of Napster, which suddenly made copyrighted files available in mass quantities to anyone who could turn on a computer. Given a choice between paying for a CD just to hear one decent song or copying that same song for free over the Internet, guess which option most people choose?

With the music industry declaring file sharing piracy as the number one reason for declining CD sales, they've taken a variety of approaches to halt piracy. They've sued file sharers, placed anti-copying technology on their CDs, and even uploaded sabotaged files disguised as ordinary music. Will any or all of these methods halt piracy? Probably not, but it's still interesting to see how the music industry keeps trying to protect itself and fight against technological changes that make piracy even easier than before.

We don't like their sound, and guitar music is on the way out.

—Decca Recording Company, rejecting the Beatles, in 1962

FILING A LAWSUIT

When in doubt, sue. Lawsuits often depend less on a question of law than on who has the most money to pay for the best lawyers over a longer period of time. Given the massive financial backing of the music industry vs. the limited resources of Napster, it was inevitable that Napster would get pummeled in the courtrooms and be forced to shut down. The mistake Napster made was having a single computer keep track of all the songs available on other people's computers. To find a song, someone first had to contact Napster's computers and then needed to connect to the personal computer that actually held a copy of the song. Because Napster played an active role every time someone copied a file over its network, the courts ruled that Napster had the legal responsibility to block copyrighted material from being traded over its network.

However, suing file sharing networks no longer works because the latest file sharing networks don't use a central computer to keep lists of available songs. Instead, the new file sharing networks simply provide people with the software to probe everyone *else's* computers for songs. Then people connect to each other's computers to copy the files they want, leaving the file sharing company itself completely out of the transaction. Because the file sharing companies play no active part in any copyright infringement, the crime is shifted to the individuals themselves.

Because it couldn't sue the latest file sharing networks, the music industry tried a new attack, suing the individuals sharing copyrighted files from its computers. This next wave of lawsuits wound up catching several hundred people, including a 71-year-old grandfather, a Yale University professor, and a 12-year-old girl who lived in project housing.

The music industry hopes that the threat of lawsuits will strike fear in users' hearts, frightening them into abandoning file sharing networks. In addition, the music industry contacted large-scale file sharers directly over different file sharing networks and sent them the following warning:

> It appears that you are offering copyrighted music to others from your computer. . . . When you break the law, you risk legal penalties. There is a simple way to avoid that risk: DON'T STEAL MUSIC either by offering it to others to copy or downloading it on a 'file-sharing' system like this. When you offer music on these systems, you are not anonymous and you can easily be identified.

While fear and intimidation might stop some people from sharing copyrighted files over the Internet, it's also fueling the popularity of new file sharing networks that protect users' identities. Making people abandon file sharing networks is completely different from making people buy more CDs.

To read the latest legal cases pending against various file sharing companies and individuals, visit the Recording Industry Association of America (RIAA) website (http://www.riaa.com), shown in Figure 17-1. To read an opposing point of view, visit the Boycott RIAA website (http://www.boycott-riaa.com), shown in Figure 17-2.

246

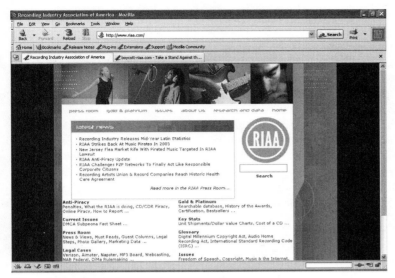

Figure 17-1

The RIAA website provides news and information about file sharing from the music industry's point of view.

Figure 17-2

The Boycott-RIAA website contains news about file sharing that tries to undermine or contradict the RIAA's claims.

EDUCATIONAL CAMPAIGNS

Fear is one tactic that the music industry hopes will sway people to their point of view. To continue their program of fear, the RIAA placed advertisements in the *New York Times* and *Entertainment Weekly* that contained foreboding headlines warning people, "Next time you or your kids 'share' music on the Internet, you may also want to download a list of attorneys."

Not all of the RIAA's campaigns focus on fear and intimidation. For young people, the RIAA hopes that a message of guilt and "education" (known as "propaganda" among dictatorships) can sway young people to its side.

By bombarding young children with "educational campaigns" to teach people why file sharing is wrong, the music industry hopes people will voluntarily shy away from any type of illegal file sharing activities. Of course, getting people to be honest is especially difficult when the rewards are high (free music) and the risks are low (the RIAA can't sue everybody).

The Motion Picture Association of America (MPAA) even launched a program aimed at educating students about the dangers of file sharing through the Junior Achievement program. A lesson plan entitled "What's the Diff? A Guide to Digital Citizenship" contains guidelines for teaching kids why they should not participate in illegal file sharing. The booklet includes quotes from famous people (Britney Spears and the Dixie Chicks) and not-so-famous people (Hollywood set painters and camera operators), explaining how illegal file sharing hurts them.

For further incentive to accept the industry's viewpoint about file sharing, the MPAA offers prizes such as DVD players, movies, theater tickets, and all-expense-paid trips to Hollywood for students who write the best essays about the illegal nature of file sharing. Presumably none of the students who won prizes turned in any thought-provoking essays that probed the reasons behind file sharing or why corporations were allowed to promote their point of view with the blessing of school teachers, who were also eligible for prizes based on the number and perceived quality of the essays their students submitted.

To approach more people than just students, various organizations have set up websites where visitors can browse through a list of questions and answers, news releases, and quotes from songwriters and artists urging people not to share copyrighted files illegally over the Internet. To see three websites that seek to educate readers about the illegality of file sharing, visit Music United (http://www.musicunited.net), the MPAA's Respect Copyrights website (http://www.respectcopyrights.org), and the Canadian Value of Music Coalition's website, Keep Music Coming (http://www.keepmusiccoming.com).

To read information supporting file sharing technology, visit the Electronic Frontier Foundation's website (http://www.eff.org) and P2P United (http://www.p2punited.org), a group of various file sharing companies that includes LimeWire, BearShare, and Blubster.

TAXING BLANK RECORDABLE MEDIA

Most big businesses write off shoplifting as a cost of doing business. The recording industry, by contrast, hopes to shore up its bottom line by adding a tax on all types of blank recordable media, such as cassette tapes, CDs, flash memory cards, and even ordinary floppy disks. The theory is that because pirates must use blank recordable media to steal copyrighted works, a tax on recordable media can at least partially compensate companies for the revenue they lose due to piracy. (Technically, this additional fee isn't a "tax" because it's not being collected by a government agency but by a recording industry representative, so it's a "levy." Either way, it's an additional cost to the consumer.)

Unfortunately, adding a tax (or "levy") to every type of blank recordable media punishes both the pirate and the law-abiding user who never records any type of music. A levy on blank recordable media is like having the police give everyone a speeding ticket for driving down a certain road whether they were speeding or not.

Forcing consumers of blank recordable media to pay extra may monetarily compensate the recording industry, but it still does nothing to address the main problem of people copying files across peer-to-peer (P2P) networks. If levies can be collected on recordable media, does that give people the right to then make copies of copyrighted files? If someone doesn't record copyrighted files, how come they can't get a refund on a levy that shouldn't affect them? From an artist's point of view, how much money does the recording industry collect through levies, and how much of that actually gets transferred to the artists, whose works are being copied in the first place? And who decides how it gets distributed?

Obviously levies by themselves won't stop file sharing, but they represent one more tactic the entertainment industry hopes can stem the revenue losses they blame on illegal file sharing.

ANTI-PIRACY COPY PROTECTION

In another attempt to protect their products, the music industry has turned to copy protection. The idea is that if the music industry can find a way to keep people from copying music in the first place, nobody will be able to share files over file sharing networks anyway. The two popular methods for implementing copy protection are copy-protecting CDs and copy-protecting individual audio files downloaded from legal music file sharing services, such as iTunes.

COPY-PROTECTING CDS

Two prominent copy-protection companies are MacroVision (http://www.macro-vision.com) and SunnComm Technologies (http://www.sunncomm.com).

In theory, copy protection might sound like the answer, until you realize that copy protection can never be foolproof. Beyond the simple fact that you can always record audio or video with the right cables connected in place of speakers or a television set, copy-protection schemes on CDs and DVDs can always be defeated because someone inevitably views copy protection as a personal challenge. They'll spend hours studying the copy-protection scheme until they find a flaw that they can exploit.

Even more embarrassing is how shockingly easy it can be to defeat some copy-protection schemes. When Sony introduced Celine Dion's *A New Day Has Come*, it embedded its key2audio copy-protection scheme, which added an extra track to the CD to prevent it from being played on a computer. People quickly found that if you just blacked out this extra track on the CD with a felt-tip marker, you could hide this track from view and allow a computer to play the CD, effectively defeating the copy-protection scheme.

When the recording industry released CDs copy-protected by SunnComm Technologies software, people discovered that if you inserted the CD into a Windows computer while holding down the SHIFT key, you could prevent the copy-protection software from even starting. Of course, if you inserted the CD into a non-Windows computer, such as a Mac OS or Linux computer, you could still play and copy the CD, because the copy-protection scheme only worked under Windows.

Copy-protection schemes often have the unpleasant side effect of keeping the CD from working in different types of players. Sometimes the copy-protection scheme may keep you from playing the CD in your computer, but it may also keep you from playing it in your car stereo. While the music industry would love nothing more than for you to buy one CD to play in your home stereo and a second CD to play in your car stereo, few people are willing to pay twice for the privilege of listening to the same music that they already paid for once. More importantly, most people feel they have the right to make backup copies of the CDs and DVDs they buy, just in case the original discs get damaged. Copy protection takes this right away from consumers, giving them *less* product for the same money.

To protest the nuisance of copy-protected CDs, many people are posting lists of known copy-protected CDs to warn others not to buy them. For information about how people are rebelling against copy-protected CDs, visit the corrupt CD list at (http://www.boycott-riaa.com/corrupt_cds) and the Don't Buy CDs site (http://www.dontbuycds.org) shown in Figure 17-3.

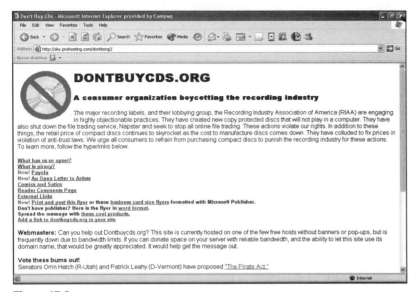

Figure 17-3
The Don't Buy CDs website offers arguments to punish the music industry by boycotting the purchase of CDs.

COPY-PROTECTING INDIVIDUAL AUDIO FILES

Legal music downloading services would go out of business if one person subscribed to the service and then started freely distributing all the songs from the legal service over illegal file sharing networks like Kazaa or Gnutella. To keep this from happening, legal music downloading services copy-protect their songs under the name of Digital Rights Management (DRM).

The idea behind DRM is that any song you download from a legal music service can only be copied and played on a limited number of computers, such as three. That way consumers have the freedom to back up and play their legally purchased songs practically everywhere they want, and the legal music downloading services protect their own assets from being stolen and spread through the illegal file sharing networks.

That's the theory, anyway. In reality, DRM often prevents people from playing their legally purchased songs on different music players, such as when they download songs from iTunes and find they can't play them on a non-iPod device. To circumvent this copy protection, hackers have developed several tools for stripping DRM away from a protected audio file. The Hymn project (http://www. hymn-project.org) provides such a free program that strips away DRM from songs downloaded from iTunes, as shown in Figure 17-4. Once you've stripped away the DRM from an iTunes file, you can play it on rival music players.

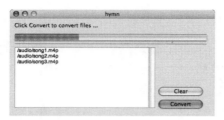

Figure 17-4
Hymn can strip away the DRM that comes wrapped
around every song downloaded from iTunes.

Perhaps the simplest way to circumvent DRM is to download a song from a legal downloading service, such as iTunes, burn it to a CD (which iTunes fully supports), and then rip those audio tracks off your newly burned CD and save them in any format you want, such as MP3.

For more information about the ongoing debate surrounding DRM and the various hacking tools, visit DRM Watch (http://www.drmwatch.com) or Freedom to Tinker (http://www.freedom-to-tinker.com).

ANTI-P2P SERVICES

File sharing has become a popular pastime. Many people spend their time at work using peer-to-peer (P2P) file sharing programs to copy their favorite songs and movies, because their work Internet connection is often much faster than their home Internet connection, and their IP address at work identifies their employer and not them. To avoid legal liability and improve network efficiency, many corporations have turned to anti-P2P services and software. These solutions scan a network to detect abnormal bandwidth usage (which could indicate file sharing activity among employees), and they can also identify specific file sharing programs on a computer, such as Grokster or Kazaa.

Anti-P2P software is likely to become as popular and necessary for corporations as antivirus software. With the continuing spread of file sharing programs, anti-P2P software could become the computer market's next growth industry. For a quick peek at some of the more prominent anti-P2P software, visit Packeteer (http://www.packeteer.com), which is shown in Figure 17-5, Allot (http://www.allot.com), or AssetMetrix (http://www.assetmetrix.com).

MONITOR TRAFFIC

update Auto (+5 sec)   Display All classes   clear stats ...   Go to Monitor Events
        Stop auto   Monitor Response Time
        Stats only

Click "clear stats ..." to reset values shown in GREEN.

May 23 2003 - 15:43:31

Traffic Class Name	Class Hits	Policy Hits	Current (bps)	1 Min (bps)	Peak (bps)	Guar. Rate Failures	Pkt Exch (ms)	Partitio Min-Ma
Inbound			71.6k	92.2k	3.8M	0	NA	uncommitted - non
/Outbound/Exchange_EMail	19	NA	58.1k	56.7k	82.0k	0	1	
/Inbound/Exchange_EMail	19	NA	51.8k	50.4k	72.7k	0	10	
Outbound			47.0k	77.9k	1.0M	0	NA	uncommitted - non
/Inbound/Gnutella_P2P	10621	NA	20.0k	20.0k	1.9M	0	911	20.0k - nonbursta
/Inbound/Default	2767	15463	7978	7925	809k	0	72	
/Outbound/Gnutella	10803	NA	7778	9644	157k	0	1584	20.0k - nonbursta
/Inbound/NetBIOS-IP	1017	NA	2555	673	3.2M	0	9	
/Outbound/Default	3650	16564	547	875	25.3k	0	383	
/Inbound/ICMP	387	NA	179	187	1303	0	NA	
/Inbound/CiscoDiscovery	57	NA	15	27	674	0	NA	
/Inbound/Localhost	2427	2427	0	25	952k	0	4	
	0	0	0	0	0	0	NA	

Figure 17-5

To uncover file sharing programs, a program like Packeteer looks at which programs are accessing a network and their bandwidth consumption.

Audible Magic (http://www.audiblemagic.com) has teamed up with Palisade Systems (http://www.palisadesys.com) to create a program that intercepts all traffic on a network, makes a copy of it, and then examines that copy to look for telltale signs of file sharing, such as Kazaa or Gnutella file sharing. If the program finds a match with Audible Magic's database of digital "fingerprints" for commonly pirated files, the program stops the file transmission.

While corporations may be interested in keeping their workers from accessing file sharing programs, other companies are targeting parents, warning that their children could be accessing pornography through file sharing networks. Media Defender (http://www.mediadefender.com) even sells a program dubbed Peer Protector, which can delete previously downloaded files and disable file sharing programs like Kazaa so they don't work at all.

SABOTAGING FILES WITH CUCKOO EGGS

Another controversial way that the recording industry has fought back against file sharing is to infiltrate the various file sharing networks themselves and plant bogus files, known as *cuckoo eggs*. (Cuckoo birds will lay an egg in another bird's nest, which tricks the other bird into thinking the cuckoo's egg is actually one of its own. Cuckoo eggs in a file sharing network are similarly deceptive because they trick people into thinking that a bogus file is actually a valid one.)

Typically a cuckoo egg is labeled with the name of a popular artist's song, and it even may have the right file size and track length. But when someone plays a cuckoo egg file, they'll hear a few seconds of the actual song followed by cuckoo clock noises and voice messages such as, "Congratulations, you must've goofed up somewhere." To deter piracy of her music, Madonna once released a cuckoo egg of her "American Life" single that contained the message, "What the fuck do you think you're doing?" By tricking people into wasting time downloading cuckoo eggs instead of actual pirated files, the recording industry hopes to discourage people from using file sharing networks.

The planting of cuckoo eggs initially began with individual musicians who tired of seeing their music appear on file sharing networks, but cuckoo eggs are now big business in the recording industry itself. Many record labels have hired the services of companies such as Overpeer (http://www.overpeer.com), Covenant (http://www.covenant-corporation.com), and MediaDefender (http://www.mediadefender.com). These companies essentially take popular copyrighted files, such as the latest hit singles, and convert them into cuckoo eggs, which they spread throughout the popular file sharing networks.

"What we do is make peer-to-peer a lot less fun and help users do the right thing," said Marc Morgenstern, CEO of Overpeer, a company with patents on altering the sound quality of a music file by dubbing in distorted sounds or voices. Based on a client's wishes, Overpeer can release thousands of cuckoo eggs that simply mimic pirated files or contain links to authorized music downloading sites.

Ironically, cuckoo eggs are not free from legal controversy. Because many cuckoo egg files contain part of the original song, trading cuckoo eggs can also violate copyrights. Even more surprising is that many of the file sharing companies have threatened to sue cuckoo egg companies for violating the terms of the agreements they supposedly read when they installed the file sharing programs on their computers.

Cuckoo eggs may discourage some people from using a file sharing network, but they often inspire others to upload the real copyrighted files just to defy the cuckoo egg distributors. Only days after Madonna released her cuckoo egg of "American Life," hackers flooded the file sharing networks with pirated copies of the actual song and hacked into Madonna's official website, leaving messages that read, "This is what the fuck I think I'm doing . . ." Next to these messages, the hackers left links directing people to pirated copies of every song on Madonna's latest album, as shown in Figure 17-6.

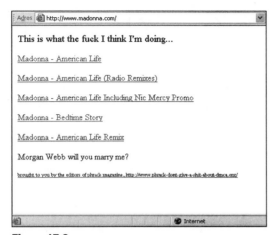

Figure 17-6
Madonna's website after it was hacked to protest her distribution
of a cuckoo egg on file sharing networks.

KILLING A COMPUTER

In other attempts to disrupt file sharing networks, the RIAA has reportedly
hired companies to try a variety of tactics that include creating fake computers
stocked with useless files of cuckoo eggs, deliberately trying to crash computers
running file sharing programs, hacking into file sharing computers and deleting
MP3 files (whether they're legal or not), and launching denial-of-service attacks
on blatant file sharing computers by continually requesting files, which prevents
other users from accessing those files.

Technically, many of these methods, such as deleting files from an offender's computer or launching a denial-of-service attack on a blatant file sharing
computer, are illegal. To fix this minor problem of legality, the recording industry's
latest attempt has been to pass a law allowing copyright holders to hack into
copyright infringers' computers and disable, block, or interfere with their activities, provided the damage doesn't exceed a certain monetary amount, such as
$50, although the specific method of hacking a copyright violator isn't defined.
One draft of this potential law, called the Berman Copyright Bill, can be viewed
at Declan McCullagh's Politech website (http://www.politechbot.com/docs/
berman.coble.p2p.final.072502.pdf).

By giving the entertainment industry the freedom to circumvent normal anti-hacking laws and to directly attack the computers of offenders, the combined music, movie, and electronic book publishing industries hope to use force to protect their copyrights where legislation, educational campaigns, levies on recordable media, and copy-protection schemes haven't had much success. (Of course, people could always upload email messages to the computers of Sony or Universal Studios, and then hack into those computers to disable them, claiming that they were only trying to prevent those corporations from distributing copies of their copyrighted email messages. If corporations can skirt the law and hack into other people's computers, hackers will likely claim the same right to hack into corporate computers, and given a battle between corporate programmers and hackers worldwide, it doesn't take much imagination to see which side will lose.)

Senator Orin Hatch of Utah went even further and suggested that all computers should be forced to include "kill switches," which would allow the authorities to remotely disable a computer whose user was breaking the law. Orin Hatch's legislation would require copyright holders to give an offender two warnings before activating the kill switch to destroy or permanently disable the computer.

"That may be the only way you can teach these people about copyright infringement," Hatch told reporters. "Requiring kill switches is an extreme step, but if the private sector can't stop piracy on its own, the government will."

Hatch further explained, "The kill switch would necessarily include an audit trail and some sort of way to prevent it from being abused by people other than legitimate intellectual property holders." Anyone who misuses the kill switch, Hatch promised, would be subjected to prosecution by the U.S. Department of Justice (assuming, of course, that the U.S. Department of Justice can find the hackers responsible, even if they happen to live in remote places like Ecuador, Libya, or Thailand).

Orin Hatch's proposal follows a similar bill by South Carolina Senator Fritz Hollings, which would require computer and consumer-electronics companies to build copyright-protection technology into future products (as if that's going to help sell more products).

The idea of crafting laws that allow copyright holders to engage in destructive hacking tactics that only benefit a handful of corporations reveals how desperate the entertainment industries must be to stem the hemorrhaging of their profits. If any of these bills ever become law, you can be sure that hackers will not only find a loophole in the legal wording, but they'll apply more destructive attacks on the corporate computers in retaliation—attacks that might well be legally protected under the entertainment industry's own "remote hacking to punish copyright infringers" law.

WHAT THE FUTURE HOLDS

There's no question that sharing copyrighted files breaks the law. The problem isn't how to stop file sharing networks. The real problem is adapting file sharing technology in a way that fairly compensates artists and corporations and yet doesn't infringe upon a consumer's right to enjoy the copyrighted information they purchased legitimately.

File sharing networks will not be forced to go away by lawsuits, copy-protected CDs, or outright sabotage by organizations that represent the music, video, or publishing industries. Rather than fight the inevitable, corporations must find a way to embrace that same technology that threatens their current business practices. If corporations fail to adapt to change, they'll simply go out of business like Montgomery Ward and Pan Am, or they will suffer lingering deaths of irrelevancy, like Kmart, Burger King, and Polaroid.

What consumers want is the right to copy and use their music, videos, or electronic books anywhere they want, whether it's on a laptop, desktop, handheld computer, MP3 player (like Apple's iPod), or even in devices yet to be created. What corporations want is fair compensation for investing in artists and taking the financial risk of publicizing and distributing a product. (What artists want is fair compensation for creating their music, but that has always been an ongoing struggle between artists and the recording industry.)

If consumers don't get what they want, they'll continue to turn toward piracy. If the corporations don't get what they want, they'll continue to fight a losing battle involving lawsuits, copy-protection schemes doomed for eventual failure, and draconian laws designed to protect their financial interests at the expense of anyone else's.

Oddly enough, the pornography industry, no stranger to embracing technological changes such as Polaroid cameras, VCRs, and webcams, may have the solution. The pornography industry is rumored to be working on a file sharing network dubbed Pornster (http://www.pornster.com). Unlike ordinary file sharing networks, Pornster will reportedly allow only copyrighted still and video images on its network and then will automatically track how many people download specific copyrighted files. Advertising and subscription revenue earned by the Pornster network will then be used to compensate the companies and porn stars for their work, based on how many people download their copyrighted images. The system allows consumers to freely share files while still giving artists and corporations fair monetary compensation in return.

The bottom line is that the corporations, who currently hold all the power and make most of the money, are going to have to change, and that's something they aren't willing to do. Unfortunately for them, their fate is already sealed and out of their hands in the same way that buggy whip manufacturers, slide rule makers, and whale-oil lamp companies found themselves wiped out by technological change. The question isn't whether file sharing technology will put today's corporate powerhouses out of business. The question is when, and that future is closer than they think.

INDEX

Z

STEAL THIS COMPUTER BOOK 3
What They Won't Tell You About the Internet

by WALLACE WANG

MAY 2003, 384 PP.
$24.95, $37.95 CAN, ISBN 1-59327-000-3

This offbeat, non-technical book looks at what hackers do, how they do it, and how you can protect yourself. The third edition of this bestseller (over 150,000 copies sold) adopts the same informative, irreverent, and entertaining style that made the first two editions a huge success. Thoroughly updated, this edition also covers rootkits, spyware, web bugs, identity theft, hacktivism, wireless hacking (wardriving), biometrics, and firewalls.

THE BOOK OF NERO 6 ULTRA EDITION
CD and DVD Burning Made Easy

by WALLACE WANG

JULY 2004, 216 PP.
$19.95, $27.95 CAN, ISBN 1-59327-043-7

If you've installed a CD or DVD writer drive, chances are that Nero came with it. Nero is great for burning music CDs, data backups, and DVDs, but it can do a whole lot more! Combining the best parts of a media player, a design program, a sound editor, and a video editor, Nero makes it possible for you to create CDs and DVDs that will knock your socks off. Best-selling computer book author Wallace Wang takes you step by step through all of Nero's capabilities, without any unnecessary jargon. You'll learn how to burn CDs, edit mixes, backup data, create slide shows, burn DVDs, design your own labels and covers, edit sound files, use Nero to play movies and music, and more.

THE SPAM LETTERS

by JONATHAN LAND

JUNE 2004, 230 PP.
$14.95, $19.95 CAN, ISBN 1-59327-032-1

From the man behind TheSpamLetters.com—featured in *Entertainment Weekly*, the *New York Times*, and Slashdot—comes a collection of brilliant and entertaining correspondence with the people who send out mass junk emailings (aka spam). Compiled from the nearly 200 entries written by Jonathan Land, *The Spam Letters* taunts, prods, and parodies the faceless salespeople in your inbox, giving you a chuckle at their expense. If you hate spam, you'll love *The Spam Letters*.

"The first funny thing I've ever found about spam." — *Detroit Free Press*

THE CULT OF MAC

by LEANDER KAHNEY

OCTOBER 2004, 376 PP., HARDCOVER, 4-COLOR
$39.95, $55.95 CAN, ISBN 1-886411-83-2

There is no product on the planet that enjoys the devotion of a Macintosh computer. Apple's machines have legions of loyal, sometimes demented fans. *The Cult of Mac* surveys the devoted following that has grown up around Macintosh computers. From people who get Mac tattoos and haircuts, to those who furnish their apartments out of Macintosh computer boxes, this full-color coffee table book details Mac fanaticism in all of its forms.

"Required reading for anyone who loves his or her Macintosh." — Guy Kawasaki, Former Chief Evangelist, Apple

APPLE CONFIDENTIAL 2.0
The Definitive History of the World's Most Colorful Company

by OWEN W. LINZMAYER

JANUARY 2004, 344 PP.
$19.95, $29.95 CAN, ISBN 1-59327-010-0

Apple Confidential examines the tumultuous history of America's best-known Silicon Valley start-up—from its legendary founding almost 30 years ago, through a series of disastrous executive decisions, to its return to profitability, and including Apple's recent move into the music business. This updated and expanded edition includes tons of new photos, timelines, and charts, as well as coverage of new lawsuit battles, updates on former Apple executives, and new chapters on Steve Wozniak and Pixar.

"If you're a member of the Mac faithful or just moderately interested in the company, you simply must buy this book." — MACDEVCENTER.COM

PHONE:

800.420.7240 OR
415.863.9900
MONDAY THROUGH FRIDAY,
9 A.M. TO 5 P.M. (PST)

FAX:

415.863.9950
24 HOURS A DAY,
7 DAYS A WEEK

EMAIL:

SALES@NOSTARCH.COM

WEB:

HTTP://WWW.NOSTARCH.COM

MAIL:

NO STARCH PRESS
555 DE HARO STREET, SUITE 250
SAN FRANCISCO, CA 94107
USA

ABOUT THE TECHNICAL REVIEWER

Ray Hoffman runs the File Sharing news and information site Slyck.com. He has been actively involved in file sharing since the early days of the Commodore 64.

UPDATES

Visit **http://www.nostarch.com/sharing.htm** for updates, errata, and other information.